Public Expenditure and Government Growth

Edited by Francesco Forte and Alan Peacock

Basil Blackwell

First published 1985

Basil Blackwell Ltd
108 Cowley Road, Oxford OX4 1JF, UK

Basil Blackwell Inc.
432 Park Avenue South, Suite 1505,
New York, NY 10016, USA

British Library Cataloguing in Publication Data

Public expenditure and government growth.
1. Expenditures, Public
I. Forte, Francesco II. Peacock, Alan, 1922–

ISBN 0-631-14182-0

Library of Congress Cataloging in Publication Data
Main entry under title:

Public expenditure and government growth.
Papers from a conference held at Cernobbio, Lake Como, Mar. 1984 and sponsored by the Fondazione Luigi Einaudi and the Istituto bancario San Paolo di Torino.
Includes index.
1. Expenditures, Public — Congresses. 2. Government spending policy — Congresses. I. Forte, Francesco, 1929– . II. Peacock, Alan T., 1922–
III. Fondazione Luigi Einaudi. IV. Istituto bancario San Paolo di Torino.
HJ2011.P8 1985 336.3′9 85-3875

ISBN 0-631-14182-0

Phototypeset by Dobbie Typesetting Service, Plymouth, Devon
Printed and bound at The Camelot Press Ltd, Southampton

Contents

Preface and Acknowledgements

The papers in this volume were first presented and discussed at a conference arranged by the editors which was held at Cernobbio, Lake Como, in early March 1984. Both the conference and the publication of the proceedings would not have been possible without the financial support of the Einaudi Centre of the Bank of Italy and the Instituto Bancario San Paolo di Torino. The editors are particularly grateful to these two institutions for their generosity.

The Fondazione Einaudi was represented at the conference by Professor Terenzio Cozzi, Vice President of the Fondazione Einaudi, Torino, who was also responsible for the administrative arrangements. The Instituto Bancario San Paolo was represented by its Chairman, Professor Gianni Zandano. Professor Franco Cavallari was strategically placed near one of the editors in Rome and collaborated in the preparation of the scientific programme. It is a pleasure to thank them for giving up their time, not least because they all took an active part in the conference proceedings.

The editors would have liked to have included all the written comments offered at the conference as well as an account of the discussion to which the papers and the comments on them gave rise, but this would have faced them with major publication difficulties. It is certainly no reflection on these comments and on the discussion that the line has had to be drawn somewhere. The very least that we can do is to thank Norman Barry, Antonio Pedone, Franco Cavallari, Domenico da Empoli, Emilio Giardina and Luc Weber for fulfilling their role so expertly – and here we speak for all the contributors.

Introduction
The Political Economy of Public-Sector Growth and its Control

Francesco Forte and Alan Peacock

It is axiomatic that if governments are concerned about the control of the growth of the public sector, they could learn much from the study of the influences on that growth. Earlier studies of that growth have been concentrated on the quite difficult tasks of defining the public sector, obtaining good-quality data of trends in public expenditure, and the testing of fairly simple hypotheses in which government expenditure (in absolute or per-capita terms) is the dependent variable and various exogenous variables are identified that exercise an influence on the dependent variable such as per-capita GDP, population, the relative price of a unit of public services and perhaps some 'catch-all' term denoted 'all other' influences.

Given this concern of governments, it is the thesis of this volume that economic analysis has to look much more closely at the underlying causes of growth before anything of operational interest can be presented to those who have the difficult task of conducting economic policy, which requires control over the size and structure of the public sector.

How this thesis is reflected in the contributions will shortly be discussed, but, additionally, the volume considers not only some of the (perhaps neglected) underlying causes of growth, but also relates the analyses to the question of whether there are 'natural limits' to the growth process or whether some form of positive action must be taken by the government to restrict the demand for its growth, bearing in mind the constraints, including the government's own objectives, that beset the introduction of growth-controlling policies.

The thesis will strike a sympathetic chord with those who have already been engaged in the extension of the earlier discussion and who have already published in the specialist literature. This volume presents a sample of new contributions to this literature with the purpose not solely of interesting fellow-specialists, but also of introducing salient features of the preoccupations of specialists to a wider and no doubt equally critical audience. It also has the purpose of reminding such an audience that the extension of the discussion is not confined to Anglo-Saxon countries. There is a deliberate 'sample bias' in the volume, arising from the fact that the host country for the conference at which the original version of the papers were presented was Italy, which is, of course, a country with a long tradition of scholarship in the field of public finance. It is a particular pleasure for the editors to introduce the work of some younger Italian scholars.

ANALYSING AND TESTING PUBLIC-SECTOR GROWTH

The chapters in part I illustrate the way in which the evolution of the discussion on the forces governing public-sector growth has incorporated the study of interest groups, in the wide sense of that term, and how the utility-maximizing propensities of these groups, and those of its members, affect the taste for public-sector expansion, given the constraints which affect the maximization process.

The programme starts with a significant extension of the public-choice approach to the analysis of the growth of government expenditure in the form of the study of the behaviour of voter interest groups by Mueller and Murrell. The process by which a party gains power in a democratic government is no longer analysed in terms of a vast spectrum of individual voters ranged along some ideological axis, in which the position of the median voter is crucial. Parties are envisaged as wooers of interest groups in which a 'core' of groups will adhere to the party in question on ideological grounds. It is unlikely that agreement over ideology would provide sufficient voting strength in order to ensure that the party would obtain office. To attract other interest groups is essential and the problem is to form agreements over the volume and pattern of public spending and its finance that have the net effect of adding to voting strength. However, the process of attraction involves considering the *net* marginal impact on voting support, for the concessions made to some additional interest group may be bought at the cost of losing the support of 'core' groups. For example, for a given level of public spending, a promise to cut the taxes of one interest group in order to gain additional voting support may imply an increase in the taxes of existing interest-group supporters, which may drive the latter to look for favours from other parties. It is intuitively obvious that parties seeking support will try to solve the conundrum of obtaining power by minimizing the perceived 'negative' impacts on voter interest groups made necessary by the need to finance the benefits derived from public expenditure. In the recent literature on public choice, parties obtaining power rely on the technique of fiscal illusion or on the transfer of the burden to the currently unenfranchised, for example, by running deficits which have to be paid off by future generations. The result will be a growth in public expenditure. What is interesting about the contribution by Mueller and Murrell (chapter 1) is that they do not rely on these arguments. They are able to show that, provided an interest group is successful in obtaining benefits 'targeted' to it (for example, transfer in money expenditure such as pensions or transfers in kind such as subsidized public housing), those who would otherwise have opposed these benefits, but have 'lost out' in the election process will not be disposed to campaign for a return to the status quo, but will favour increased total government spending. To add to the considerable interest which this contribution should arouse is an attempt to test a number of hypotheses derived from this general conclusion.

The structure of the Italian system of government (including the recent devolution of spending functions to lower layers of government as well as the methods of voting in members of the legislature, the Cabinet structure and the legislative procedures), highlights in particular the division into interest groups not only among the voting population, but also within the process of government itself. Martelli is that rare person, a sociologist who is fully at home in economics, and the crux of his contribution in chapter 2 lies in the idea that if a government performs its task of 'giving political and legislature coherence to legislative output', it will be made painfully aware of the financial consequences of its choices. Because of the fear of the external as well as the internal consequences of growing fiscal deficits, governments will be constrained by their own 'deficit aversion' and will be forced to limit themselves in the extent to which they will buy support simply by expanding government expenditure. This still leaves governments with sufficient 'goods', which Martelli calls 'representation goods', to trade for parliamentary support and which collectively amount to the forms of patronage which a government in power can command. In return for patronage favours, representatives in parliament are expected to deliver more electoral votes than would be lost through their support for containing public spending. However, to be fully effective, the government must have a formidable array of representation goods to deliver and must be sure that secret ballots in passing legislation do not block the process of exchange. This summary does less than justice to a subtle analysis, which, incidentally, requires the author to offer a useful critical view of the economic analysis of representative government in order to illustrate his main thesis by the use of the prisoner's dilemma model.

The next two contributors (chapters 3 and 4) consider the effects on the growth of public spending of an important institutional change which has occurred in a number of Western countries, namely the growth of central government grants as a proportion of lower-layer government revenue and with it the separation of spending and taxing decisions. The rationale of this change is a major subject of discussion in the literature of fiscal federalism, but is not the concern of this volume. The positive issue which arises is how far such an institutional change of the sort resulting from the Italian tax reform of 1971, which abolished the principal taxes levied by local authorities, has an expansionary or contractionary effect on public-spending growth. Intuitively, one might argue that centralization of decision-making would improve control over overall spending by the concentration of the power to tax and the allocation of grants by a general formula decided by the central legislature. However, as Brosio emphasizes, this form of centralization engenders the growth of countervailing power in the form of various local pressure groups, and coalitions between regional interests. To take one example, where bargaining power is important, grant formulas must depend on the production of detailed information on regional economic and social conditions, but both the production and control of such information may be in the hands of the local government themselves. Furthermore, the devising of the formulas may cut across party differences at the central level, with poorer regions demanding a 'needs-based' grant formula and richer regions a 'tax-effort-based' one. Such a situation is ripe for political compromises which requires that there must be prizes for all. After a review, not only of Italian conditions, but those in a number of federations, Brosio concludes that the introduction of a system of grants can foster the growth in public expenditure, but that the magnitude and the duration of this effect is a matter for further speculation. He is surely right to stress that in the longer run 'deficit aversion', as Martelli has called it, may force the public authorities at different levels to seek some more effective method of control of public expenditure. Such may be revenue-sharing schemes, which clearly stipulate that any transfer of resources from richer to poorer regions is quite explicitly laid out in the grant formula and that spending levels at regional level about some 'norm' can only be increased by raising local taxes or charges still left in regional hands.

The complementary contribution by Rizzo performs the useful function of testing a particular version of the Brosio analysis. Her statistical data suggest a close relation between growth in total public expenditure and local public expenditure in Italy in the last two-decades, which is also associated with a period when there was a narrowing in regional economic disparities. She offers two related hypotheses to explain these trends. The first follows the Peltzman thesis that the self-interested behaviour of politicians leads them to expand public spending through voter pressure to redistribute income through the public budget, with regional authorities taking the place of voters in the hypothesis. The narrowing of regional income disparities will promote coalitions between the regional authorities in regions with similar income levels, designed to promote expenditure programmes. The second hypothesis explains the influence of decentralization of expenditure decisions (but not of revenue decisions) through the circumstances which favour collusion between voters seeking access to local services with politicians who 'facilitate' access in exchange for voter support and with bureaucrats who have a bias towards expansion of services anyway. With the budget constraint on expansion operating through the central budget, voters in particular regions are not 'charged' directly for local services, and politicians and bureaucrats will more readily accede to their wishes. A particular feature of this contribution is the discussion of the procedures for testing these hypotheses and careful appraisal of the results which offer support for them.

The final contribution in part I by Zandano (chapter 5) links the first part of the book with part II. His analysis of the evolution of the study of public-expenditure growth offers support for the study of the political 'linkages', which is a particular feature of this work, but in seeking to understand how public-expenditure analysis bears on policy questions, he rightly stresses that more attention needs to be paid to the evolving composition of that expenditure and also to the mode of its finance. To take only one of his examples, the ratio represented by the growth of public spending to GDP clearly depends on the ways in which public spending and taxation produce changes in the composition of national expenditure between consumption and investment, including the government's allocation of its own spending between the two. The pressures to increase public-consumption spending programmes plus the 'crowding out' of private investment created by the continuing use of public deficits as a means of financing these programmes creates an enormous problem of readjustment, so he believes, for countries such as his own, because of the threat to future economic growth. To Zandano, anticipating some later discussion, 'the task of controlling public expenditure, while maintaining a satisfactory level of welfare, can best be achieved by more selective control of entitlement programes'.

PUBLIC CHOICE AND THE CONTROL OF PUBLIC-SECTOR GROWTH

Having identified the forces which determine the growth of government spending, in so far as that is possible, what, if anything, need be done to control those forces? Clearly the answer depends on a set of value judgements about the tasks of government and how these are translated into budgetary provisions; and there is no reason to suppose that all sets of value judgements would imply that public expenditure in any democratic Western country should cease to grow. However, it is a well-known fact that governments of very different political persuasions are currently concerned about the possibility that public spending may get out of control, and seek guidance on how to control it. As we shall observe in part II, economists have suggested and analysed in detail various possible ways of doing so, but leave to others to decide whether or not any particular technique of control is feasible in a particular political or administrative content. This is perfectly natural and it may be that, for the economist, 'modesty is the best policy' when it comes to practical implementation. However, we believe that we should go further than this, for it may be that the economic analysis of government can shed some light on how interest groups will react to these measures, given their utility-maximizing propensities. This may stimulate further discussion of how strategies designed to circumvent and even to defeat the control measures may be countered.

A good starting-point for such discussion is to consider the question: are there any 'natural' limits to the growth of the public sector? In chapters 6 and 7, by Frey and Schmidt, respectively, the important point is made that it is no use seeking an answer to this question by considering budgetary transactions alone, for the same set of government objectives, for example, standards of welfare services, may be promoted by the use of government regulation of the private sector. It is therefore necessary to consider the growth in regulation alongside the growth in the absolute and relative size of the public budget. Frey considers that a useful indication of the natural limits is provided by the incentives given to individuals both to evade payment of taxes to finance ever-growing public expenditure and to evade regulations. His associated models of evasion, which contain highly original features, add a further dimension to the range of weapons open to individuals and interest groups in order to maximize their utility, subject to the constraints imposed by the bargaining environment. Using the Hirschman terminology, his models concentrate on 'exit', rather than on 'voice', which has been the characteristic of the political bargaining processes identified in part I. There are, as he recognizes, formidable obstacles encountered in testing hypotheses regarding the relationship between the growth of government and the growth in evasion of taxes and regulations, and therefore it would be optimistic to expect that even a guess can be made as to the extent and timing of any 'braking effect' exercised by evasion tactics. Economists, if not practical men, will be pleased with his results, if only because of the number of interesting fields of research which are laid before them for further exploration.

Schmidt, on the other hand, lays much more stress on limits to public-expenditure growth that operate within the constitutional structure. He already discerns a change in taste for public services in the Federal Republic of Germany, where growth in public expenditure markedly accelerated in the 1970s, which is traced to the learning process undergone by the electorate and political parties as a result of the experience of being subjected to more public control over those goods which determine the size of real income. However, it cannot be assumed that this reversal of view will necessarily be translated into a reversal of trend in public spending, because of the familiar 'isolation paradox', that is to say, the uncertainty that individuals perceive is not knowing whether a demand for reduction in public services from which they benefit will be translated into a reduction in the taxes which they pay in order to finance them. With the caution bred by long experience as both a scholar and a government adviser, Schmidt understandably does not stick his neck out.

The lack of precision with which any 'natural' checks on public-spending growth might work means that policy-makers must look elsewhere for control devices than the pressures emanating from the system of representative government. At the same time, how are such devices and the associated rules of action generated through the system of representative government itself? Peacock argues in chapter 9 that there is a presumption that a rule designed to control overall spending is more likely to command agreement than rules which presuppose a clear identification of gainers and losers, before the political process gets to work in making public-spending decisions. After an extensive critique of the qualified majority principle supported by Buchanan and Tullock, Forte argues in chapter 8 that governments forced to accept the realities of economic policies that are subject to the constraint of external events are pushed against their will to inflate public expenditure and to use deficit finance, if simultaneously they have the further constraint of having to assemble a large majority to support those policies. As a former Minister of Finance and now the Minister for EEC Affairs in the Italian Cabinet, he has had close encounters with situations of this kind. It is therefore all the more significant that he favours quite detailed constitutional rules, and notably a constitutional limit on the issue of internal and external debt. Peacock is rather pessimistic about the possibility of having such a rule accepted, perhaps influenced by his own experience in government, and that, if acceptance is achieved, for example, for some expenditure-growth rule coupled with debt limitation, he doubts whether any government intent on circumventing the rule could be prevented from doing so. But he does agree with Aaron Wildavský that 'limits on total spending do not guarantee control, but without limits on total spending there can be no control'.

Both editors had some doubts about whether it was worth exploring the connection between monetary policy and public expenditure, but these were soon dispelled when the contributions from Tanzi and Wellink and Halberstadt were received. In several Western countries, whatever the constitutional position, the central bank plays an independent role, or at least offers an influential source of economic advice. Monetary policy, according to Tanzi, which allows inflation to become established and therefore expected, induces pressures to increase the share of public expenditure in GDP. An important reason is that the relative price of both government capital goods, heavily biased towards construction, and of government purchases of labour services, often covered by indexation, rises in response to monetary expansion. Inflationary expectations engendered by such expansion lead to a deterioration of the budgetary process, for programme managers will press hard for money-expenditure increases based on the higher end of the probability distribution of price rises. These factors are less commonly stressed than the effect of inflation on interest rates, which increases the interest burden on government debt. In chapter 11, Wellink and Halberstadt implicitly accept this analysis, though recognize that it is controversial: however, they add a point which is particularly relevant to a public-choice approach, namely that it is important to know how the monetary authorities perceive their role and how they relate their actions to the fiscal authorities. Certainly, control of public-expenditure growth has been one of the considerations that has led them to devise monetary targets which, among other things, are intended to place strict limits on the growth in public deficits. However, fixing of monetary targets and reaching them is not an easy matter, and in consequence the influence that these targets will exercise on public expenditure will be difficult to determine precisely and indirect. Perhaps the most significant result of determined action by the monetary authorities to control deficit financing is that it may force the fiscal authorities to conduct a dialogue with them, which, hopefully, could produce a consistent and sustained policy of public-expenditure control.

An obvious extension of the study of control would embrace the traditional areas of budgetary planning and control, and project appraisal, which were very much to the forefront of discussion in the 1960s and 1970s. However, given constraints on space, it seems more sensible to the editors to accept that such subjects, though important, have had adequate attention, and to concentrate on more recent attempts to improve the allocative and technical efficiency of goods supplied by the public sector by the use of market forces. In chapter 12, Blankart sets out in systematic fashion the gradations of public control which are associated with the application of market principles. At one end of the spectrum, the application may simply consist of facilitating entry into the provision of goods and services already supplied by the public sector through, for example, deregulation. In the middle, so to speak, lie such measures as outside contracting for services, for which the government is still responsible for delivery. At the other end of the spectrum will be the outright sale of government-owned industries and services to private operators. Blankart neatly contrasts the logical stance of the economist, based on principles of welfare economics, which determine the scope and the form of deregulation, with the willingness of politicians to respond to such ideas, which will be based on their 'vote-production function'. On the whole, he argues, the politicians' horizons are likely to be very restricted because deregulation and privatization are associated more with the loss of votes through loss of patronage than with the gain in votes from increasing consumer satisfaction and even extension of private ownership through the sale of public assets. Chapter 13, by Byatt, a senior British Treasury official who has made a close analysis of the problems, offers an authoritative commentary on the ambitious programme of privatization embarked upon by the British Conservative government in the early 1980s, illustrating very clearly the technical problems of how, in practice, governments can ensure that privatization is going to improve the prospects of greater competition, rather than merely to substitute private for public monopoly.

The choice between public control of production, and operation, in so far as it rests on economic reasoning, depends on the view taken of the feasibility of simulating competition in the former case and stimulating it, for example through deregulation, in the latter. The study by Marchese (chapter 14) has two interesting features, amongst others. The first is her exploration of transactions cost theory as a way of throwing light on the problems of making the choice. The second is the examination of the problem encountered in making comparisons of public and private performance in the same industry.

In the latter case, she draws attention to the earlier work of Giovanni Montemartini, one of the first writers on the problem of public-goods provision, who more than eighty years ago attempted to compare the relative efficiency of local public and private enterprises, to the detriment of the latter in the case of English electricity generation. Marchese's own empirical work is concerned with another problem of more relevance to the theme of this volume, namely the relationship between charging for public services and the level of public spending. Although commendably cautious in her statistical analysis, she demonstrates that the share in GDP for collective consumption plus sales of goods and services by government is negatively correlated with the percentage share of receipts from sales by the public sector. She is careful to add that other policy considerations will obviously be brought into play concerning whether or not pricing should be extended, such as the effects on income distribution and on inflationary pressures where systems of indexation are in operation.

CONCLUDING REMARKS

This review of the individual contribution leads to an obvious conclusion about the advice to be given by economists to policy-makers about how to contain the growth of the public-sector, *if that is what they want to do.* It is to introduce more competition in all 'markets' in which the public sector is involved. Constitutional rules which place a limit on the growth in public debt and on the relation between government expenditure and GDP growth have the function not only of limiting public-sector growth, but also of encouraging competition between bureaucrats in the supply of policy services to politicians, so that the former may be induced to give much more information about their activities, leading to questioning of their efficiency. As Martelli stresses, removing the imperfections in the political bargaining process within the legislature would make it more likely that governments, once committed to control of public-sector growth, can obtain the necessary political support. The severing of the nexus between taxes and the services for which they represent payment has led several contributors, in keeping with the well-established Wicksellian tradition in public finance, to call for a restoration of 'tax competition' between lower levels of government as well as hypothetication of revenues in a form which restores some link, however rough, between the level of services provided and the finance available. Following the same reasoning, Byatt and Marchese have illustrated the thinking behind putting out government services to competitive tender, but where the level of provision is still a government responsibility. The 'ultimate deterrent' to government-sector growth is to introduce privatization of public enterprises, but with careful attention paid to the need to combine privatization with removal of restrictions on freedom of entry into the relevant market for the previously nationalized or municipalized good or service (see chapters 12 and 13).

Several of the contributors have shared the experience of trying to persuade policy-makers that economic ideas are translatable into useful policy instruments, but none would wish us to underestimate the difficulties encountered in trying to do so. At least it can be claimed by the contributors that however far economists fall short as salesmen for their own ideas, at least there must be ideas to present in the first place. It may be claimed for this volume that its emphasis on the economic analysis of the political process, in a somewhat wider sense than that normally understood in public-choice theory, may promote a better understanding not only about how government grows, but also how that growth may be contained.

Part I
Analysing and Testing Public-Sector Growth

1

Interest Groups and the Political Economy of Government Size

Dennis C. Mueller and Peter Murrell

The size of government, both absolutely and as a percentage of gross national product, has in the last decade reached unprecedently high levels in all Western countries (Nutter, 1978). Although in most cases growth in government began long before the Second World War, it is only in recent years that the level of government activity has reached such proportions as to cause widespread concern and discussion in the political arena and in academia. In the economics literature, this concern has led to an increasing interest in positive analysis of the size of government (Borcherding, 1977; Brunner, 1978; Meltzer and Richard, 1978, 1981; Peltzman, 1980; Frey, 1982; Fratianni and Spinelli, 1982). This chapter is a contribution to that analysis.

Public choice is the natural framework in which to investigate the question of government size, and most economists have made use of propositions from this literature, such as the median-voter theorem, when examining this question. Mention is often made of the potential role of interest groups in expanding government. The implicit argument here is that interest groups favour government outlays of a quasi-private good nature and that log-rolling leads to a coalition of interest groups, which introduces a package of quasi-private goods into the public budget in the manner first described by Tullock (1959). Hence, the size of government becomes excessive. However, Breton (1974, pp. 192–3) has noted the possibility that there might be under-investment in government activities. Because interest groups favour targeted tax reductions, log-rolling resulting in 'Christmas-tree tax bills' decorated with numerous loopholes might then be expected to reduce government size, at least over time, by eroding the tax base. Thus it is still an open question whether the existence of effective special-interest groups leads to greater government expenditure.

Given the frequency with which interest groups are mentioned as a possible cause of excessive government spending, it is surprising how little has been done to develop and test hypotheses regarding the impact of interest groups on the size of governments (but see McCormick and Tollison, 1981). This chapter begins to remedy this deficiency. First, we analyze the fiscal concerns of interest groups as they relate to the size of government. Next, we explore the relationship between interest groups and the political process. Building on the theory developed in these sections, the hypotheses to be tested are then formulated and the results follow; the chapter concludes with brief comments on the findings.

THE FISCAL CONCERNS OF INTEREST GROUPS

The pioneering contribution to the size of government literature might be regarded as Lindahl's famous essay of 1919, for its objective was to determine the level of government output that would arise under a 'just' set of taxes. Ironically, perhaps, Lindahl's answer to the question has had an important influence on the public finance and public choice literature not because of the inherent justness of the outcomes at the Lindahl equilibrium, but due to their efficiency properties and the analogy between the Lindahl equilibrium with public goods and a competitive equilibrium with private goods. At the Lindahl equilibrium, each individual's marginal rate of substitution between public and private goods equals the ratio of (tax) prices paid for these goods, and the outcome is Pareto optimal.

The 'process' by which the equilibrium is reached in Lindahl's essay has been the subject of searching criticism at least as far back as Musgrave's first paper (1939). Much of modern public choice might be regarded as an effort to add realism to Lindahl-type discussions of government output determination, by modelling more explicitly the institutions through which decisions are made. Typically, a particular aspect of the collective decision process is taken up, for example, log-rolling, and the impact of introducing this part of reality into the discussion is examined. As might be expected from such a partial introduction of reality into a complex world, the results vary considerably, depending on precisely which institution is being modelled: the Lindahl equilibrium may not be attained, Pareto optimality may not be attained, no equilibrium may be attained, the government is 'too big', the government is 'too small', and occasionally a set of assumptions is even made under which the Lindahl equilibrium reappears as the outcome of a political process.[1]

A full modelling of all the institutional complexities of modern political systems has yet to be presented, and is not attempted here. Instead, this chapter is in the tradition of the existing literature, in that it examines deviations from the Lindahl equilibrium which are induced by the introduction of but one subset of the institutional factors determining the size of government. In modelling this subset – interest groups in the context of a parliamentary representative system – we abstract from other institutional factors characteristics that might affect the size of government. We do so, not in the belief that they are irrelevant, but in the hope that they are largely additive, and that a fuller modelling of political reality will leave our partial equilibrium predictions of the impact of interest groups intact.

Given that we have chosen to analyse movements away from the Lindahl equilibrium when examining the influence of interest groups,[2] we must first model the equilibrium which exists before those groups obtain undue influence on government decisions. This case is most easily envisaged by assuming the existence of *latent* interest groups, that is, groups of individuals with identical demands for public goods.[3] We can then analyse the behaviour of an interest group in terms of the decisions of a representative member who has income Y_i and a utility function, $U_i(G,X_i)$, defined over a public good (G) and a private good (X). Assume that the tax price of the public good for the representative member of interest group i is t_i, where the summation of all t_i over interest groups and individuals equals 1. In a Lindahl equilibrium, the tax prices t_i and government spending G are such that all members of society maximize their utility, given their budget constraint, $Y_i = t_i G + X_i$ (Johansen, 1963). The equilibrium is defined by the condition that:

$$\frac{U_{iG}}{U_{iX}} = t_i \qquad (1)$$

for all i, where $U_{iG} = \partial U_i / \partial G$.

We now proceed to analyse how government expenditures deviate from this equilibrium,[4] when interest groups can exert separate influence on government policy.

Changes in taxes

It is obvious from equation (1) that a reduction of t_i increases interest group i's preferred quantity of public good, if the public good is a normal good. Thus, an interest group which succeeded in lowering its tax price would favour an increase in the quantity of the public good. Of course, if one tax price falls, others must rise. Those individuals or groups whose tax prices rise will favour reductions in G. Thus, after the change in tax prices, there no longer exists a Lindahl equilibrium. Some groups must consume a quantity of the public good other than their most preferred quantity, given their tax shares.

With conflicting demands for G, the outcome will depend on the aggregation rule for combining individual preferences. It is reasonable to assume, at least for parliamentary systems, that an interest group that can exert sufficient influence to lower the taxes its members pay can also influence the level of government outlays. The plausibility of this assumption is argued below. If true, this assumption implies that interest-group action to reduce the taxes of its members will be combined with the expansion of government, even when all government expenditures go to finance pure public goods.

One might object to the above conclusion by noting that most taxes are not defined as a percentage of the cost of the public good, but as percentages of income, sales, property values or some such variable. Thus, a reduction of one group's tax rate *need not* be offset by a rise in another's. We agree, but maintain our assumption that an interest group that is successful in lowering its taxes will want and obtain higher taxes on other groups to finance the higher government expenditures it favours, given its lower tax outlays. Reductions in one source of tax revenue will be accompanied by increases from another. The introduction of new tax loopholes accompanies the closing of old ones.[5] Here it is worth noting that even in the USA, where this assumption is likely to be the weakest, log-rolling-type legislation opening up new loopholes often emerges out of tax-reform efforts that close other loopholes.

Changes in output characteristics

We now examine what happens to the level of government expenditure when the tax shares remain at the levels obtaining at the original Lindahl equilibrium, but an interest group is able to influence the nature of public output. Suppose that the interest group succeeds in changing the characteristics of the basket of public outputs to include a good whose benefits are targeted towards its members. One obvious form of targeted good is a direct cash transfer, allowing the interest group's members to increase their consumption of private goods. This case can be analysed by simply adding the targeted good, Z, to an individual's consumption by private good X_i, and rewriting U_i as $U_i(G,X_i+Z)$. Frequently, however, targeted public outlays are not pure transfers, but are in the form of redistribution in kind, like public housing, subsidized education or medicine, etc. These public expenditures, although having an obvious private-good characteristic for the recipients, also have spillover effects that make them partially of a public-good nature. These joint public and private-good properties of targeted public outlays can be most conveniently captured by assuming that a proportion θ of Z has public-good characteristics, whereas the proportion $(1-\theta)$ is equivalent to a private good. For a given targeted good Z going to interest group i, we can then rewrite U_i as $U_i(G+\theta Z,X_i+(1-\theta)Z)$, and for all other groups j, $U_j=U_j(G+\theta Z,X_j)$. The polar cases of Z being a pure private or public good are captured by θ being equal to zero or one, respectively.

Now let us examine the choice of Z and G. It is natural to assume that there is a constraint on the interest group's choice of Z: the nature of which constraint, imposed within the political system, depends upon the bargain struck between a political party and the interest group (see pp. 18–20 below). Here, we model this constraint by assuming that Z must be less than some maximum level m. Under the foregoing assumptions, the following two results can be obtained by maximizing

$$U_i(G+\theta Z, X_i+(1-\theta)Z)$$

subject to the new budget constraint, $Y_i=t_i(G+Z)+X_i$.

1. Interest group i always favours a level of targeted good Z equal to the maximum level m.[6]
2. The higher the upper bound, m, set on the provision of Z, the greater the amount of total government outlays $(G+Z)$ favoured by interest group i.[7]

Thus, an interest group which succeeds in introducing a quasi-private good into the public budget will favour an increase in the total size of government.

Now consider those individuals who consume Z only as a public good, that is, those with utility functions $U_j(G+\theta Z, X_j)$. One can establish the following two propositions for them.

3. Interest group j always favours imposing a limit of zero on the amount of the good Z targeted to interest group i.[8]
4. More important, given that a positive quantity of Z has been introduced into the basket of public outputs (i.e. $Z=m>0$), interest group j always favours an increase in the total amount of government expenditures $(G+Z)$ over what they would have wanted had $Z=0$.[9]

Proposition (3) is quite intuitive. To see the intuition behind proposition (4), recall that we start from a Lindahl equilibrium in which $U_{jG}/U_{jX}=t_j$. Now suppose that G would fall by just enough, following the provision of m units of Z, so that the new level of total government outlay just equalled the old. Each member of interest group j would then be consuming $(1-\theta)m$ units less of the public good and the same number of units of the private good. If $U_{iG}/U_{jX}=t_j$ at the original level of G, then if total government expenditure does not rise after Z is introduced, $U_{iG}/U_{jX}>t_j$. Members of j will favour giving up some private goods to replace the lost public goods which the introduction of Z into the budget produces.

Thus, we reach the perhaps surprising conclusion that once an interest group has succeeded in introducing a private or quasi-private good into the public budget, *all* members of society will agree that there should be an increase in total government expenditure over what it would have been (at the Lindahl equilibrium) without the new good. Conflict occurs only on whether a (quasi-) private good should be introduced at all, and, once it has been, perhaps over the magnitude of the increase. An interest group always favours the introduction of goods into the public budget, part of whose benefits are targeted directly at its members. The rest of the polity always opposes the provision of such goods.

INTEREST GROUPS IN THE POLITICAL PROCESS

Since the rest of the polity is a majority, in most cases, the question is how do interest groups succeed in winning special tax favours and targeted public outlays for their members?

We envisage a political process in which the government, the executive that is, is formed by the winning majority coalition in parliament. When a single party wins a majority of the seats in parliament in an election, it forms the government itself. When no party secures a majority, a coalition of parties with a majority of seats must come together to form a government. This type of system characterizes most democracies in the world today, the most important exception being the USA.

Interest groups attempt to win favours for their membership by offering to supply a party with votes. An interest group may endorse a party, supply campaign volunteers, or contribute funds to the party's campaign. Each of these translates into votes, which the interest group attempts to 'trade' with a given party in exchange for a promised tax reduction or redirection of public output, should the party succeed in becoming the government, or a part thereof.

Parties are assumed to maximize the number of votes they expect to win by agreeing to supply interest groups with special favours (see Downs, 1957). Alternatively, we might posit a party objective function containing votes and other 'ideological' variables (see Wittmann, 1973; Frey and Schneider, 1975). We prefer, however, to embed the ideological variables into the party's vote function. When the number of interest groups supporting the party is zero, the number of votes given by the vote function is the party's electoral support, based solely on its stance on ideological issues or on the package of pure public goods it proposes. We abstract from issues of competition for votes using ideology by assuming that that competition is independent of the competition for votes supplied by interest groups.

The above assumptions lead to a vote function for party i in a two-party system of the following form: $V_i = V_i(N_i, N_j)$, where V_i is the number of votes for the ith party, and $N_k, k = i, j$, is the number of interest groups supporting the kth party. In deciding which interest groups and how many to form agreements with, each party must consider the *net* marginal impact on V_i from adding a given interest group. Each interest group can both add and subtract votes from a party's expected total vote. A promise to cut one group's taxes, for example, may imply an increase in the taxes of some existing supporters of a party, driving them to another party.

In striking bargains, a party can be envisaged as ordering potential supporting interest groups from highest net increase in votes to lowest. Because some interest groups naturally lie closer to a party's ideological position than others, more voters may be added, and fewer driven away, after a bargain is concluded with these groups. Similarly, the interests of a given possible additional interest group could be more complementary to existing supporters than are those of other potential supporters. Thus, the support of this additional group will have a greater net effect than the support of other groups. As the number of interest groups supporting a party increases, however, eventually the party confronts interest groups whose interests are so far removed from the party's position on basic ideological issues and so much in conflict with the interests of groups already supporting the party that no mutually beneficial agreement can be reached. These considerations lead to the following predictions about the vote function, V:

$$V_{iN_i} \geq 0 \text{ and } V_{iN_iN_i} \leq 0$$

with strict inequalities for N_i in some neighbourhood of zero.

The opposing party's agreements with interest groups naturally affects a party's votes. Since individuals are often members of several groups, the support of interest groups for the opposition reduces the votes of a party: $\partial V_i/\partial N_j < 0$. The larger the number of interest groups supporting the opponents, the more those opponents encroach on the natural (in an ideological sense) voters for a party. Thus, the larger the number of interest groups supporting the opposing party, the easier it is for a party to increase (regain) support by adding another interest group:

$$V_{iN_iN_j} > 0$$

The above considerations suggest a competition for interest-group support among parties in which, at least in the early phases, each party is induced to increase the number of interest groups supporting it in response to an increase in the number of interest groups supporting its opponents. Whether this competition would lead to the absorption of all interest groups into the list of supporters of one or the other parties cannot be deduced without making more restrictive assumptions about the nature of the V functions, the form of competition, etc. What seems quite intuitive, however, is that the number of interest groups absorbed into the political process is an increasing function of the number of interest groups existing in the population. To see the intuition behind this assertion, assume that an equilibrium in the competition for interest groups has been reached in which M of the N interest groups in the population have formed (tacit) agreements to supply support to the existing parties ($M \leq N$). Now suppose the total number of interest groups in the population increases. Some of the new interest groups will most certainly be able to make promises of campaign support (that is, of votes) to one or more of the existing parties, upsetting the previous equilibrium. Given the characteristics of the V functions, the support of new or previously unattached interest groups will become more valuable to the other party(ies). A renewed competition will then ensue and will continue until a new equilibrium is attained in which a greater number of interest groups has struck bargains, exchanging votes for favours with the parties.

Competition for interest groups takes place prior to an election. After the election, one or more of the parties controlling a majority of the seats of parliament forms a government. This party or coalition of parties governs until the next election. During this period the party(ies) in the majority control both the executive and the parliament. In contrast to the United States, where winning coalitions on issues can vary within a session of the parliament (Congress), and thus one coalition can offset by, say, a tax change the gains of an interest group through an expenditure, in a parliamentary system *the* government lasts only so long as the majority control of the parliament does. Thus, in 'paying off' interest groups for their previous support, the winning party(ies) can assure that a combination of taxes and expenditure is effected that does leave its supporting interest groups better off. Given the arguments of the previous section, this coalition is almost certain to favour a level of government expenditure in excess of that which would occur at a Lindahl equilibrium.

The next election brings a new competition for interest groups, most likely some reshuffling of interest-group support among the parties, perhaps a new government. Almost certainly, the set of interest groups represented in the new government will not be identical to those in the previous one. Some of these may have felt the previous level of government expenditure excessive. Thus, one cannot predict that this new set of interest groups represented in parliament favours an increase in expenditure over the previous level. One can predict, again on the basis of the previous section's analysis, a *level* of government outlays in excess of the Lindahl equilibrium. Our theory of interest-group politics predicts excessive *levels* of government expenditure, not necessarily excessive *growth* in the size of government.

By analogy with oligopoly models, one might expect competition for interest groups to be more intense, the greater the number of political parties. The more parties there are, for example, the closer any one interest group is likely to come to the ideological position of a given party, and the more likely it is that an agreement between *a* party and the interest group is reached. Thus, we expect the absorption of interest groups into the political process to be greater, the greater the number of parties in a polity, and thus the influence of interest groups on the size of government to increase with the number of political parties.

A full development of the outcomes of a competition for interest-group support is beyond the intention of this chapter. Our purpose in this section is simply to motivate the empirical work by showing why an absorption of interest groups into the political process can be expected, and why the number of interest groups having an influence on political outcomes can be expected to be positively related to the number of interest groups in a society. Beyond this we have suggested a positive link between the number of political parties and the influence of interest groups. We turn now to the specific models to be tested.

SIZE OF GOVERNMENT EQUATION

In discussing the impact of interest groups on the size of government, it has been conceptually useful to employ the familiar Lindahl equilibrium as a reference point. However, we now confront the difficulty of attempting to estimate the level of government expenditure at the Lindahl equilibrium. The theory tells us that the cost of public output relative to private goods is important, as well as income, and these two variables (or proxies thereof) figure importantly in our equations. Beyond these, we are left with 'tastes' as the key explanatory variable.

In our equation, we shall include several variables gleaned from the public choice/government expenditure literature that do not assume an interest group–party competition–parliamentary system as posited here. We do so not in the pretence that we are testing these alternative models of government against our own, but, as stated above, under the assumption that the impact of these other factors may be additive. We thus make the strong prediction that the effect of interest groups on the size of government will remain as predicted in the presence of additional institutional complexity, and begin to test this additional assumption by adding several of the variables which other studies have posited to be determinants of the size of government.

The basic equation

We seek to explain the relative size of government across countries. No single measure can capture fully the concept of governmental size. We shall therefore employ several alternative dependent variables that measure government size as a percentage of total economic activity. These variables are listed and defined in table 1.1, together with all the other variables used in this study. The data are for 1970, unless otherwise noted.

The traditional discussion of the role of government views government as a provider of public goods. By definition, public goods have significant scale-economy attributes. The price per capita of an army, of a judicial system, of central government should fall as the population of a country increases. Thus, as population increases the relative cost of public goods should decline. As the demand for public goods is likely to be price inelastic, probably infinitely so for variables such as legislative costs, the fraction of total income devoted to government should decline as population increases.

McCormick and Tollison (1981) assume all government activity consists of wealth transfers. They hypothesize that interest groups have more success using government to make these transfers, the less that diligent citizens are policing government, that is, the more citizen free-riding there is. Since free-riding increases with population, they predict a positive correlation between population and government size. The coefficient on population can be used

Table 1.1 *Variables in the size of government equation*

	Variable name	*Concept measured*	*Predicted sign of coefficient*	*Variable definition*
1.	EXP	Size of government		Total outlays of government as a percentage of GDP
2.	TAX	Size of government		Total tax revenue as a percentage of GDP
3.	CONS	Size of government		Government final consumption as a percentage of GDP
4.	EXPNP	Non-payroll government size		Variable 1 minus public payroll expenditures as a proportion of GDP
5.	TAXNP	Non-payroll government size		Variable 2 minus public payroll expenditures as a proportion of GDP
6.	MINC	Median income	+	Variable 8 multiplied by variable 13
7.	PROG	Tax price/progressivity	−	Average income plus social security tax rate of an average production worker divided by total tax revenue as a proportion of GDP[1]
8.	INC	Mean income	+	Per-capita GDP as a percentage of US per-capita GDP
9.	POP	Population	−	Population in millions
10.	EFRC	Ethnic fractionalization	−	Probability that two randomly selected members of the population will not be from the same ethnolinguistic group
11.	NIG	Number of interest groups	+	Count of the number of interest groups listed for each country in a standard reference work
12.	PFRC	Political fractionalization	+	Probability that two randomly selected members of parliament will not be from the same party
13.	SKEW	Skewness of income distribution	+/−	Total income of the middle quintile of households in the income distribution as a proportion of average household income divided by 5[2]
14.	VOTE	Degree of enfranchisement	+	Percentage of adult population voting in a general election
15.	PUEM	Size of bureaucracy	+	Public employees as a percentage of total workforce
16.	DATE	Start of modernization		Year in which a country began the modernization process

[1] Since, to our knowledge, no information is available on the tax levels of the median voter in the OECD countries, we took the 'average production worker with a wife and two children' as a proxy for the median voter. The figures are for 1974, the earliest data available.

[2] Definitions of income, households, etc. vary a great deal between countries. For most countries, data are based on pre-tax post-transfer income.

Sources: Numbers refer to variable numbers.

1. OECD, 1982a, p. 59.
2. OECD, 1980a, p. 43.
3. OECD, 1982a, p. 58.

4. & 5. Payroll expenditure as a proportion of GDP were constructed by using variable 15 and information on earnings in the public sector relative to those in the private sector (OECD, 1982b, pp. 34–6).

7. OECD, 1980b, p. 123, table 35 and OECD, 1980a, p. 43.
8. Kravis, Heston and Summers, 1978, pp. 232–7, col. (5).
9. United Nations, 1972, pp. 140–4.
10. Taylor and Hudson, 1972, pp. 271–4.
11. *Internationales Verzeichnis der Wirtschaftsverbände*, 1973. All groups listed in this work were included in the data. The groups are industry and trade associations, labour unions, and chambers of commerce.
12. Taylor and Hudson, 1972, p. 48. The data refer to some point in 1963–8.
13. Sawyer, 1976, pp. 14, 23–5.
14. Taylor and Hudson, 1972, pp. 54–6. The data refer to some point in the 1960s.
15. OECD, 1982b, p. 12.
16. Black (1966) has identified periods during which the 'consolidation of modernizing leadership' and 'economic and social transformation' took place. DATE is the average of the beginning years of these two periods.

to test whether total government activity appears more as a public good or a wealth transfer.

In addition to relative cost (as proxied by population), theory leads us to expect a positive relationship between income and public-good demand. Since we seek to explain the relative size of national government expenditure, a positive relationship between income and government in fact implies that the income elasticity of a nation's demand for public goods exceed the income elasticity of its demand for private goods, which is the assumption usually made and is typically referred to as Wagner's law (see, Pryor, 1968, p. 50). Traditionally, empirical studies of government expenditure have employed the mean income of the policy as the explanatory variable for testing Wagner's law, and we do so also, in part, because it is available for more countries than other income measures.

We employ a second, demographic variable besides population to capture the degree of ethnic fractionalization in a country. Ethnic fractionalization might be viewed as a form of tastes variable, but we view it as more related to the transaction costs of reaching collective decisions. The greater the ethnic fractionalization, the greater the difficulty of reaching collective decisions, and the smaller is the expected size of government.

We turn now to those variables that emerge explicitly from the public-choice literature.

Public-choice variables

Our main concern is with the impact of interest groups on the relative size of government. We therefore seek a measure of interest-group strength. The discussion in the previous section indicates that parties trade political favours for votes. The more votes an interest group can promise, the larger the political favour it can demand in exchange. The logical choice of a measure of the ability that an interest group has to influence government expenditure is the number of votes it can promise.

There are severe difficulties in trying to construct an appropriate weight for each interest group. What determines the terms of the bargain is the *net* number of votes an interest group can provide. This number depends on which party the interest group supports, what other interest groups support that party when the bargain is struck, and the constellation of interest-group support across other parties. A method for distilling the net marginal impact of an interest group across a wide variety of countries is not readily apparent.

It should be noted that the most obvious choices of measures of strength of an interest group are not satisfactory. For example, strength is not a function of the number of members in any simple way. An industry trade association may have relatively few members, but exert a large impact through substantial financial contributions to a party. Citizens' groups of similar size may vary greatly in their impacts, depending on the intensity of the members' concerns.

For the foregoing reasons and due to the non-availability of suitable alternative data, we have chosen to use the absolute number of interest groups formally operating in a country as the measure of interest-group strength. In doing so, we make the implicit assumption that the expected impact of a single interest group is the same across countries.

The second variable that emerges out of our discussion of political competition and the size of government is the number of political parties. As with interest groups, there are different ways to weigh parties when counting them. We use as our measure political fractionalization, the probability that two randomly selected members of parliament do not belong to the same party.

The most frequently used public-choice model in studies of local government expenditure is the median-voter model (see Bergstrom and Goodman, 1973; Borcherding and Deacon, 1972; Deacon, 1978; Pommerehne, 1978). To apply this model to explain total government expenditure at the national level, one needs to make several rather heroic assumptions.[10] Nevertheless, keeping in mind that our objective is to ensure that our tests of the effects of interest groups are not biased by the omission of relevant variables, we shall include proxies for the key variables contained in this model.

The median-voter literature forces two basic modifications to the list of variables so far compiled. It replaces mean income with the income of the median voter, and adds the median voter's tax price. Ideally, the tax-price variable should measure the cost to the median voter of one unit of the public good (Bergstrom and Goodman, 1973, p. 293). Thus, the tax price should take into account both the relative price of public goods and the tax share of the median voter. As we do not have information on relative price, our tax-price variable captures only the tax-share aspect of tax price. Our variable is an estimate of the progressivity of the tax structure and is used on the assumption that, *ceteris paribus*, the more progressive the tax structure, the lower the relative tax price of the median voter, and the higher the expected relative size of government expenditures.

Two additional studies have appeared that rely on the median-voter theorem and explicitly seek to explain the size or growth in size of government. Both assume that all government activity involves only redistribution and that the amount of redistribution is related to the skewness of the distribution of income. Meltzer and Richard (1981) use the median-voter theorem to argue that more redistribution takes place (and thus more governmental activity) the lower the income of the median voter, relative to average income. Peltzman predicts the reverse sign and claims empirical support for his hypothesis. Thus, we include a measure of the relative income of the median voter. Our intention, however, is not to conduct a test of these rival theories, but rather to ensure that our results on interest-group influence are not biased by omitting relevant variables.

An important element of Meltzer and Richard's account of the growth in government is the extension of the voting franchise to increasing numbers of voters, whose income falls below the mean. We test for this enfranchisement effect directly, by including as a separate explanatory variable the percentage of the adult population which votes. Our supposition here, based on considerable empirical support (see Frey, 1971; Verba and Nie, 1972; Tollison and Willett, 1973; and references therein) is that lower-income groups tend to be disproportionately excluded from voting *de facto*, if not *de jure*. Thus, higher percentages of voters in a population means higher percentages of low-income voters relative to high-income voters, and should lead to greater redistribution and government size.

Following Niskanen (1971), many economists have argued that the strength of the bureaucracy is important in determining the size of the government. As a crude measure of bureaucratic strength, we have chosen the proportion of government workers in the workforce. Of course, greater numbers of government workers are associated with larger government size, purely because government payrolls are one element of government expenditure. To avoid embodying this tautological effect in the regressions when the strength of bureaucracy was included as an independent variable, the dependent variables were redefined by netting out the size of the government payrolls.[11]

Before presenting the results, two points must be emphasized. First, some of the variables we have constructed are very imperfect measures of the concepts they are supposed to represent. Such imperfections are inherent in cross-national research. Second, the variables discussed in this section are viewed as complements, not substitutes, to interest-group strength in explaining government size. Our purpose in including these additional variables is not to test their underlying theories *against* the interest-group hypothesis, but *along* with it. Thus, we have decided that, even though some concepts are measured highly imperfectly, it is better to include the relevant variables in the tests rather than omit them. By including these variables, we can ensure that any positive results we find for interest groups are not spuriously derived due to the omission of some relevant variable.

THE RESULTS

Ordinary least squares estimates

The hypothesis put forward pertain to developed countries in which interest groups have the potential for influencing government decisions. A natural choice of sample meeting this criterion is the OECD countries. Although data for these countries are more plentiful than for most others, even for these, observations on all countries are not available for each variable. We thus confront a trade-off between number of observations and number of variables in any equation. Rather than arbitrarily select a given subset of variables and subsample of countries, we have chosen to present a spectrum of results running from maximum number of observations and fewest explanatory variables to fewest observations and maximum number of variables. The reader is thus free to make his own trade-off.

The first three equations in table 1.2 provide the benchmark for measuring the influence of interest groups and the other public-choice variables on the relative size of government. Population has a negative coefficient in each equation, consistent with the hypothesis that total government output has, on average, public-good characteristics.[12] Both income and ethnic fractionalization have the predicted signs in all three equations, although only income is statistically significant in each.

The fit is improved considerably by the inclusion of our two public-choice variables, number of interest groups and political fractionalization. The former is significant at the 99 per cent level in all three equations, political fractionalization is significant at the 5 per cent level (one tail test) in one equation. The performance of both population and ethnic fractionalization is noticeably improved by the addition of the number of interest groups and political fractionalization. The performance of mean income is worsened.

For 21 countries, we were able to measure median income and skewness of the income distribution. When median income is introduced, its coefficient is positive in all three equations and significant in two. In those three equations, and the following five, we tried mean income and median income as alternatives, and median income performed better, in terms of *t*-values, all eight times. This suggests perhaps that there may be some weak, superior predictive power in the median-voter theorem, even at this level of aggregation.

Both the Meltzer–Richard and Peltzman theories posit a relationship between the pre-transfer skewness of the income distribution and government size. Our skewness measure is post-transfer, and thus our results are biased away from the negative coefficient the Meltzer–Richard theory predicts and toward the positive coefficient Peltzman expects. The consistently negative coefficient on this variable, in spite of this bias, might be regarded as some support for the Meltzer–Richard hypothesis. The statistical performance of this variable remained weak in the remaining equations also, and it is omitted to save a degree of freedom.

The performance of the other variables in equations 7–9 is similar to that in equations 4–6, but with lower *t*-values, as can be expected, given the addition of a variable which performs poorly. The number of interest groups remains significant in all three equations, however.

To add VOTE, the percentage of the population which votes, another three countries must be dropped from the sample. Equations 10–12 present the results with the VOTE variable included. Its coefficient is positive as predicted, large and significant in all three equations. Its inclusion increases $\bar{R}^2$ visibly, and generally increases the *t*-statistics on the other variables. For the first time, the intercept is not significantly different from zero, as one's intuition suggests it should be. Equations 10–12 are clearly the best specifications of the government-size equation in the table.

Table 1.2 *Regression results using ordinary least squares (t-statistics in parentheses)*

Dependent variable	Number of observations	$\bar{R}^2$	Intercept	*POP*	*EFRC*	*PROG*	*INC*	*MINC*	*NIG*	*PFRC*	*SKEW*	*VOTE*	*PUEM*
1. EXP	24	0.24	18.4	−0.045	−0.117		0.29						
			(3.30)	(−1.35)	(−1.55)		(3.04)						
2. TAX	24	0.42	15.5	−0.055	−0.106		0.30						
			(3.66)	(−2.17)	(−1.85)		(4.22)						
3. CONS	24	0.11	8.03	−0.003	−0.019		0.11						
			(2.96)	(−0.21)	(−0.52)		(2.35)						
4. EXP	24	0.51	24.2	−0.137	−0.161		0.06		0.006	0.109			
			(5.03)	(−3.29)	(−2.50)		(0.59)		(3.44)	(1.70)			
5. TAX	24	0.67	20.6	−0.136	−0.149		0.14		0.005	0.065			
			(5.92)	(−4.55)	(3.21)		(1.83)		(4.03)	(1.40)			
6. CONS	24	0.32	10.8	−0.051	−0.050		0.07		0.003	0.008			
			(4.19)	(−2.30)	(−1.47)		(1.18)		(2.76)	(−0.25)			
7. EXP	21	0.55	29.0	−0.144	−0.201	−6.52		0.0001	0.006	0.101	−0.003		
			(2.16)	(−3.42)	(−3.02)	(−1.40)		(0.67)	(3.31)	(1.45)	(−0.02)		
8. TAX	21	0.69	32.1	−0.141	−0.174	−4.80		0.0002	0.005	0.077	−0.137		
			(3.27)	(−4.61)	(−3.60)	(−1.41)		(2.11)	(3.75)	(1.51)	(−0.97)		
9. CONS	21	0.47	16.9	−0.054	−0.061	1.09		0.0002	0.002	−0.006	−0.120		
			(2.61)	(−2.65)	(−1.90)	(0.49)		(2.36)	(2.45)	(−0.17)	(−1.28)		
10. EXP	18	0.70	3.44	−0.124	−0.107	−2.89		0.0001	0.005	0.122		0.258	
			(0.267)	(−3.61)	(−1.67)	(−0.84)		(1.23)	(3.48)	(1.04)		(3.02)	
11. TAX	18	0.82	−2.94	−0.109	−0.072	−0.225		0.0002	0.004	0.135		0.224	
			(−0.34)	(−4.79)	(−1.70)	(−0.10)		(3.17)	(3.98)	(1.73)		(3.94)	
12. CONS	18	0.54	−4.70	−0.033	−0.387	3.97		0.0001	0.002	0.019		0.119	
			(−0.65)	(−1.72)	(−0.01)	(2.07)		(2.58)	(1.75)	(0.29)		(2.49)	
13. EXPNP	14	0.93	−20.1	−0.181	−0.231	−14.1		0.0003	0.009	0.304		0.182	0.017
			(−3.01)	(−7.24)	(−6.99)	(−6.30)		(2.00)	(8.98)	(4.13)		(2.75)	(0.04)
14. TAXNP	14	0.64	−14.0	−0.147	−0.210	−7.53		0.0000	0.007	0.361		0.013	0.057
			(−1.01)	(−2.95)	(−3.19)	(−1.69)		(0.08)	(3.83)	(2.46)		(0.10)	(0.80)

The last two equations in table 1.2 include the public employment variable. Given the scant number of degrees of freedom, and the crudeness of the test, the insignificance of this variable should not be interpreted as strong evidence against the bureaucratic-influence theory of government size. Our main concern is to ensure that this variable does not detract from the explanatory power of the interest-group and political-party variables. It does not and, if anything, the performance of the interest-group variable is enhanced. This improvement could be due to the change in the dependent variable used. The new dependent variable is government expenditure exclusive of personnel costs. This is exactly the part of expenditure that interest groups would be most eager to influence. Thus, the results in the last two lines of table 1.2 are reassuring, in that the interest-group variable performs well in explaining these two new dependent variables.

Since the scale of the interest-group variable will not be known to most readers, it will be useful to give more information to facilitate interpretation of coefficient estimates. This information is best conveyed through elasticity estimates. Thus, in equation 10, for example, the elasticity at the sample mean of the interest-group variable is 0.18. (The equivalent statistic for equation 11 is 0.15 and for equation 12, 0.12.) This indicates that, *ceteris paribus*, in a country which is at the sample mean (government expenditure 35 per cent of GDP), a 10 per cent increase in numbers of interest groups will lead to an extra 0.7 per cent of GDP flowing through the government sector.

Simultaneous equation estimates

Objections to the foregoing results could arise from the possibility of two-way causation and therefore simultaneous equations bias. It has been hypothesized that increases in the size of government spur the formation of interest groups (Eckstein, 1963, p. 413). Although Murrell (1983) has shown that there is some doubt that this hypothesis is correct, our intention is not to debate its veracity, but to show that our results hold, even if it is correct. Thus, we seek exogeneous variables which can be used in two-stage least squares estimates of the equations explaining government size.

In a study examining the factors affecting the number of interest groups in a country, Murrell (1983) has found population and 'the beginning year of modern economic development' to be the most important variables. The use of the latter variable has sound theoretical underpinnings in the work of Olson (1982). Given that population is already included in the equations predicting government expenditure, the 'beginning year of development' variable (DATE – see table 1.1) was used as an exogeneous variable when deriving two-stage least squares estimates of the equations explaining government size (see table 1.3). These estimates are completely consistent with those of table 1.2. There is some slight reduction in the *t*-statistics for the interest-group variable, but nevertheless of eleven statistics, five are

Table 1.3 *Regression results using two-stage least squares (t-statistics in parentheses)*

Dependent variable	*Number of observations*	$\bar{R}^2$	*Intercept*	*POP*	*EFRC*	*PROG*	*INC*	*MINC*	*NIG*	*PFRC*	*SKEW*	*VOTE*	*PUEM*
EXP	24	0.47	26.4	−0.172	−0.182		0.001		0.008	0.120			
			(4.67)	(−2.81)	(−2.54)		(0.10)		(2.59)	(1.76)			
TAX	24	0.61	22.8	−0.174	−0.171		0.009		0.007	0.076			
			(5.39)	(−3.78)	(−3.19)		(0.93)		(3.10)	(1.49)			
CONS	24	0.31	10.5	−0.047	−0.048		0.007		0.002	−0.010			
			(3.62)	(−1.48)	(−1.30)		(1.11)		(1.45)	(−0.28)			
EXP	21	0.54	29.7	−0.156	−0.208	−6.60		0.000	0.007	0.104	−0.003		
			(2.16)	(−2.68)	(−2.94)	(−1.41)		(0.47)	(2.23)	(1.47)	(−0.01)		
TAX	21	0.67	33.5	−0.162	−0.186	−4.95		0.002	0.006	0.081	−0.137		
			(3.24)	(−3.73)	(−3.52)	(−1.41)		(1.53)	(2.75)	(1.53)	(−0.93)		
CONS	21	0.47	16.8	−0.052	−0.060	1.10		0.002	0.002	−0.006	−0.120		
			(2.56)	(−1.89)	(−1.78)	(0.49)		(2.14)	(1.43)	(−0.18)	(−1.29)		
EXP	18	0.69	3.61	−0.130	−0.112	−2.93		0.001	0.006	0.130		0.257	
			(0.28)	(−2.99)	(−1.65)	(−0.852)		(0.95)	(2.43)	(1.06)		(2.99)	
TAX	18	0.81	−2.5	−0.125	−0.086	−0.34		0.0002	0.005	0.155		0.221	
			(−0.28)	(−4.11)	(−1.81)	(−0.144)		(2.18)	(3.10)	(1.81)		(3.68)	
CONS	18	0.54	−4.75	−0.031	0.001	4.00		0.001	0.001	0.016		0.120	
			(−0.66)	(−1.27)	(0.37)	(2.08)		(2.30)	(1.03)	(0.24)		(2.49)	
EXPNP	14	0.93	−21.0	−0.182	−0.231	−14.1		0.002	0.009	0.305		0.182	0.018
			(3.01)	(−6.98)	(−6.92)	(−6.22)		(2.00)	(8.46)	(4.11)		(2.75)	(0.05)
TAXNP	14	0.64	−13.7	−0.139	−0.204	−7.13		0.000	0.007	0.353		0.015	0.542
			(−0.98)	(−2.67)	(−3.06)	(−1.57)		(0.11)	(3.40)	(2.38)		(0.12)	(0.76)

significant at the 99 per cent level, three at the 95 per cent level, and two at the 90 per cent level.

SUMMARY AND CONCLUSIONS

This essay is a first attempt to develop and test the hypothesis that interest groups increase the size of government. The theoretical results show that the formation of bargains between parties and interest groups leads to an increase in government size. The sign of the expected effect on government size is independent of whether an interest group influences its own tax rate or the direction of public expenditure. The empirical results support the theory in that the number of interest groups is positively related to the relative size of government. This relationship is robust with respect to substantial changes in both the composition of the sample of countries and the explanatory variables in the equation.

The two most important explanatory variables other than the number of interest groups proved to be population and the percentage of the population voting. The consistently negative relationship between relative government size and population is noteworthy, since several recent public-choice theories of government size have assumed that the *only* government output is redistribution. However, the negative relationship, implying that an increase in population leads to a less than proportionate increase in the size of government, shows that government expenditure exhibits a most basic public-good characteristic.

The percentage of the population voting, which probably is closely related to the proportion of voters with incomes below the median, consistently has a positive and significant impact on the size of government. The Meltzer–Richard hypothesis that greater participation by low-income voters leads to more redistribution and greater government size is strongly supported.

Other variables perform less consistently and/or with lower statistical significance. Since most of these variables are included to account for determinants of government size unrelated to the interest-group hypothesis, this performance does not reflect on that hypothesis. The one exception to this generalization is the consistent, but somewhat weak positive contribution of the party-fractionalization variable. We argue that the number of political parties and the number of interest groups have complementary, positive impacts on the size of government. But the effect of the number of political parties is obviously dependent on many economic and political factors in a country. Perhaps identification of these factors is necessary to isolate the impact of this variable on government size. However, such a task is beyond the scope of this chapter.

Given the level of aggregation, the number of observations and the rough measurement of some concepts, our results must be regarded as tentative. However, these results do indicate promising approaches to further research.

In particular, the substantial contribution of the public-choice variables to explaining government size indicates a potentially high pay-off from developing this line of research. Especially intriguing would be further investigation of the effects of two variables we found to be consistently significant: voter participation and number of interest groups.

The theory underlying both voter and interest-group influence points to redistributive activities. The voter-participation variable is related to rich-to-poor redistribution and posits a direct responsiveness of government outcomes to voter preferences through the operation of the median-voter theorem. In contrast, the interest-group variable is included on the presumption that voter preferences are transmitted indirectly via interest groups and interparty competition, and makes no predictions about the direction in which redistribution flows. However, since the largest single category of interest groups in most countries is, by far, industry trade associations,[13] one might posit poor-to-rich redistribution as the most likely consequence of interest-group influence. Thus, the possibility exists that the influence of the two variables on the distribution of income might be largely offsetting, while their influence on the size of government is cumulative. Disaggregating the effects of these and other public-choice variables is a promising avenue for future research.

NOTES

1 With respect to the last, see Bowen (1943) and Bergstrom (1979). Other results in the literature are surveyed by Mueller (1979).

2 The most obvious alternative-solution concept to use as a benchmark is the government output favoured by the median voter. But to apply the median-voter model to this question, we must assume taxes are fixed and government output has a single dimension. Neither of these assumptions seems plausible when analysing interest-group behaviour, which is assumed to affect government outcomes either by changing taxes or adding private goods (dimensions) to public output.

3 An interest group can be regarded as a club, whose members have common characteristics. If the population is large enough, individuals will sort themselves into common interest clubs whose members have homogeneous demands for public goods (Pauly, 1967, 1970; McGuire, 1972, 1974). We can thus assume that interest groups make their collective decisions via the unanimity rule and analyse the behaviour of interest groups in terms of a representative member.

4 Our benchmark Lindahl equilibrium is assumed to be the one corresponding to the pre-tax, pre-expenditure distribution of wealth.

5 For a similar analysis, see Buchanan and Pauly (1970).

6 Treat $m \geq Z$ as an additional constraint and maximize the following expression (i subscripts omitted):

$$U(G+\theta Z, X+(1-\theta)Z)) + \lambda(Y - t(G+Z) - X) + \eta(m-Z) \qquad (1')$$

Taking partial derivatives of equation (1′) with respect to G and X we obtain, as before:

$$U_G/U_X = t \tag{2'}$$

Taking partial derivatives of equation (1′) with respect to Z we obtain:

$$\theta U_G + (1-\theta)U_X - \lambda t - \eta = 0 \tag{3'}$$

Substituting from equations (2′) and (3′) and rearranging, we have:

$$(1-\theta)U_G[(1/t)-1] = \eta \tag{4'}$$

and by the Kuhn–Tucker theorem:

$$(\eta > 0) \rightarrow (Z = m) \tag{5'}$$

In this proof, we have ignored the constraints $G \geqq 0$ and $X_i \geqq 0$. If these constraints were introduced, the results would show that $Z < m$ is possible, if m were larger than the initial levels of either public or private spending. Such a case seems of no interest.

7 From the previous note we can rewrite U as:

$$U(G+\theta m,\ X+(1-\theta)m) \tag{6'}$$

Taking the total differential of equation (2′) and substituting from equation (6′) we obtain:

$$U_{GG}(\mathrm{d}G+\theta\mathrm{d}m) + U_{GX}(\mathrm{d}X+(1-\theta)\mathrm{d}m) = tU_{XG}(\mathrm{d}G+\theta\mathrm{d}m) + tU_{XX}(\mathrm{d}X+(1-\theta)\mathrm{d}m) \tag{7'}$$

Using the total differential of the budget constraint to remove $\mathrm{d}X$ and some algebra, one obtains:

$$\frac{\mathrm{d}G}{\mathrm{d}m} = -1 + (1+\theta)\left[\frac{U_{GG} - U_{GX}(t+1) + tU_{XX}}{U_{GG} - 2tU_{GX} + t^2 U_{XX}}\right] \tag{8'}$$

The numerator of the factor in brackets can be shown to be negative if G and X are both normal goods. The denominator is negative by the second-order conditions. Thus, $\mathrm{d}G/\mathrm{d}m > -1$, implying:

$$\mathrm{d}(G+m)/\mathrm{d}m > 0 \tag{9'}$$

8 Proceeding as in note 6 except that η is now the multiplier attached to the constraint $Z \geqq 0$, we obtain as the analogue to (3′):

$$(\theta - 1)U_G = -\eta \tag{10'}$$

so that, again, using the Kuhn–Tucker theorem:

$$(\eta > 0) \rightarrow (Z = 0) \tag{11'}$$

9 Proceeding as in note 7, using $U(\mathrm{G}+\theta m, X)$ we obtain:

$$\frac{\mathrm{d}G}{\mathrm{d}m} = -1 + (1+\theta)\left[\frac{U_{GG} - tU_{XG}}{U_{GG} - 2tU_{GX} + t^2 U_{XX}}\right] \qquad (12')$$

as the analogue expression to equation (8′). Since the denominator is negative, from the second-order conditions, and $(U_{GG} - tU_{XG})$ is negative if X is a normal good, equation (12′) implies $\mathrm{d}G/\mathrm{d}M > -1$, and equation (9′) again holds.

10 See note 2. For a lengthy critique of the median-voter literature as applied to explaining levels of local government expenditures, see Romer and Rosenthal (1979).

11 This was only possible for two of the dependent variables. Final consumption expenditure is only a part of total government expenditure and there exist no data showing how many public employees are connected solely with this part.

12 McCormick and Tollison (1981, ch. 3) find that population size is positively related to regulation activities at the state level, and that it is consistent with their hypothesis that large population size leads to less vigilant citizen policing of government and thus more wealth transfer activities by government. The two results need not be contradictory. Some government activities of a particularly redistributive nature may grow larger as population increases, whereas those with public-good characteristics become relatively smaller. Our results indicate that the latter tendency dominates for total government output at the national level.

13 Interesting in this connection is Fratianni and Spinelli's (1982) observation that special government programmes catering to business interest groups are becoming increasingly important in Italy.

REFERENCES

Bergstrom, T. C. (1979), 'When does majority rule supply public goods efficiently?', *Scandinavian Journal of Economics*, vol. 81, pp. 217–26.

Bergstrom, T. C. and Goodman, R. P. (1973), 'Private demands for public goods', *American Economic Review*, vol. 63, pp. 280–96.

Black, C. C. (1966), *The Dynamics of Modernization: A Study in Comparative History*, New York: Harper and Row.

Borcherding, T. E. (ed.) (1977), *Budgets and Bureaucrats*, Durham: Duke University Press.

Borcherding, T. E. and Deacon, R. T. (1972), 'The demand for the services of non-federal governments', *American Economic Review*, vol. 62, pp. 891–901.

Bowen, H. R. (1943), 'The interpretation of voting in the allocation of economic resources', *Quarterly Journal of Economics*, vol. 58, pp. 27–48.

Breton, A. (1974), *The Economic Theory of Representative Government*, Chicago: Aldine.

Brunner, K. (1978), 'Reflections on the political economy of government: the persistent growth of government', *Schweizerische Zeitschrift Volkswirtschaft und Statistik*, vol. 114, pp. 649–80.

Buchanan, J. M. and Pauly, M. V. (1970), 'On the incidence of tax deductibility', *National Tax Journal*, May, pp. 269–76.

Buchanan, J. M. and Wagner, R. R. (1977), *Democracy in Deficit: The Political Legacy of Lord Keynes*, New York: Academic Press.

Deacon, R. T. (1978), 'A demand model for the local public sector', *Review of Economics and Statistics*, vol. 60, pp. 184–92.

Downs, A. (1957), *An Economic Theory of Democracy*, New York: Harper and Row.

Eckstein, H. (1963), 'The determinants of pressure group politics, in H. Eckstein and D. E. Apter (eds), *Comparative Politics: A Reader*, New York: Free Press.

Fratianni, M. and Spinelli, F. (1982), 'The growth of government in Italy: evidence from 1861 to 1979', *Public Choice*, vol. 39, pp. 221–43.

Frey, B. S. (1971), 'Why do high income people participate more in politics?' *Public Choice*, pp. 101–5.

Frey, B. S. (1982), 'The public choice approach to the explanation of collective consumption', in R. C. O. Matthews and G. B. Stafford (eds), *The Grants Economy and Collective Consumption*, London: Macmillan.

Frey, B. S. and Schneider, F. (1975), 'On the modelling of politico-economic interdependence', *European Journal of Political Research*, vol. 3, pp. 339–60.

Internationales Verzeichnis der Wirtschaftsverbände (1973), Munich: K. G. Saur Verlag.

Johansen, L. (1963), 'Some notes on the Lindahl theory of determination of public expenditures', *International Economics Review*, vol. 4, pp. 346–58.

Kravis, I. B., Heston, A. W. and Summers, R. (1978), 'Real GDP per capita for more than one hundred countries', *Economic Journal*, vol. 88, pp. 215–42.

Lindahl, E. (1919), 'Just taxation – a positive solution', (first published in German), English translation in R. A. Musgrave and A. T. Peacock (eds), (1967), *Classics in the Theory of Public Finance*, London: Macmillan and New York: St Martin's Press.

McCormick, R. E. and Tollison, R. D. (1981), *Politicians, Legislation, and the Economy*, The Hague: Martinus Nÿhoff.

McGuire, M. (1972), 'Private good clubs and public good clubs: economic models of group formation', *Swedish Journal of Economics*, vol. 74, pp. 84–99.

McGuire, M. (1974), 'Group segregation and optimal jurisdictions', *Journal of Political Economy*, vol. 82, pp. 112–32.

Meltzer, A. H. and Richard, S. F. (1978), 'Why government grows (and grows) in a democracy', *Public Interest*, vol. 52, pp. 111–18.

Meltzer, A. H. and Richard, S. F. (1981), 'A rational theory of the size of government', *Journal of Political Economy*, vol. 89, no. 5, pp. 914–27.

Mueller, D. C. (1979), *Public Choice*, Cambridge: Cambridge University Press.

Murrell, P. (1983), *An examination of the factors affecting the formation of interest groups in OECD countries*, Berlin: International Institute of Management.

Musgrave, R. A. (1939), 'The voluntary exchange theory of public economy', *Quarterly Journal of Economics*, vol. 53, pp. 213–38.

Niskanen, W. A. Jr. (1971), *Bureaucracy and Representative Government*, Chicago: Aldine-Atherton.

Nutter, G. W. (1978), *Growth of Government in the West*. Washington: American Enterprise Institute.

Olson, M. (1982), *The Rise and Decline of Nations: Economic Growth, Stagflation, and Social Rigidities*, New Haven, Conn: Yale University Press.

Organization for Economic Co-operation and Development (1980a), *Revenue Statistics of OECD Member Countries*, Paris: OECD.

Organization for Economic Co-operation and Development (1980b), *The Tax/Benefit Position of Selected Income Groups in OECD Member Countries: 1974–78*. Paris: OECD.

Organization for Economic Co-operation and Development (1982a), *Historical Statistics: 1960–80*. Paris: OECD.

Organization for Economic Co-operation and Development (1982b), *Employment in the Public Sector*. Paris: OECD.

Pauly, M. V. (1967), 'Clubs, commonality, and the core: an integration of game theory and the theory of public goods', *Economica*, vol. 35, pp. 314–24.

Pauly, M. V. (1970), 'Cores and clubs', *Public Choice*, vol. 9, pp. 53–65.

Peltzman, S. (1980), 'The growth of government', *Journal of Law and Economics*, vol. 23, no. 2, pp. 209–88.

Pommerehne, W. W. (1978), 'Institutional approaches to public expenditures: empirical evidence from Swiss municipalities', *Journal of Public Economics*, vol. 9, pp. 163–201.

Pryor, F. L. (1968), *Public Expenditures in Communist and Capitalist Nations*, London: George Allen and Unwin.

Romer, T. and Rosenthal, H. (1979), 'The elusive median voter', *Journal of Public Economics*, vol. 12, pp. 143–70.

Sawyer, M. (1976), *Income Distribution in OECD Countries*, OECD Occasional Studies, Paris: OECD.

Taylor, C. L. and Hudson, M. (1972), *World Handbook of Political and Social Indicators*. New Haven, Conn: Yale University Press.

Tollison, R. D. and Willett, T. D. (1973), 'Some simple economics of voting', *Public Choice*, vol. 16, pp. 59–71.

Tullock, G. (1959), 'Some problems of majority voting', *Journal of Political Economy*, vol. 67, pp. 571–9.

Verba, S. and Nie, N. H. (1972), *Participation in America – Political Democracy and Social Equality*. New York: Harper and Row.

Wittmann, D. A. (1973), 'Parties as utility maximizers', *American Political Science Review*, vol. 67, pp. 490–8.

United Nations (1972), *Demographic Yearbook*. New York: United Nations.

2

Legislative Choice and Public-Spending Growth

Paolo Martelli

INTRODUCTION

In modern representative democracies, the process of collective decision to choose, finance, produce and distribute public goods can be sketched in the following ways:

Voters send through their votes messages to the political system about their preferences;
Representatives, as a legislative body made up of one or more assemblies and/or committees, organize this demand in the form of spending legislation;
Government assembles this demand in a more or less coherent system of inputs and outputs of public finance. From the interaction between the representatives and government stems the definition of the state budget;
Public administration has to transform the decision of the government administrative acts, and also to inform it of the difficulties of the process of their implementation.

The basic intuition of the economic theory of representative democracy is that the decision-makers in the model act rationally in order to pursue their own interests. The theory must look for these interests in the elements more suitable to the optimal maintenance of the role of the various subjects, and make those elements the arguments of their utility functions. Some of these are, for example, maximizing the net balance between public goods and tax prices for the voters, maximizing the votes necessary to enhance the probability of re-election for politicians (Downs, 1957), maximizing the size of the office budget for the bureaucrats (Niskanen, 1971).

It then becomes important for the working of representative democracy that the institutions that rule the interaction of these decisional subjects act for the positive association of their utility functions, in order to reach an optimal firm integration of their interests. Among these institutions there is the *electoral law* which puts into legal form the relationship between voters and politicians, and which also defines, together with the decision-making procedures of legislative assemblies, the link between collective needs and bureaucracy. There are, then, institutions which rule the relations inside the bureaucracy (Breton and Wintrobe, 1982) and between the various subjects of the model (Buchanan and Tullock, 1962; Riker, 1962; Breton, 1974).

In this chapter, I intend to examine a particular aspect of this complex institutional system, that is, the techniques and procedures adopted by the legislative body to reach decisions about public policies, in order to understand the effects that these techniques and these procedures have on public-spending control. For this purpose I shall first sketch some theoretical results which stress the weak efficiency and effectiveness of the majority decision method (MDM), and the reasons which, nevertheless, account for its general acceptance as a collective decision rule. It will therefore be necessary to consider some other aspects of legislative choice. After dealing separately with parliamentary activity, I shall try to sketch an interaction between parliament and government, showing a process of public-spending control endogenous to the representative system.

CONSTITUTIONAL VOTING RULES

In many democratic states constitutional rules exist requiring qualified majorities in the legislative assemblies in order to take particularly important political decisions. In Italy, for instance, this is true for the election of the President of the Republic and for approval of constitutional amendments. As one can guess, this serves to protect particularly relevant decisions from hasty choices, at the cost of reducing the possibility, or at least the timeliness, of innovative decision. A theory of constitutional choice is contained in the idea of James Buchanan and Gordon Tullock of calculating the optimal level of consent. As is well known, it associates in every subject the increase in the costs of decision-making with the increase in the majority necessary for collective decision, and the increase in the external cost with the risk of not being considered in the decisional output. The external cost is a decreasing function of the required majority, and therefore the problem of the constitutional choice is reduced to that of minimizing the total costs (Buchanan and Tullock, 1962, ch. 6).

A comparable decision rule, however, does not seem to exist for the most important questions of public economy, so that, for example, a state budget can be approved, even if it reduces the utility of almost half the representatives. In this case, the system of election of single-place constituencies can even lead to a worsening of the situation of the majority of voters (Buchanan and Tullock, 1962, pp. 220–2).

The founders of methodological individualism soon pointed out this weakness of the MDM. In fact, Vilfredo Pareto believed that two social situations cannot be compared, if the first is preferred by an individual and the second is preferred by another, because this would imply the introduction of an unacceptable superindividual value judgement (Pareto, 1906). Knut Wicksell, in his turn, proposed a 'new principle of just taxation', according to which legislative assemblies should adopt, for public finance and spending, a decision rule as inclusive as to be a sort of 'relative unanimity' so that any relevant social group might not be displeased (Wicksell, 1896). As is well known, these contributions have been formalized in the 'Paretian' criterion of comparison between social alternatives, in relation to which the collective situation develops in a socially efficient way if it improves everybody's condition, or at least somebody's condition without worsening that of others.

Until a few decades ago, the individualistic analysis stuck to normative ground, without explaining why actual assemblies use the MDM, although it is the most socially inefficient of the electoral rules that avoid contradictory decisions. This has certainly been a serious limitation of the individualistic paradigm capacity of explaining constitutional reality. In their classic study, Buchanan and Tullock have nevertheless pointed out that the efficiency of MDM, in the Paretian sense, can be increased if the committee members are allowed to exchange or trade their votes (Buchanan and Tullock, 1962, chs 10–12). In this way, the excluded minorities can attract some members of the majorities with profitable offers, undermining their stability and re-entering the decision-making game. If in a committee, besides log-rolling and vote-trading, full side payments are allowed, the equilibrium solution of this game is on the Pareto-efficient frontier, so that MDM obtains for the public economy what the competitive-market institutions obtain for the private economy.

Legislative assemblies are made up of a not very large number of members able to obtain information about each other's preferences and to use them for their own ends. This fact leads to the consideration that the political representatives are rationally oriented to log-rolling in order to reduce the social inefficiency of MDM. The economic theory of representative democracy makes it possible to infer some consequences concerning decisions on public finance from this tendency of the legislative body. If in fact one considers that the representative process induces the members of parliament to safeguard sectoral interests, agreement on reciprocal legislative support of these interests allows a mutual advantage to the representatives who defend them before the voters. In their turn, these agreements will legitimate the desire of every voter to maximize the difference between public goods enjoyed and the tax prices paid for them. There will therefore be a tendency to increase the number and the intensity of the items of public spending, and to limit their sources of financing. Inside this dangerous tendency of representatives towards the loosening of public-spending control, there is also a further distortion: the expenditures interesting particular constituencies tend to multiply, whereas the ones of general interest tend to be contained (Tullock, 1967).

The situation can be described by means of the game model known as the *prisoner's dilemma.* Let us suppose that two representatives, A and B, both necessary for achieving a parliamentary majority, are respectively interested in the assembly approval of two amendments, X and Y. Each votes for his/her amendment, after evaluating the opportunity to vote or not for the other's amendment. We have therefore two strategies for each player, and this gives rise to the situation shown in table 2.1.

Table 2.1 *Representatives' pay-off matrix*

	B votes for X and for Y	*B votes for Y and against X*
A votes for X and for Y	1, 1	−1, 2
A votes for X, against Y	2, −1	0, 0

Each is in the best situation when his/her amendment, but not the other's, is passed, because then the benefits are concentrated on his/her voters, although the costs are shared by all. Obviously the worst situation is the opposite. On the other hand, the approval of both amendments still gives a partial advantage to each of the two constituencies, and thus to each of the two representatives. The matrix pay-offs refer to the case when each amendment gives a benefit of 3 and a cost of 1 to the one who proposes it, and a benefit of 0 and a cost of 1 to the other one. If the legislative choice were taken only once, the solution of the game would be non-cooperative, and the expenditures proposed with the amendments would be rejected by the assembly. The agreement instead becomes rational in the iteration of the game, which stimulates the continuous flow of legislative activity with greater realism. The possibility offered by iteration to control and to punish the free-rider, excluding him/her from further trades, makes it rational to vote for both the amendments, and to reach the Paretian efficiency with log-rolling and the rise of public spending. This consequence is stressed by the electoral system of proportional representation, which in general allows a wider presence in the house of the claims of the voters.

REPRESENTATIVE DEMOCRACY AND THE DEMAND FOR PUBLIC SPENDING

The tendency of the government in power to reach the goal of re-election through the approval of expenditure that can guarantee differential advantages to a group of voters explains how the increase of the total spending tends to escape parliament's collective control. It is not sufficient, however, to rule out the possibility that such control can be obtained by means of constraints governing the legislative output. These constraints can be due to parliamentary institutions themselves, and/or to the influence of the institutions which link parliament with other decision-makers connected with the regulation of demand (voters) and supply (government, bureaucracy) of public goods, and/or to the existence of constitutional rules which embody a sort of moral code of the public economy. I shall now discuss, within the limits already outlined, some of these institutions.

The examination of the specific parliamentary institutions connected with public-spending control first implies a thorough study of MDM. Beyond the fact that it is particularly inefficient, this decision rule cannot in many cases actually produce a collective choice. This limitation of MDM was pointed out long ago during the eighteenth century by such writers as Condorcet (1785) and Borda (1781), and reappeared more recently under the name of the 'voting paradox' (Black, 1958). Thus, given a set of more than two alternatives on which the voters establish a transitive system of personal preferences, it can happen that the majority of voters display a cyclical system of preferences and that therefore MDM is not fit for selecting the collectively preferred alternative. Duncan Black has formulated a restrictive hypothesis on the system of preferences which side-steps what I will call the 'decisional ineffectiveness' of MDM. However, his hypothesis suggests that the alternatives can be in an objective scalar order on which each voter has a single-peaked preference curve (Black, 1958, p. 7), but this seems generally to be an over-restrictive condition in the case of the problem of budget confrontation, so that a voting paradox appears as an impassable limit of the MDM capacity for decision-making.

The analytical solution of the problem of MDM 'decision effectiveness' requires a deeper analysis of assembly activities. Thus it has been discovered that MDM is not a decision rule, but a simple method of collective comparison between couples of alternatives. To become an operational rule it must be supported by procedures concerning the presentation of motions, the number of amendments and the order in which these must be voted. Some of these decisions are generally stated by the assembly regulation, whereas others are decided by the chairman or by the office which has the power to settle the agenda. The study of these questions has recently led to two theorems demonstrated under rather general conditions. The first states that if agenda power does not exist, and therefore each member can propose an amendment at any time, MDM does not offer stable solutions for collective choice, in the sense that every motion can be beaten by majority voting (Plott, 1967). The second demonstrates that if there is absolute agenda power which governs the nature of motions and the voting order, the majority decision process can be piloted in order to reach a predetermined collective decision, whatever the initial situation may be (McKelvey, 1976). In other words, MDM without agenda power produces the same decision block as anarchy, whereas MDM with absolute agenda power is equivalent to dictatorship. More recent results (Shepsle and Weingast, 1982) show that intermediate levels of agenda power lead to a restriction of choice possibilities with MDM, but without giving the chairman alone the power to determine the outcome. To sum up, legislative choice is a game ruled by a complex institution. The relation establishing social preference between alternatives (that is the majority rule) is only a part of it, and is not sufficient to settle the effectiveness of its decision, nor even its democratic character.

If MDM can become a decision rule only through the two alternative ways of effectiveness and democracy, it is important to determine a more inclusive optimal rule of social preference between alternatives. This recalls, at a more concrete level of analysis, the distinction made by Buchanan and Tullock between decision costs and external costs, the minimal sum of which should select the constitutional rule of collective choice. In the economy theory of representative democracy, however, the constitutional choice that Buchanan and Tullock encapsulate in the determination of optimal consent becomes a more complex and flexible determination of rules, where majority decisions, agenda power and log-rolling are associated so as to produce variable levels of rule representation and democracy and of stability of outcomes. This accounts for the fact that political consent in legislative decisions tends, on average, to exceed the constitutionally necessary minimum, and also for the fact that the width of parliamentary support varies with different legislative initiatives.

In the public economy, collective decisions are taken by simple majority, so that political exchange cannot go below the level which guarantees its achievements, given the assembly regulation and agenda power constraints. Where assemblies elect their own chairman, as in Italy, they are not likely to permit strong agenda power. If to this is added an assembly regulation which gives way to a strong initiative of every representation in the House, parliamentary efficiency produced by log-rolling does not encounter any obstacle to demands for the increase in public spending. In this sense, an institutional reform which in some way ties the assembly chairman to the bodies supplying public policies would have, as we shall see, positive repercussions on public-spending control. In any case, assembly regulations can be modified by the assembly itself, which should guarantee that agenda power will not grow to the point of transforming the chairman into a dictator.

Among the institutions that can influence the legislative outcome is the unicameral or bicameral composition of the legislature. In general, it can be said that the bicameral legislature reflects the complex historical nature of the process which has led from monarchy to democracy. The Upper House takes its origin from the feudal conflicts between crown and aristocracy, whereas the Lower House are typically established when the representation becomes elective and spreads to wider strata of the population. The statute of the Kingdom of Italy, for instance, added an elective chamber to a senate appointed by the king. Another historical reason for bicameral legislature is to be found in the foundation of a union of states or provinces. In this case, a chamber equally representing the constituents of the union, which stipulated the renunciation of full sovereignty, is added to a chamber elected on a state-wide formula. Thus it can be said that, in general, the addition a second House is found to be convenient when the social basis of the old assembly is no longer sufficiently representative of the changes that have occurred in unification of a state.

In modern democratic states representation is assured by elections, and the basis of representation assumes the technical meaning of the criterion adopted for the definition of the electoral constituencies. Buchanan and Tullock point out that a randomized basis for representation raises the uncertainty of the electoral result and induces the voters to go to the polls, whereas a functional basis, which aggregates the electorate by social roles and thus presumably by political preferences, virtually determines the electoral result, and causes the shifting of political debate at representative level (Buchanan and Tullock, 1962, ch. 16).

Buchanan and Tullock observe that, if the two Houses have the same basis of representation, both the functional and randomized elements of the basis will tend to act in an identical way in the two assemblies, producing a useless duplication of the decision structure. The logic of a bicameral legislature consists, in fact, in the search for a point of balance between decision and external costs, weighted comparatively more in favour of the latter and thus giving the legislature a more representative decision procedure. The problem is, however, to minimize the sum of the two costs, and it cannot be said that this result is attained by two Houses with totally different bases of representation. In this case, the decision costs are in fact likely to rise so much that rational persons are no longer interested in containing the risk of suffering others' preferences. In other words, it can occur that the greatest advantages of a second House are achieved when the basis of regulation is only 'a little' different from that adopted in the first. This is also because to the difference in the basis of representation must be added the differences of the regulation and the chance by which the agenda power marks the two parallel legislative tracks. The importance of these aspects, for the legislative outcome, has already been stressed.

What I have so far outlined can be exemplified by the public-spending decision. If the second House is elected on the same basis, the representation of the legislative body remains unchanged, as well as the tendency to political exchange and to public-goods demand. The coexistence of two parallel decision paths, with different procedures and obviously different agenda, can therefore produce a slowing down of public-spending demand, instituting a compulsory re-examination of the decisions of the first House. When, on the contrary, the basis is different, the wider representation increases the necessity for political exchange, because of the combination of sectoral interests. This can lead to an increase in demand for public spending by the legislature, which can exceed the contrary tendency produced by the parallel path. All this induces one to consider the Italian system of two Houses elected on a similar basis more indulgently than is usually done, and anyway to look for other institutional causes of the difficulty in our democracy of controlling public spending.

The number of representatives can influence directly or indirectly the model of increase of public spending already described, according to whether the electoral law is that of a single-vote constituency or a proportional one. In the first case, in fact, in order to increase the number of representatives it is necessary to increase the number of constituencies (for example, by reducing the geographical area). Obviously this tends to reduce the general political value of the parliamentary debate, while multiplying the occasions for political exchange. In the case of proportionality, on the other hand, the fundamental interests of a constituency are represented in parliament independently of the number of representatives. If these increase, however, the number of contacts between representatives and voters will grow, and this will generally increase the personal expectation of voters in the political system, and with that the probability that this system will satisfy a wider range of sectoral requests. In general, therefore, the 'degree of representation', to use the words of Buchanan and Tullock, seems to have a negative influence on public-spending control. The case of Italy would make an interesting study in this context, because of its plethoric parliament unequalled in any other country.

The members of parliament are generally organized in parties and coalitions, whose formation and stability are due to forms of traditional affinities (idealistic, ethnic, religious) and/or convergence of economic interest among voters, which are reflected at a representational level. The members of parliament are therefore only allowed to form those coalitions that do not too openly violate these formally organized groups, and this is an impediment to the formation of certain channels of political exchange, because it binds the representatives to pre-established alliances and oppositions. Added to this is the fact that more than a few representatives owe their election to lobbies and associations which control groups of voters whose interests cut across the parties, making an explicit formation of a majority coalition virtually impossible.

The *secret-ballot* rule accentuates these difficulties: on the one hand, it protects this system of multiple loyalty, to which many representatives are bound, allowing them to behave contrary to their declared position. On the other hand, it frustrates this opportunity for political exchange, because it prevents policing of any agreement. It is difficult to establish the effects of all this on the parliamentary demand for public spending, but one can presume that it reduces the certainty of utilitarian results derived from log-rolling and, eventually, has a negative influence on the rise of public spending.

The analysis of the effects of the parties and the secret ballot will be taken up later, in dealing with the supply of public spending. However, one can say at this juncture that parliaments generally have produced within themselves institutions that have proved capable of overcoming the aforesaid difficulties to a large extent. These are the *parliamentary committees*, which debate specific questions among relatively small groups of representatives. The work of the committees is less apparent to the whole electorate than that done in the House, but it is subject to more influence by the interests of specific sectors of voters. Furthermore, the members of the various committees tend to be selected on the basis of professional competence, and this to a great extent frees the debate from the constraints of ideological positions and predisposes it to find 'technical' solutions. Finally, the limited number of members makes it easier to discover how the individual members have voted in the secret ballot, and harder for them not to keep to agreements. The Italian system allows the parliamentary committees to deliberate as a legislative body. In effect, this happens very frequently, all the more because a failure to agree by the committee brings the matter into the House, greatly reducing the representative power of its members. Here, furthermore, the attention of the press and public opinion hardens their positions and reduces the possibility of optimal agreements.

It is now possible to summarize, from the point of view of the economic theory of representative democracy, the effect of the institutions examined so far on the demand for public spending. As the aim of the representatives is primarily that of maximizing the electoral votes, they direct their activity to satisfying the voters' demand for public services. This is achieved by log-rolling, whereby a representative offers his vote for a pressing request for expenditure by a colleague in exchange for the vote of others for his own request of equal intensity. Thus there is a tendency towards 'Paretian efficiency' within parliament, but, at the same time, accompanied by the loss of global spending control. The institutions which increase 'efficiency', such as the second chamber, the high degree of representation, and the parliamentary committees, all promote the increase of the public-spending demand, whereas those which tend to restrain political exchange, such as agenda power and, partially, the secret ballot and the formal groups of representatives, lead the assemblies to sub-optimal agreements.

IMPORTANCE OF THE RELATIONSHIP BETWEEN PARLIAMENT AND GOVERNMENT

In the economic theory of democracy, the relationship between parliament and government has been largely neglected. The latter, in fact, is generally thought to coincide, as an economic subject, with the supporting parliamentary majority (see Downs, 1957; Breton, 1974). The idea which stands behind this assimilation is that the common fate of the government and the majority, bound to the electoral votes, renders their interests and behaviour identical. It is worth noting that this identification itself stems from the attempt of the theory to explain the empirical fact of the uncontrolled rise in public spending. Let us, in fact, maintain the hypothesis that the voters' utility rises with the net balance between public goods and tax prices, and that this fact induces the representatives to press for more and more expenditures and less and less taxes. In these conditions the government adjusts its policies to their requests, having the same utility function which increases with the electoral votes. Hence it uses its monetary, fiscal and administrative power to side-step or sweep away the balance constraint, leading to 'democracy in deficit' (Buchanan and Wagner, 1977).

In my view, however, this model is too unilateral. It is an empirical fact that parliamentary support of the government varies widely so far as public finance as well as other questions are concerned. In other words, a government may sometimes be supported by a steady and certain majority with which it can then be identified, but more often it has to be content with inconstant and precarious support, which must be achieved day by day as legislative programmes are presented. This can be explained by saying that the government adjustment to the parliamentary pressurs for a rise in spending is not immediate and uncritical, but reluctant. The government's institutional function of giving political and administrative coherence to legislative output makes it aware of the serious consequences of the choices which it is still forced to take. In other words, the government utility function is not completely expressed solely by the voting preferences of the representatives, but also induces a certain 'deficit aversion', which hinders the pursuit of parliamentary consent. This 'deficit aversion' characterizes the government in the model, so that it becomes an autonomous decision-making unit within representative democracy, searching for that majority coalition which maximizes its utility as the occasion demands.

The idea of decision autonomy of the executive body in the field of public finance is certainly not a new one. It is in fact central to the classical theories of democracy, especially to those that emphasize the role of the state. Furthermore, the idea is also hinted at in Down's theory, when he claims that the government must 'carry out its specialized role in the division of labour' with the legal means of 'constituted elections or *legitimate influence*' (Downs, 1957, p. 24). There are, however, at least two conditions necessary for a model of a government able to regulate the legislative output which is consistent with an economic theory of representative democracy. The first is the existence of a 'commodity' which the government can offer to representatives in order to obtain their support in reducing the deficit. The second, which I will return to later, is that the structure of the groups of representatives effectively allows the activity of exchange between government and parliament.

As far as the first condition is concerned, one can observe that there are many ways in which the action of the government can have a positive influence on the status of the political representative. I will call *representation goods* those possibilities at the disposal of the government by virtue of its privileged relationship within the political and administrative setting. These goods can be, for example, appointments such as vice-minister, support for the chairmanship of, or a place on, a desired committee, technical support of administration granted informally for political activity, publicity of representatives' activity among public officials, and political support through favourable press and mass media in general.

To acquire these goods in exchange for government support the representatives must bring in more electoral votes than would be lost by their support for contained public spending. On the one hand, this would encourage a representative to agree to collaborate on the reduction of some general expenses, but to oppose similar intervention in his own constituency, accentuating the already observed distortion of the budget towards the relative expansion of the sectoral expenditure. On the other hand, 'representation goods' could act positively on the argument of the voters' utility function, which is independent of the net balance between public goods and tax prices. To support this hypothesis, let us suppose that the utility of the voter depends inversely on the *costs of acquiring information* necessary to the rational expression of his vote. (See Downs, 1957, pt III; Tullock, 1967, chs 6–7.) Also, these goods, through the notoriety they offer to the representatives who receive them, reduce voters' costs in choosing representatives. The government would then be in a position to offer some resistance to the expansion of the public deficit, bargaining with part of the representatives' restrictive policies against goods with part of the voters' information economies against votes. Figure 2.1 shows the variation flows of political exchange taken into consideration in this chapter. The representatives promote the exchanges on the upper part of the figure that generate the expansion of the deficit, whereas those on the lower part allow the government some form of control. The two log-rolling loops indicate the ambivalence of this practice in respect to spending control: on the one hand, as is seen, this facilitates the formation of majorities in favour of spending expansion; on the other, it allows those who receive representation goods to agree to 'break them up'.

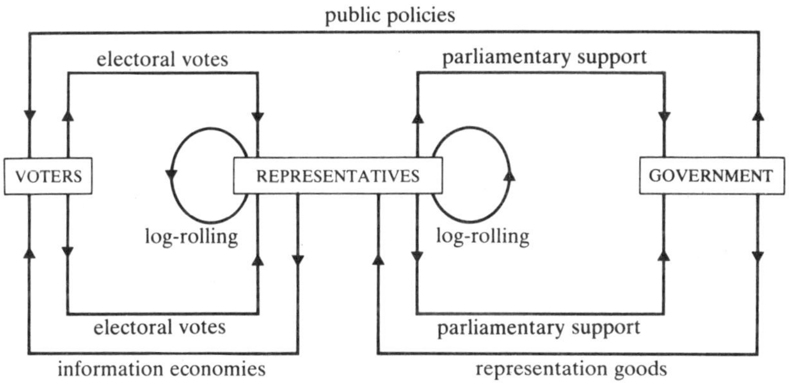

Figure 2.1 Flows of political exchange between government, representatives and voters.

In principle, the mechanism described is perfectly reversible and can allow the government to oppose the expansion of public spending in an efficient manner. In practice, its success depends on the correspondence between the various arguments that appear in the utility function of the three subjects. If, for example, the utility of the voters is much more sensitive to the positive variations in public spending than to the negative ones in the costs of information, the government will end up exhausting its stock of representation goods before receiving in exchange adequate support for a policy of a balanced budget. In this way the model can be used simply to describe the difficulties and uncertainties of the action of a government in obtaining parliamentary consent for the control of public spending, but not directly to offer norms for the solution of this problem.

On the other hand, it seems evident that in general the exchanges between government and parliament for the control of public spending are less fluid than those which tend to expand it. It therefore becomes important to analyse the condition necessary for their establishment. An example is opportune in this context. Let us suppose that a representative agrees with the government to vote in favour of the proposal to reduce adjustments of salaries with the increases in the cost of living, in exchange for the position of vice-minister. After the agreement, each of the contracting parts has two strategies open to it – the representative to vote for or to vote against, the government to give or not to give the position of vice-minister. Whatever is a benefit for the representative is obviously a cost for the government, which cannot give the position to anyone else, whereas the favourable vote that the government adds to its 'balance' is a cost for the representative who supports an unpopular law. Here, as in the case of log-rolling, a situation of the prisoner's-dilemma type exists and may be represented by the matrix shown in table 2.2.

Table 2.2 *Government and representative pay-off matrix*

	Government gives the position	*Government does not give the position*
Representative votes for	5, 3	−3, 5
Representative votes against	8, 0	0, 2

The representative estimates that the position of vice-minister will have more effect on his re-election than the bad reputation he will get for having voted for an anti-union law (5 to 1 in arbitrary units), whereas the government values the vote in its favour more highly than the opportunity cost of having given away a position of vice-minister (3 to 2 in the same units). The non-cooperative strategies are dominant and the market agreement is not rational. But, as one must suppose, a continual reiteration of these exchanges and, as in a market like this without a coercive system of sanctions, the worst sanction is the loss of credibility. The cooperative solution, and with it a programmed diminution of public spending, is rational in the precise sense that it optimizes the long-term strategic preferences of the contracting parties. This implies, however, the possibility that the government can control the representative's vote. The role of the secret ballot in legislative choice with regard to public spending is therefore ambivalent: on the one hand, it discourages log-rolling and with it the 'Paretian efficiency' of parliament, and contributes to containing public spending. On the other hand, it blocks the exchange of representation goods for supporting votes and the efficiency of the government–parliament system, preventing the government from assembling the consent of the representatives for a policy of public-spending control. In fact, this institutional reform would allow all the requests for expenditure, including those from minorities, to declare themselves openly in inter-parliamentary contracting, making it possible for the government to order this mass of spending according to priorities and criteria agreed with parliament. The political exchange that allows the most intensely felt needs to make themselves known in the House through log-rolling, offers the government the means of convincing parliament that it should give up the less orthodox requests when planning its own comprehensive budget.

Let us now look at how the nature of organized groups of representatives influences the relationship between the government and parliament. If, in parliament, the formal groups of parties and groups leave room for the formation of strategic coalitions that do not ask the government for anything other than social policies and representation goods, the government, somewhat precarious perhaps, remains in a position of being able to influence the political exchange with one coalition or another, optimizing its own utility in each transaction. If, on the other hand, the formal groups are diffused and rigid to the point of not allowing the rise of other distinct strategic coalitions, then it is the parties who, as decision-makers, will determine government action in accordance with their support. Two cases can be given: first, consider a party that is strong enough to make up a majority coalition on its own. In this case the government will have a stable and certain support with which it can be identified, as Breton and, to a certain extent, Downs suggest. The second case is that in which the government's parliamentary support arises from a coalition of many parties so that the strategic conflicts of the parliamentary majority will dominate the government's action. Downs considers this possibility, but he excludes it from his treatise because he holds that this case ceases to be that of a democratic 'government', but rather becomes that of a democratic 'paralysis'. With a greater adherence to the spirit of the 'economic theory', one can say that in this case the government's activity makes up the output of a complex strategic game where the parties forming the majority have an interest in increasing their votes, not only to the detriment of opponents, but also to allies. The results of this competition among government supporters on the matter of public spending is twofold: on the one hand, the offer of social policies expands so that they widen the deficit and, once allocated, are registered among the government's merits;

on the other hand, the supply of representation goods is contained because these are assigned to single individuals as positional goods and, as such, their offer is limited.

In the case of a coalition government, an open vote, although necessary in principle, is no longer sufficient to control public spending. The preliminary need is for the government to re-establish itself as a decision-maker, which implies that a system of institutional rules must be adopted to prohibit the use of the most conflicting strategies among the members of a majority coalition. The current discussion concerning the necessity of a fiscal and/or monetary constitution can in fact be interpreted as the attempt to reformulate in contractarian terms the role of the government in the representative system. However, this important topic is not the subject of this chapter.

CONCLUSION

Legislature and government are respectively agencies of demand and supply, exchanging between themselves votes against policies of public spending. Votes do not have any cost for the representatives, who are thereby urged by their interest to purchase that amount of public policies that will give them the highest probability of re-election. By acting on legislative institutions, such as agenda power, degree of representation, committees, secret ballot, second House, it might be possible to curb the public-spending demand, and eventually to stop it completely. The government alone might be given the possibility of increasing the opportunity cost of the representative's votes spent in public-policies purchasing, offering them representation goods for some governing policies of public-spending control. This requires, at the very least, the repeal of parliamentary secret ballot and, furthermore, the ability of the government to offer and distribute representation goods. This ability, however, is likely to be affected by the government's need to be supported by a coalition of parties. In this case, a social contract must be established as a prior condition in order to limit the strategies of the allied parties to those which recognize the role of the government as a decision-maker in charge of the bureaucracy and competing as an equal with parliament.

REFERENCES

Black, D. (1958), *The Theory of Committees and Elections*, Cambridge: Cambridge University Press.

Borda, J. C. de (1781), 'Mémoire sur les élections au scrutin', *'Mémoires de l'Académie Royale des Sciences.*

Breton, A. (1974), *The Economic Theory of Representative Government*, Chicago: Aldine Treatises and London: Macmillan.

Breton, A. and Wintrobe, R. (1982), *The Logic of Bureaucratic Conduct*. Cambridge: Cambridge University Press.

Buchanan, J. M. and Tullock, G. (1962), *The Calculus of Consent, Logical Foundations of Constitutional Democracy*. Ann Arbor, Mich: University of Michigan Press.

Buchanan, J. M. and Wagner, R. E. (1977), *Democracy in Deficit: The Political Legacy of Lord Keynes*, New York: Academic Press.

Condorcet, M.-J. A. N. de (1785), *Essai sur l'application de l'analise à la probabilité des décisions rendues à la pluralité des voix, de l'imprimerie Royale*, Paris.

Downs, A. (1957), *An Economic Theory of Democracy*, New York: Harper and Row.

McKelvey, R. D. (1976), 'Intransitivities in multidimensional voting models and some implications for agenda control', *Journal of Economic Theory*, vol. 12, pp. 472–82.

Niskanen, W. A. Jr (1971), *Bureaucracy and Representative Government*, Chicago: Aldine-Atherton.

Pareto, V. (1906), *Manuale di economia politica*, Milan: Società Editrice Libraria.

Plott, C. R. (1967), 'A notion of equilibrium and its possibility under majority rule', *American Economic Review*, vol. 57, pp. 787–806.

Riker, W. H. (1962), *The Theory of Political Coalitions*, New Haven, Conn: Yale University Press.

Shepsle, K. A. and Weingast, B. R. (1982), 'Institutionalizing majority rule: a social choice theory with policy implications', *American Economic Review, Papers and Proceedings*, vol. 72, pp. 367–71.

Tullock, G. (1967), *Towards a Mathematics of Politics*, chs 6–7. Ann Arbor, Mich: University of Michigan Press.

Wicksell, (1896), *Finanztheoretische Untersuchungen*, Fischer, Jena. Partially published in English under the title 'A new principle of just taxation', in R. T. Musgrave and A. T. Peacock (eds) (1959), *Classics in the Theory of Public Finances*, London: Macmillan and New York: St Martin's Press.

3

Fiscal Autonomy of Non-Central Government and the Problem of Public-Spending Growth

Giorgio Brosio

INTRODUCTION

In recent decades we have witnessed a growing tendency in almost all industrial countries towards the reduction of the part played by local taxes in total revenues of local government and the growth of various kinds of transfer from the central government. There are many reasons for this phenomenon, their relative importance varying from country to country. Frequently local taxes have been shown to be less elastic to income than centrally administered taxes, whereas the demand for public services has shown the opposite pattern. Real or presumed economies of scale in the collection of taxes have stimulated the centralization of administration. Greater reliance on fiscal policies for stabilization purposes has also played an important role in this tendency. The aim of reducing tax competition between local jurisdictions, which was fostered by the increased spatial mobility of resources, may also have played a certain role.

In the same period, local government expenditure in most industrialized countries has exhibited a faster rate of growth than central government expenditure. This becomes even more evident if we consider expenditure only on goods and services. It is tempting to hypothesize a direct relationship between the two trends, which is supported by a basic tenet of public finance theory. When the link between taxation and spending decisions is weakened or severed, the perception of the real cost of public services is affected. If perception of a lower cost prevails, the demand for public services will increase, exerting a positive and systematic influence on the growth of the public sector.

If we look at the relationship between the growth of local expenditure and the degree of fiscal independence (measured in terms of the proportion of total tax revenue raised at the local level), however, we find that the evidence does not support this hypothesis. In general, the growth of local expenditure appears to be positively correlated with the degree of fiscal independence (see Gould (1983) for a preliminary analysis of these trends). This evidence is too general, however, to be considered an adequate test of the hypothesis of effects of separation of tax gathering and spending.

The aim of this chapter is to throw some light on the effects of separation. Therefore, I do not consider the stimulative effects on expenditure of the various forms of transfer from higher government levels. I am perfectly conscious that the differential impact of various categories of transfers can be substantial.

The chapter develops only a positive approach to the problem. In other words, no attempt is made to develop a model of a system of local governments oriented towards the minimization of the size of the public sector. If this were to be the only objective of such a system, the recipe would not be difficult to find: small, monofunctional units financed by means of Lindahl-type taxes. But other problems in terms of allocation and distribution would arise, that can more than offset, even in terms of the dimension of the total public sector, the advantages derived from such a system of local governments. We must think, for example, on the allocative side, of the scale economies in expediture and in tax collection that are foregone, or of the need for vast coordination activities.

The building of a model for a full analysis of these problems is clearly outside the scope of this chapter, and probably of my capabilities.

THE MODEL

In order to simplify the problem, let us assume that a central government decides, for one of the reasons previously mentioned, to take over the administration of a general tax from the local governments, but to give them the revenue raised. Let us also suppose that the revenue is distributed among the individual jurisdictions in proportion to the sums that were previously raised by each of them. We can thus eliminate the effects arising from the redistribution of funds among the various jurisdictions.[1]

We can now imagine that the possible expansionary effects on the expenditure levels of the local governments stemming from this change in the financing system would be of three distinct orders. The first two relate to the separation of the taxation and spending decisions. We may distinguish an immediate effect concerning the spending of the grant and a further effect concerning the securing of the grant, that is, its future expansion and distribution. The third effect relates to the loss of competition in tax rates between local jurisdictions caused by the centralization of the tax.

We shall begin with the problem of the spending of the grant. According to standard economic theory, variations in the system of finance of local governments, in our case the substitution of their own taxes with transfers, should not have any effect on their expenditure. This can be demonstrated by applying indifference curve analysis to a fully informed median-voter model. In figure 3.1 private goods are shown along the ordinate and the public goods on the abscissa. *MN* is the pre-modification budget line. The local tax is then abolished and the grant, *G*, is introduced.

In order to make the problem clearer, we can suppose that in the year the modification has taken place, the revenue has increased due to an expansion of the tax base, and the fiscal pressure has thus not changed. *M'N'* will be the new budget line. The income of the community is increased, but not the relative prices. *E* was the equilibrium point before the change. If both public and private goods have positive income elasticities, the community will move toward a point such as *E'*, where $<\Delta L/\Delta G<1$. The increase in the local expenditure, ΔL, will be determined by the income elasticity of the demand for the public good of the median voter. Following this line of reasoning, the same result would occur if sometime later the central government were to repeal this tax or cut its other taxes by the exact amount of the grant, leaving more scope for local government to increase its own taxes and expenditure. Disconnected taxation and spending decisions have no influence on the growth of the public sector.

The results may be different, however, if conditions other than those assumed above prevail. That is, if the median voter is not fully informed –

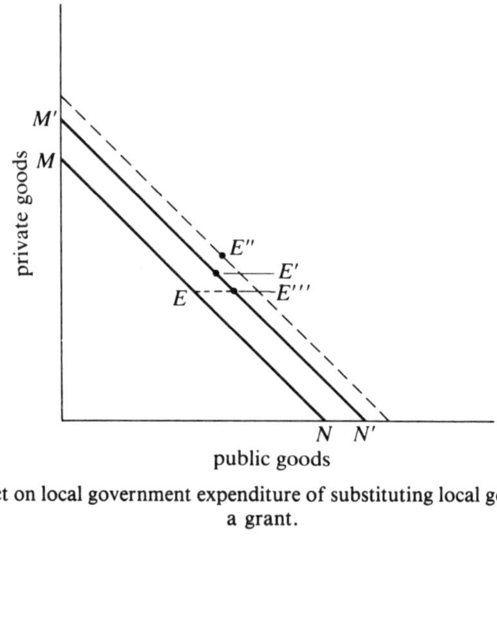

Figure 3.1 Effect on local government expenditure of substituting local government taxes with a grant.

there is fiscal 'illusion' – and/or the political decision-making process is other than that implied by the median-voter model (for example, local governments act as revenue-maximizers).

The effects stemming from the introduction of fiscal illusion can be analysed in the context of the previous indifference model. The 'illusion' simply means that the perceived level of public services, and of the revenue that finances them, may be different from the effective level

$$S^* = \beta S; \; T^* = d_1 T \text{ and } G^* = d_2 G$$

where the perceived dollar share of local service is β, of locally raised taxes is d_1, and d_2 is the perceived per dollar share of the central taxes required to pay for the grant. The opportunity set then becomes

$$Y^* = X - d_1 T - d_2 G$$

Y^* is the perceived disposable income (for private goods) and X is the gross income, which is perfectly known.

Then, if $d_1 > d_2$ – that is, if the voter believes that he can pass onto another jurisdiction part of the cost of the grant – the opportunity set will move towards the right and the equilibrium point, if the income elasticities of private and public goods do not change, will be E'', implying a higher level of public services.

The same result will obtain if the local government is somewhat outside the control of its electorate and if it attempts to get a bigger budget to administer, as in models embodying greedy politicians or politicians as revenue-maximizers. In this case, we remain on the opportunity line $M'N'$ of figure 3.1. The equilibrium point simply shifts toward E''' – 'the money sticks where it hits', as the 'flypaper theory of incidence' says (see Fisher, 1982). So far so good with the theory. But in practice we can ask, how great is this effect and, more important, how long will it last? I doubt whether the mere fact that a tax has been allocated to a higher level of government can substantially and persistently reduce the perception of the real burden of the taxes the citizens pay. The evidence on the persistence of the effect is still scarce, but not contrary to the hypothesis that the spending effect can be reabsorbed with the lapse of time.

Winer (1983) has applied the model of fiscal illusion mentioned above to the case of the Canadian provinces. His data cover a long enough time-span (17 years) for this testing of the persistence of the illusion. The evidence he provides shows that the separation of the decisions created by the equalization grants does increase local expenditure. This also emerges from the enormous number of studies carried out on the USA (see, among others, Gramlich (1979) for a review). But the effect tends to diminish over time, even if it does not disappear completely in the period observed.

The present author, in a joint paper (Brosio, Nyman and Santagata, 1980), tried to test the effect of the separation produced by the Italian tax reform of

1971. This reform abolished the principal taxes administered by the local authorities. In their place a system of practically 100 per cent revenue-sharing was introduced. The particular characteristics of Italian institutions, especially the lack of effective sanctions to prevent local authorities from incurring debts, restrict the generality of the results. However, they show a substantial increase in the real level of per-capita expenditure over and above what one would have expected after adjusting for the changes affecting the demand and the supply of local public services over the period observed (five years). This effect was immediate, then subsequently it declined in intensity, due also to the financial stringency of the local governments.

FISCAL COMPETITION

Leaving aside for the moment the second effect, that of securing the grant, which is more closely connected with the last part of this chapter, I come to the competition issue. When taxes are transferred from the local to the central level, uniform rates will be imposed across all jurisdictions. As a consequence, competition among local authorities will be eliminated. In other words, the reduction of local tax autonomy eliminates one possible check on the expansion of revenue.

Obviously, the fiscal competition is *per se* a neutral mechanism as far as the size of the public sector is concerned. The assertion that an increase (decrease) in competition can check (or foster) the growth of revenue and expenditure relies to some extent on the hypothesis that local administrators are revenue-maximizers, in addition to that of a substantial mobility of the citizens. The potential extent of competition is correlated directly with the mobility of resources and individuals, and inversely with the size of jurisdictions (not only because size reduces mobility, but because of the number of potential competitors).

How much the opportunity for competition is or has been exploited becomes the relevant question. It can be looked at in two distinctly different ways. The first consists of the observation of the pattern in various countries of the assignment of taxes between levels of government. If taxes more suited to competition are assigned to the central level, this indicates that the political system, as a whole, does not intend to use this instrument. The second is through empirical tests.

For a large group of countries, including the USA, Britain, Canada, Australia, France (and also Italy as regards the discussions on future reform), the role of personal income tax, which offers a high potentiality of competition, has been reduced (or at least not increased), whereas the taxes on real property still form the bulk of local tax revenue. Worries about the disruptive effects of competition on revenue seem to have been the main cause and these are widely reflected in literature on the subject. Maxwell and Aronson (1977 p. 137) typically maintain: 'Local taxation of income, sales, or business would induce shrinkage in the tax base and, therefore, bring serious injury to the locality. But real property is quite immobile.... In short real property offers a base on which local governments can safely levy taxes.

On the other hand, in the Scandinavian countries personal income tax represents the totality of tax revenue for the local authorities. But here the behaviour of local authorities seems to have been more oriented to the exploitation of the revenue potential offered by the residents, rather than to attracting new tax base through competition. In fact as Løtz (1981) states: 'In Norway the central government has, for fear of growth in public expenditure, done away with local income taxes by setting a maximum rate so low that everybody must use it. Also in Denmark there have been ad hoc attempts to stop the growth in local government expenditure by imposing limits for tax increases'.

Summing up, it appears that, at least from the experience of the industrialized countries, where possibilities of competition did exist (that is, some of the actors of the game tended to use it), they were prevented from doing so by the imposition of a cartel, in the form of centralization of taxes with a wide agreement between local and national politicians.[2] Taxes that do not allow disruptive effects of competition were like the property taxes left to the local authorities.

Brennan and Buchanan (1980, pp. 183 – 4) suggest this interpretation of the recent trends in the assignment of taxes to the various levels of governments. There are, of course, other concomitant, but not entirely coincidental explanations. I would simply like to mention that the assignment of broad-based taxes to the central government has been considered essential for the purpose of the stabilization policies. It reflects thus the popularity of the Keynesian policies in the post-war period.

Empirical studies on the intensity of competition are not very numerous to my knowledge, and in any case do not show cases with a really high degree of competition. The extent and the intensity of competition has been measured indirectly by observing the relationship between the income elasticity of local taxes and the growth of the expenditure. A strong correlation between the two should indicate the absence of competition, because every government is trying to increase its expenditure, and is limited only by the availability of resources. On the contrary, a weak correlation can be taken to indicate the existence of competition and the operating of a Tiebout effect.

Oates (1975) and Craig and Heins (1980) show that tax elasticity has an important effect on the growth of expenditure, even if their results do not exclude the existence of some competition. The results obtained by Di Lorenzo (1982) seem to indicate, on the contrary, that the Tiebout effect is somewhat more operational.

On a simply descriptive level of analysis, Swiss cantons demonstrate against the plausibility of the restraining effect stemming from the competition. In fact, they present the proper operation conditions for the working of the competition effect. First, they are reasonably small. Second, taxes on income and wealth represent 50 per cent of their total revenue. From 1950 to 1981, however, the share on the GDP of the expenditures of the cantons increased by 64, 9 per cent, whereas the share of the federal government, that relies much more on the indirect taxation, rose only by 8, 4 per cent. (See Weber (1984) for a concise description of this experience.)

Tax autonomy does not only foster competition, but it can also allow the exploitation of location rents – with opposite effects on the size of the public sector. Tax rates can be raised without loss (or at least with no immediate loss) of the tax base, when resources are not mobile, when the tax payers (or rather the tax bearers) do not vote in the same jurisdiction, and the tax burden can be shifted to other jurisdictions. We can even imagine, where the tax burden can be shifted, a process of retaliation by which taxes are continuously increased.

Fiscal exploitation of the locational rents is obviously not a purely theoretical case, but a reality. It operates mainly with property taxes and with business taxes (first, firms are attracted by lower rates and then burdened). The dispute on 'rate-capping' in the UK in the early 1980s represents the best illustration. The attempts of the Treasury to limit the growth of local authorities by penalizing overspending by means of a reduction to zero of the block grant are circumvented by the huge increase of the burden on non-domestic tax payers (business property). The government sees only one way open: to impose a ceiling on the growth of expenditure[3] (a measure already unsuccessfully attempted in Italy in the last few years).

In conclusion, we cannot assert from a positive point of view that the substitution of taxes with grants has *per se* an impact on the size of the public sector, in so far as it diminishes the tax competition. The impact will depend on the type of taxes abolished. The consideration of the tax competition issue, however, is essential from a normative point of view. It gives useful indications on the assignment of taxes between various levels of government, if the limiting of the size of the public sector is a primary objective of policy.

EFFECTS OF SECURING THE GRANT

I come now to what I have called the effects of 'securing the grant'. Let us recall the initial example. A locally raised tax has been substituted with a grant which is distributed according to the previous revenue in each jurisdiction. Because we can neither assume that the revenue provided by the tax will always evolve at the same rate at which the demand for local services will increase, nor that this demand will show the same pattern in each jurisdiction, the national government will necessarily be faced with two different choices. The first one concerns the amount of the grant, the second its distribution. Whether this centralization of the decision will or will not exert a positive influence on the growth of the public sector is hard, if not impossible, to ascertain.

I do not believe that we can go a long way in modelling these effects using a median-voter model. This kind of model is more suited to the analysis of budget processes in a simple decision-making context such as a direct democracy dealing with a restricted range of issues. The impact on the local expenditures will depend on the rules that govern the decision-making process in the nation. At parliamentary level, it will depend, in those countries where a bicameral parliamentary system operates, on the type of representation provided by the Upper House. What is certain, however, is that when the system of financing of local government is radically modified through revenue being centralized, the system of representation of interests will also be modified: first, in an informal (non-statutory) way, and then, it is likely (and I think it will be necessary), at a formal (legislative) level.

I thus feel obliged to follow a more inductive kind of reasoning. The arguments I will develop are strongly influenced by recent experience in Italy. (It shows, however, in many respects a strong similarity to the process of adoption of the American revenue-sharing system.)

When local taxes are substituted to a large extent with grants, the availability of more or better local public services will depend not only on the residual local taxes, user charges and increases in centrally administered taxes, but also on the formula introduced for the distribution of the grants.

In our modern systems, where the tax burden is distributed according to some form of the 'ability to pay' principle (even through it is not very clearly defined as such), the role of personal wealth in determining the voter's attitude on the various issues (for example, the increase or decrease of local services and the accompanying taxes) becomes less important than the voter's geographical location.

A new form of representation with the central government is in fact recognized by the local politicians and a bargaining situation is set up which has, on the one side, the central government and, on the other, a great mass of local representatives (mayors, councillors, etc.).

The representation of local interests is obviously partitioned along many overlapping dividing lines: small and big, rich and poor, rural and urbanized, agricultural or industrial jurisdictions. The fact that each member of the local representative front is thus a supporter of a particular interest enhances the intensity of the interest in participation in the bargaining process, thus reducing the free-rider problems usually associated with mass movements.

One might imagine that these cleavages would reduce the bargaining power of the local front and allow the central government to exploit the golden rule of 'divide and rule'. But we have to take into account that in a representative democracy the national and local representatives are not real counterparts. Their political careers or simply their electoral stakes are interwoven because of mutual patronage. Is it more important in electoral terms for a national representative to support a reduction of taxes, or to get the support of the local politicians of his constituency?

In any case, new pressure groups are created and old groups revitalized. For example, in Italy we have the Association of Municipalities, the Union of Provinces, the Conference of the Heads of Regional Governments (other countries often show a wider variety). This gives way to what Beer (1975) has defined 'the public-sector politics' – a system in which influences on the choices of government arise autonomously within government itself. I suspect that in this bargaining process the power of local politicians can reveal itself to be more decisive than that of politicians who operate at the central level, because the former produce and/or control much of the information that is relevant for this process.[4]

What do these changes amount to? Certainly to a reduced power of control over the entire process of spending and taxing on the part of the individual voter, accompanied by an increase in the element of fiscal illusion. Even though I still believe that it is not possible 'to fool the people' all the time, the adoption of a system of revenue-sharing introduces a period of 'turmoil' at the political-representative level, which facilitates some sort of displacement of expenditure toward an higher level.

Disagreement over the form of distribution is likely to be solved by increasing the amount of the grant, which will allow everyone to get what he is asking for or needs; that is, by adoption of a distribution formula that will take into account the different situations and needs.

DISTRIBUTION FORMULAS

I should like to focus now on the distributive issue. The normative theory of grants gives two alternative criteria of distribution, which correspond to the two main concepts of distributive justice. The first is based on the criterion of merit, the second is based on the criterion of need. Applied to intergovernmental relations, the first criterion maintains that the grant should be distributed according to some index of tax effort; the second criterion says it should be distributed according to an evalution of the difference between the need for public services and fiscal capacity (if it still exists).

In the debate about the reform of local and regional finance in Italy, we can observe a gradual alignment of these opposing criteria according to the relative wealth of the various jurisdictions. In particular, the northern and richer regions and municipalities (more and more independently of partly differences) clearly support a fiscal effort-rewarding formula, whereas the southern and poorer jurisdictions advocate a need-based formula.

Something very similar happened in the USA with the adoption of revenue-sharing. The allocation formula which was finally adopted in the USA has combined the two criteria, thus partially offsetting their effects. The final result is very similar to an equal per-capita distribution.[5] Beer calls this result 'a third criterion of populistic distributive justice'. In fact every jurisdiction gets something.

Italy at present represents the best application of this criterion. Every municipality or province has been allowed in recent years to increase its expenditure every year by a fixed percentage, which (except for a small difference between north and south) is equal in all jurisdictions. This percentage is applied to the previous year's expenditure. In addition, in order to reduce the existing inequalities in per-capita expenditure derived from the past, an equalization grant, calculated for the dimensional class of reference, is paid to those jurisdictions that are below the national average.

What is the implication of giving each jurisdiction something, in terms of the growth of the grant? The 'populistic formula' can be more growth-inducing than a formula based on needs. In fact, the first is less redistributive than the latter, because even the rich jurisdictions have access to the grant. They thus have less incentive to oppose themselves to the increases of the grant demanded by the poor jurisdictions. It represents a clear example of pork barrel politics and, by reducing the opposing interest, it possesses a big potentiality for increasing the grant. The populistic formula is, on the other hand, less growth-indicing than the formulas that reward the fiscal effort, but these formulas, being very demanding, have very few changes of being adopted.[6]

A second, long-term, effect of the populistic (localistic) formulas is the fact that they tend to keep the number of local authorities unchanged. If even the smallest units are granted with some transfers, this becomes an implicit recognition thay they have a role to play in they system of local government, even though they are totally inefficient because of their small size, which leads to higher per-capita costs.

CONCLUSION

I come now to the conclusion. If I have correctly identified the effects stemming from the separation of the spending and tax decision, the analysis I have made shows that in fact the introduction of a system of grants can foster the growth of public expenditure. The intensity and the duration of these effects depend on the degree of fiscal illusion that the separation introduces and on the role that the new fiscal arrangements allow local and national politicians to play.

Surely the process of centralization of the taxes is not an irrevocable one. Most of the arguments that were used for justifying centralization both by politicians and by scholars are clearly overstated. If the centralization of local taxes is considered to be absolutely necessary, then financial arrangements that limit the extent of fiscal illusion and the discretionary role of politicians – other than the revenue-sharing schemes which have been adopted in recent years in some countries – can be devised.

In fact there are at present systems of financing local governments with centralized taxes that allow more control on the size of the public sector. Take, for example, the case of the states (*Länder*) in the Federal Republic of Germany (see Hunter, 1973; ACIR, 1981), where most of their revenue (and also of local governments) is a fixed percentage of the three main taxes; that is income tax, corporation tax and value added tax. The *Länder* are not empowered to vary the rates of these taxes. The taxes therefore cannot be considered as local, contrary to what is done in the international statistics. Revenues are distributed according to the sums collected in each jurisdiction. There are thus very few elements, if any, of fiscal illusion.

A system of equalization that functions at the *Länder* level is added. The *Länder* that have per-capita revenues above a certain percentage of the national average have to transfer resources to the *Länder* that are below the average. The system is thus symmetrical. Poor *Länder* can get a bigger share only at the expense of the rich. This system too contains very few elements of fiscal illusion. The rich (and also the poor) *Länder* can increase their spending only by raising their own residual taxes. The amount of the equalization grant is not affected by these decisions.

I do not know if this system has in fact constituted a check on the growth of local spending in the Federal Republic of Germany. We have to take into account that such a system eliminates the possibility of tax competition among the states (and local governments). But intergovernmental financial arrangements do not, to a large extent, influence the growth of local expenditure.

NOTES

1 The centralization of the tax implies that uniform rates are imposed throughout the country. If rates were previously differentiated – the central government has to calculate the tax rate (or structure) that insures the equivalence of revenue – we have a redistribution of income at the individual level that may influence the spending decisions. We are thus obliged to suppose that these effects are modest or that the rates were not previously differentiated.

2 In Italy the total centralization of the local taxes put into effect with the tax reform of 1971 did not meet opposition from local authorities, which considered the fact that the centralization could put an end to the 'unfair' competition among local governments an advantage.

3 See Kay and King (1983, pp. 138–9) and '*The Economist*', 14–20 January 1983.

4 I do not consider here the problem – which we can clearly observe in the Italian and British experience in the early 1980s (see Bennett, 1982 on this latter case) – of the incapacity of the central government to impose the respect of the limits on local expenditure it has introduced. This incapacity is an important factor for explaining the overspending of local authorities, especially in Italy, where there are so many of them. What is relevant for this account is the determination of the limit itself, that is, the amount of resources left to the local governments.

5 With regard to the allocation among states, Nathan, Manvel and Calkins (1975, p. 92) 'The statutory elements of relative capacity and effort work at cross purposes in the allocation formula'.

6 The formulas that reward fiscal effort are the most growth-inducing because they

introduce competition among local authorities to increase the rates of their taxes. Moreover, like the categorical matching grants, they reduce the price of acquiring new services. These formulas are usually supported in the literature on the basis of their orthodoxy, as they stimulated the financing of local services with increases in compulsory revenues.

REFERENCES

Advisory Council on Intergovernmental Relations (ACIR) (1981), *Studies in Comparative Federalism: Australia, Canada, the United States and West Germany*. Washington, DC: ACIR.

Beer, S. H. (1975), 'The adoption of revenue sharing: a case study in public sector politics', mimeo.

Bennett, R. S. (1982), *Central Grants to Local Governments. The Political and Economic Impact of Rate Support Grants in England and Wales*. Cambridge: Cambridge University Press.

Brennan, G. and Buchanan, J. M. (1980), *The Power to Tax. Analytical Foundations of a Fiscal Constitution*. Cambridge: Cambridge University Press.

Brosio, G., Nyman, D. N. and Santagata, W. (1980), 'Revenue sharing and local public spending: the Italian experience', *Public Choice*, vol. 35, no. 1, pp. 3–15.

Craig, E. D. and Heins, J. A. (1980), 'The effect of tax elasticity on government spending', *Public Choice*, vol. 35, no. 3, pp. 267–75.

Di Lorenzo, T. J. (1982), 'Tax elasticity and the growth of local public expenditure', *Public Finance Quarterly*, vol. 10, pp. 385–92.

Fisher, R. C. (1982), 'Income and grant effects on local expenditure: the fly-paper effect and other difficulties', *Journal of Urban Economics*, vol. 12, pp. 324–45.

Gould, F. (1983), 'The development of public expenditure in western industrialized countries: a comparative analysis', *Public Finance/Finances Publiques*, vol. 38, no. 1, pp. 38–70.

Gramlich, E. M. (1977), 'Intergovernmental grants: a review of the empirical literature', in W. E. Oates (ed.), *The Political Economy of Fiscal Federalism*. Lexington: Lexington Books.

Hunter, G. S. H. (1973), 'Revenue sharing in the Federal Republic of Germany'. Canberra, Australian National University.

Kay, J. A. and King, M. A. (1983), *The British Tax System*. Oxford: Oxford University Press.

Løtz, (1981), 'Local government taxation: recent trends and issues', in K. W. Roskamps and F. Forte (eds), *Reforms of Tax Systems*. Wayne State University Press.

Maxwell, J. A. and Aronson, R. J. (1977), *Financing State and Local Governments*. Washington, DC: Brookings Institution.

Nathan, R. P., Manvel, A. D., Calkins, S. E., *et al.* (1975), *Monitoring Revenue Sharing*. Washington, DC: Brookings Institution.

Oates, W. E. (1975), 'Automatic increases in tax revenue – the effect on the size of the public budget', in W. E. Oates (ed.), *Financing the New Federalism*, Baltimore, Md: Johns Hopkins University Press.

Weber, L. (1984), 'Does fiscal autonomy of non-central government contribute to the growth of the public sector?', comment to this paper presented at the Cernobbio Conference (unpublished).

Winer, S. S. (1983), 'Some evidence on the effect of the separation of spending and taxing decisions', *Journal of Political Economy*, vol. 91, pp. 126–40.

4

Regional Disparities and Decentralization as Determinants of Public-Sector Expenditure Growth in Italy (1960–81)

Ilde Rizzo

The purpose of this essay is to examine the impact of decentralization and the effects of regional disparities on the public-sector share in domestic output in Italy for the period 1960–81. First, the main features of the growth of the public sector in Italy are outlined, stressing the correspondence between trends in aggregate public administration expenditure, local authorities expenditure shares and regional disparities in the period under consideration. Hypotheses are then reviewed that trace a connection between decentralization, regional disparities and public-sector growth with a view to formulating an hypothesis relevant to the Italian case. This hypothesis is then tested and the results of the tests are commented upon. Finally, some tentative conclusions are offered.

MAIN TRENDS IN THE GROWTH OF PUBLIC EXPENDITURE

As a point of departure, it may be useful to look at the main features of the growth of the public sector.[1] In accordance with many studies in the field, the size of government is measured in relative terms and is given by the share of public expenditure[2] in domestic output (TPE : GDP). This ratio, as well as the others listed below, is expressed in current prices, although I am well aware that constant price measures would avoid the 'illusion of growth', derived from the assumed 'productivity lag' existing between private and public sector (see Baumol, 1967). However, the choice of a suitable deflator for public-expenditure components is difficult and does not have to be made in this chapter.[3] In fact, my purpose is not to measure public-expenditure growth in order to evaluate if it is 'too low or too high', but

Table 4.1 *Public and local administration expenditure in absolute size and as a percentage of GDP*

		Public administration							*Local administration*						
Year	*GDP*	*Current expen-diture*	*(3)/(2)*	*Capi-tal expen-diture*	*(5)/(2)*	*Total public expen-diture*	*TPE/ GDP (7)/ (2)*	*Final con-sump-tion*	*Current expen-diture*	*Capi-tal expen-diture*	*Total expen-diture*	*(12)/ (2)*	*LPE/ TPE (12)/ (7)*	*Final con-sump-tion*	*LFC/ TFC (15)/ (9)*
(1)	*(2)*	*(3)*	*(4)*	*(5)*	*(6)*	*(7)*	*(8)*	*(9)*	*(10)*	*(11)*	*(12)*	*(13)*	*(14)*	*(15)*	*(16)*
1960	23 207	6 086	26.22	1 012	4.40	7 098	30.59	2 959	1 277.6	403.45	1 681	7.24	23.67	996.6	33.78
1961	25 810	6 569	25.46	1 065	4.12	7 634	29.58	3 272	1 393.1	416.85	1 810	7.01	23.70	1 097.4	33.54
1962	28 998	7 682	26.50	1 219	4.20	8 901	30.70	3 787	1 597.8	452.2	2 050	7.06	23.02	1 267.4	33.47
1963	33 215	9 150	27.54	1 236	3.72	10 386	31.27	4 614	1 943.8	519.24	2 463	7.41	23.71	1 568	33.98
1964	36 360	10 239	28.16	1 392	3.83	11 631	32.00	5 213	2 172.7	625.28	2 798	7.69	24.05	1 744.2	33.46
1965	39 124	11 988	30.64	1 514	3.87	13 502	34.51	5 915	2 374.6	659.41	3 034	7.75	22.47	1 892.5	31.99
1966	42 391	13 031	30.74	1 595	3.77	14 626	34.50	6 301	2 681.7	692.32	3 374	7.95	23.06	2 066.1	32.79
1967	46 695	14 026	30.04	1 809	3.87	15 835	33.91	6 726	2 929	724.01	3 653	7.82	23.07	2 202.5	32.75
1968	50 614	15 691	31.00	1 993	3.94	17 684	34.94	7 331	3 387.4	738.63	4 126	8.15	23.33	2 451.6	33.44
1969	55 876	17 083	30.57	2 134	3.82	19 217	34.39	7 947	3 674.8	825.17	4 500	8.05	23.41	2 682.5	33.75
1970	62 883	18 993	30.20	2 843	4.52	21 836	34.72	8 664	4 261	969	5 230	8.31	23.95	3 125	36.07
1971	68 510	22 672	33.10	2 641	3.85	25 313	36.95	10 608	5 146	1 066	6 212	9.06	24.54	3 705	34.93
1972	75 124	26 294	35.00	2 978	3.96	29 272	38.96	12 077	6 197	1 213	7 410	9.86	25.31	4 469	34.62
1973	89 746	30 871	34.40	3 245	3.61	34 116	38.01	13 907	7 248	1 377	8 625	9.61	25.28	5 161	37.11
1974	110 719	38 087	34.40	4 459	4.03	42 546	38.43	16 714	8 933	1 949	10 882	9 82	25.58	6 125	36.65
1975	125 378	48 028	38.31	6 430	5.13	54 458	43.44	19 362	11 416	2 656	14 072	11 22	25.84	7 814	40.36
1976	156 657	59 573	38.03	7 150	4.56	66 723	42.59	23 133	13 666	3 621	17 287	11.03	25.91	9.080	39.25
1977	190 083	73 276	38.55	8 734	4.59	82 010	43.14	28 991	16 570	4 375	20 945	11.01	25.54	11 080	38.22
1978	222 254	92 735	41.72	10 097	4.54	102 832	46.27	35 257	19 010	6 333	25 343	11.40	24.64	13 514	38.33
1979	270 198	110 859	41.03	12 423	4.60	123 282	45.63	43 890	26 859	7 869	34 728	12.85	28.17	17 782	40.54
1980	339 068	140 495	41.43	16 444	4.85	156 939	46.28	55 636	35 926	10 095	46 021	13.57	29.32	22 773	40.93
1981	398 125	183 643	46.13	19 873	4.99	203 516	51.12	71 985	47 309	11 763	59 072	14.84	29.02	31 640	43.95

Figures in columns (4), (6), (8), (13), (14) and (16) are percentages; figures in columns (2)–(3), (5), (7), (9)–(12) and (15) are in billion lire at current prices.
Source: Based on ISTAT, National Accounts, 1974 I and 1982).

Table 4.2 *Local administration receipts*

Year	*Tax receipts*	*Grants*	*Other receipts*	*Total receipts*	*Borrowing*	*Total receipts +borrowing*	*(2)/(7)*	*(3)/(7)*
(1)	*(2)*	*(3)*	*(4)*	*(5)*	*(6)*	*(7)*	*(8)*	*(9)*
1960	671	528.1	199.9	1 399	282	1 681	39.92	31.42
1961	695.9	593.4	226.7	1 516	294	1 810	38.45	32.78
1962	730.8	792.1	158.1	1 681	369	2 050	35.65	38.64
1963	857.8	1 012.6	90.6	1 961	502	2 463	34.83	41.11
1964	967.4	932.3	278.3	2 178	620	2 798	34.57	33.32
1965	1 060.7	1 120.1	268.2	2 449	585	3 034	34.96	36.92
1966	1 128	1 290.3	234.7	2 653	721	3 374	33.43	38.24
1967	1 225.1	1 260.3	465.6	2 951	702	3 653	33.54	34.50
1968	1 343.3	1 618.3	416.4	3 378	748	4 126	32.56	39.22
1969	1 430.5	1 593.8	586.7	3 611	889	4 500	31.79	35.42
1970	1 489	1 817	651	3 957	1 273	5 230	28.47	34.74
1971	1 634	2 408	809	4 851	1 361	6 212	26.30	38.76
1972	1 878	2 818	895	5 591	1 819	7 410	25.34	38.02
1973	1 535	3 985	1 066	6 586	2 039	8 625	17.79	46.20
1974	1 113	5 651	1 216	7 980	2 902	10 882	10.23	51.93
1975	1 098	6 743	3 663	11 504	2 568	14 072	7.20	47.92
1976	1 489	10 188	1 982	13 660	3 627	17 287	8.61	58.94
1977	1 752	10 689	3 725	16 166	4 779	20 945	8.36	51.03
1978	1 796	20 485	4 596	26 877	1 534	25 343	7.09	80.83
1979	2 207	25 830	3 508	31 545	3 183	34 728	6.35	74.38
1980	3 247	37 690	4 081	45 018	1 003	46 021	7.05	81.90
1981	4 336	44 280	6 403	55 019	4 053	59 072	7.34	74.96

Figures in columns (8) and (9) are percentages; figures in columns (2)–(7) are in billion lire at current prices.
Source: Based on ISTAT, National Accounts, 1974 I and 1982 I.

to investigate the likely causes underlying such growth. This is not to deny that the existence of a disparity between the growth in nominal and that in real terms may offer useful insights for the analysis. In fact, the relative price effect may reflect features of government production – technological and especially institutional ones – affecting the growth itself.

Between 1960 and 1981, the ratio of TPE : GDP in Italy increased by 20.53 percentage points, from 30.59 per cent in 1960 to 51.12 per cent in 1981. Table 4.1 summarizes this growth. The pattern in this growth is not uniform in the period under review. In fact, between 1960 and 1970, the ratio of TPE : GDP increased by only 4.13 percentage points. On the contrary, between 1970 and 1981, the ratio increased by 16.4 percentage points and, more precisely, within this decade, by 7.68 percentage points in the period 1975–81. Table 4.1 also provides an outline of this growth in the public-sector

Table 4.3 *Industry value added (IVA) at factor cost for north–central and southern Italy*

Year	IVA_s	IVA_{nc}	IVA_{nc}/IVA_s
(1)	*(2)*	*(3)*	*(4)*
1960	1 139.4	6 179.6	5.42
1961	1 260.2	6 936.8	5.50
1962	1 409.5	7 874.5	5.58
1963	1 717.8	9 039.2	5.26
1964	1 896.7	9 765.3	5.14
1965	2 077.5	10 148.5	4.88
1966	2 289.4	10 972.6	4.79
1967	2 555.1	12 126.9	4.75
1968	2 780.2	13 409.8	4.82
1969	3 115.4	15 031.6	4.82
1970	4 285.1	18 783.9	4.38
1971	4 595.5	19 805.5	4.31
1972	4 927.1	21 945.9	4.45
1973	6 014.0	27 452.0	4.56
1974	7 890.0	35 319.0	4.48
1975	9 175.9	39 001.1	4.25
1976	11 363.9	50 355.1	4.43
1977	13 418.4	59 834.6	4.46
1978	15 849.8	69 232.2	4.37
1979	19 833.5	84 966.5	4.28
1980	24 482.3	106 175.7	4.34
1981	28 992.8	119 268.2	4.11

Figures in columns (2) and (3) are in billion lire at current prices; figures in column (4) are percentages.
Source: ISTAT National Accounts, 1974 II and 1982 II.

share broken down by its two main components: current and capital expenditure. As may be seen, over the whole period capital expenditure accounted for only 0.63 percentage points of the total increase, whereas current expenditure accounted for 19.90 percentage points.

Local administration expenditure (as defined in national accounts, that is, including all the sub-central spending)[4] shows a very similar trend.[5] In fact, local public expenditure, as a ratio of the domestic product (LPE :GDP), increased by 7.60 percentage points in the period 1960–81 (see table 4.1), from 7.24 per cent in 1960 to 14.84 per cent in 1981.

In comparing total and local public-expenditure trends, it is clear that in Italy there has been a tendency towards decentralization, at least in terms of expenditure:[6] in fact, local expenditure as a share of total public expenditure (LPE : TPE)[7] has increased by 5.35 percentage points, from 23.67 per cent in 1960 to 29.02 per cent in 1981. The pattern of this increase

Table 4.4 *Agricultural value added (AVA) at factor cost for north–central and southern Italy*

Year	AVA_s	AVA_{nc}	AVA_{nc}/AVA_s
1960	986.2	1836.9	1.89
1961	1 243.4	2 048.9	1.65
1962	1 299.8	2 313.9	1.78
1963	1 569.9	2 270.0	1.44
1964	1 479.0	2 601.4	1.76
1965	1 681.6	2 640.5	1.57
1966	1 695.6	2 786.7	1.64
1967	2 085.1	2 819.9	1.35
1968	1 934.7	2 715.6	1.40
1969	2 215.7	2 936	1.32
1970	2 275.0	3 081.0	1.35
1971	2 540.6	3 056.4	1.20
1972	2 372.5	3 242.5	1.37
1973	3 257.1	4 058.9	1.25
1974	3 765.7	4 590.3	1.22
1975	4 477.0	5 644.0	1.26
1976	4 642.0	7 016.0	1.51
1977	5 967.7	8.075.3	1.35
1978	6 671.0	9 830.0	1.47
1979	8 220.0	11 305.0	1.37
1980	4 745.0	12 886.0	1.32
1981	10 518.0	13 966.0	1.33

Figures in columns (2) and (3) are in billion lire at current prices; figures in column (4) are percentages.
Source: ISTAT National Accounts, 1974 II and 1982 II.

is rather uneven: there was a small decrease between 1960 and 1969 (0.26 percentage points) and a rapid increase after 1970 (5.77 percentage points). Moreover, this increasing trend is enhanced if a specific public expenditure component such as final consumption is inspected. In fact, local final consumption, expressed as a share of total final consumption (LFC : TFC) increased by 10.17 percentage points, though unevenly distributed throughout the period under consideration.

In the period under review, another interesting feature is the changing composition of local revenues.[8] Because of lack of data, tax revenue and grants are the only componenets we can examine (see table 4.2). Considered as shares of total local financial resources (i.e. total local receipts plus borrowing), they show an opposite trend. The ratio of local tax revenue : total local revenue sources decreased by 32.58 percentage points, from 39.92 per cent in 1960 to 7.34 per cent in 1981, whereas the ratio of grants : total local revenue sources increased by 43.54 percentage points, from 31.42 per cent in 1960 to 74.96 per cent in 1981.[9] These figures show the decreasing

Table 4.5 *Gross domestic product per capital in north-central and southern Italy*

Year (1)	GDP_s/POP_s (2)	GDP_{nc}/POP_{nc} (3)	$(GDP_{nc}/POP_{nc}) \div (GDP_s/POP_s$ (3)/(2) (4)
1960	262	533	2.03
1961	295	586	1.99
1962	325	655	2.01
1963	386	735	1.90
1964	417	795	1.91
1965	462	841	1.82
1966	491	905	1.84
1967	546	985	1.80
1968	580	1 056	1.82
1969	640	1 150	1.80
1970	791	1 378	1.74
1971	888	1 473	1.66
1972	956	1 608	1.68
1973	1 129	1 906	1.69
1974	1 375	2 333	1.70
1975	1 573	2 609	1.66
1976	1 876	3 284	1.75
1977	2 274	3 962	1.74
1978	2 624	4 627	1.76
1979	3 231	5 581	1.73
1980	4 029	6 997	1.74
1981	4 820	8 147	1.69

Figures in columns (2) and (3) are in thousand lire at current prices; figures in column (4) are percentages.
Source: ISTAT National Accounts, 1974 II and 1982 II.

importance of tax revenue within total local revenue and may be considered as indicators of the progressive divergence between expenditure and revenue decisions at local level, that is, the decreasing accountability of local authorities.

During the period under review, as may be seen from tables 4.3–4.5, the disparities between the two major statistical regions – the north-central and the south–narrowed. Such disparities may be represented by the following indicators:

1. the ratio between industry value added in the north–central region and industry value added in the southern region ($IVA_{nc} : IVA_s$);
2. the ratio between agricultural value added in the north–central region and agricultural value added in the southern region ($AVA_{nc} : AVA_s$);

3. the ratio between the gross domestic product per capita in the north–central region and the gross domestic product per capita in the southern region $(GDP_{nc}/POP_{nc}) : (GDP_s/POP_s)$.

The first ratio decreased by 1.31 percentage points, from 5.42 per cent in 1960 to 4.11 per cent in 1981 (table 4.3). Smaller variations characterize the other two ratios: $AVA_{nc} : AVA_s$ decreased only by 0.56 percentage points, from 1.89 per cent in 1960 to 1.33 per cent in 1981 (table 4.4) and $(GDP_{nc}/POP_{nc} : (GDP_s/POP_s)$ decreased by 0.34 percentage points, from 2.03 per cent in 1960 to 1.69 per cent in 1981 (table 4.5). These indicators, however, are to be considered only as crude measures of the inequalities existing among political regions because they do not allow for the presence of other relevant differences within the above-mentioned major statistical regions.[10]

THE HYPOTHESES

In the previous section it was seen that there is a close relation between trends in total public expenditure and local public expenditure. Moreover, another association has been detected between the growth in public expenditure and the narrowing of regional disparities. In this section, these hypothesized relationships are examined, before being tested by multiple regression analysis.

The hypothesis of a relationship between interregional disparities and public-sector share has been considered before (for example, Peltzman, 1980, pp. 249–51), but within the framework of a broader approach which tries to explain growth in public expenditure through demand influences in the political market.[11] More precisely, given self-interest behaviour, politicians are assumed to compete with each other with the object of maximizing voter support. To pursue this objective, they include politically 'dominant'[12] redistributive programmes in their platform. Given these assumptions, distribution of income is considered a relevant force shaping the size of government.[13] More precisely, Peltzman reaches the conclusion that 'a reduction in within-beneficiary-group inequality stimulates the growth of government, whereas reduced inequality between groups retards it'.

In this context, inequality between legislative constituencies is a special case. In fact, in such a case, bargaining among politicians would be more closely focused on the constituencies' average interests than on the interests of income groups who have members everywhere. The legislator would still have to take into account the disparity of interests within his constituency, but he would easily ally himself with a legislator from a district with, for instance, a similar average income that is, one belonging to the same 'ideal' group. Thus, greater equality between legislative constituencies is likely to facilitate legislative agreement to implement the expansion of expenditure. It follows that the effects of interdistrict disparities may be assimilated within the above-mentioned 'within-group' inequalities effects; in fact, as long as differences among constituencies are reduced, they can join – through their representatives – an 'ideal' group of beneficiaries from government expansion.

Empirical analysis has not produced unambiguous results concerning the role of interregional disparities in explaining public-sector growth. In the United States these do not seem to have had a perceptible effect on the growth of government. By contrast, in Canada the narrowing of inequalities is positively correlated with the size of government. As such results show, the relevance of this factor varies across countries; it is likely that it depends on the specific social and economic conditions in each of them.

Regional disparities deserve attention in Italy. In fact, this country is characterized by historically marked inequalities between regions, though these inequalities are narrowing as data presented in the previous section show. Therefore, it may be interesting to investigate whether this narrowing of interregional disparities has contributed to the growth of government.

Let us consider the second hypothesis to be tested: the positive role of decentralization of expenditure on the size of government. The *a priori* reasons for such a relationship may be found in the supply-oriented explanations of public-sector growth (Peacock and Wiseman, 1979). Following this approach, demand-oriented explanations are to be considered unsatisfactory because goverments cannot be assumed to act only as passive adjusters to citizens' preferences. Shifting attention from demand to supply, 'institutional' factors become important; the growth may be explained by a close examination of utility-maximizing behaviour of those demanding public services and those supplying them (voters, politicians and bureaucrats). Bureaucrats' bias for overproduction, inefficiency and labour intensity is considered to be a good point of departure to explain patterns in public expenditure. Bureaucrats' strategy is bound to be successful because it is likely to be supported by legislators;[14] in fact, bureaucratic organizations promote the services that voters want.

In my opinion, the relevance of the voter–legislator–bureaucratic nexus may be considered stronger if applied to decentralized levels of government rather than to the central level, given the closer relationships existing among these different actors.[15] In fact, the complex *bargaining* characterizing public-service supply at all levels of government assumes precise characteristics at the local level, where the identification of *contractors* is easier. Therefore, in such a situation, politicians are able to supply voters not only with the services and policies they want, but also with 'facilitation services', in order to reduce the voters' cost of access to services (Fiorina and Noll, 1978).

This view calls for further comment. As long as sub-central governments are endowed with new functions – as has happened in many Western countries – the local spending share in total spending increases. The production of local services is likely to be characterized by the above-mentioned institutional features, which are widely recognized as relevant determinants of the size of government. Thus it may be hypothesized that the increasing share of local public expenditure in total public expenditure (as expressed by the ratio of LPE : TPE) influences the growth of government itself, precisely because of the existence of the already mentioned institutional factors.

Such a conclusion, however, must be strongly affected by the method of financing local expenditure growth. In fact, if increasing local expenditure can be financed without levying additional taxes within the jurisdiction (for instance, through central government grants), such a conclusion seems even more plausible. In such a case, local administrators do not need to match the benefits of increasing public output with its cost. In so doing, they give only the benefits from expenditure to voters, without charging them directly; therefore, voters will not have a true perception of the cost of a unit of service. As a consequence, given that popular support for further public growth will not diminish at the local level,[16] politicians and bureaucrats are likely to agree on increasing local expenditure.

This conclusion might be questioned on the grounds that voters cannot be fooled all the time, and that therefore the extent of fiscal-illusion argument should be reduced. However, given the specific hypothesis we are examining, it seems fairly rational, from the voters' point of view, to support increasing local expenditure. In fact, not only are they supposed to share with a large community the cost of the expenditure they receive, as members of a small community, but also they do not know how the other local jurisdictions will behave. Indeed, they are likely to be beset by the isolation paradox: a reduction of expenditure within a jurisdiction does not necessarily lead to a decrease of taxes levied at national level, unless all the jurisdictions move in the same direction. Therefore, supporting the reduction of expenditure within one jurisdiction might imply a decrease of benefits for the members of that jurisdiction without any relevant gain for them in terms of cost, that is, taxes to be paid at national level.

Given these considerations, it might be concluded that a greater decentralization of expenditure, coupled with increasing fiscal illusion among local taxpayers and the loss of accountability of local government to their electorate (both depending upon the local financing system), may positively affect the growth of government, especially when sub-central governments are entrusted with a growing range of functions.

This hypothesis may be considered as the 'other side of the coin' with respect to the thesis supported by Peacock and Wiseman,[17] that a growing concentration – measured by the proportion of total government expenditure which is centrally financed – facilitates the growth of government. In fact, this statement is based on the idea that in the presence of growing concentration, government can behave rather like a monopolist, without the restraints on taxes provided by competition among localities. This statement assumes that local governments are responsible for their financing, and therefore that they cannot expand expenditure without increasing the tax burden within their constituencies. Of course, such an increase finds a limit in the existing competition among local governments.[18] This limit disappears if we assume that local authorities can increase expenditure simply by seeking transfers (or through borrowing) from higher levels of government; in such a case, they will be stimulated to incur as much expenditure as possible,[19] without becoming less competitive.

These considerations may provide useful insights in interpreting the Italian experience. In fact, since the 1971 tax reform, communal administrators have lost their power to tax their constituents and, at the same time, they have not been limited in any effective way in their power to supply public services and to borrow, at least until the late 1970s. Moreover, in the same decade, relevant institutional changes took place and several functions were transferred from central government to sub-central authorities,[20] without giving the latter any financial autonomy. Therefore in Italy, a strong decentralization of expenditure – as a consequence of the above-mentioned transfer of functions – has been coupled with a local financing system based on grants, the primary effect of which has been to reduce considerably the fiscal responsibilities of sub-central government.[21]

EMPIRICAL RESULTS

In order to test the hypothesis that the decentralization of expenditure and the narrowing of regional disparities affect the size of government positively, the least square method has been applied to equations expressed in linear and logarithmic forms and expressing decentralization in terms of total expenditure as well as in terms of final consumption. The results are as follows:

$$\frac{\text{TPE}}{\text{GDP}} = \underset{(2.06)}{30.20} + \underset{(4.66)}{1.64}\,\frac{\text{LPE}}{\text{TPE}} - \underset{(4.55)}{7.07}\,\frac{\text{IVA}_{\text{nc}}}{\text{IVA}_{\text{s}}} \tag{1}$$

$\bar{R}^2 = 0.85$
$F = 62.68$
$\text{DW} = 1.37$

$$\log\frac{\text{TPE}}{\text{GDP}} = \underset{(2.29)}{2.19} + \underset{(4.06)}{0.93}\,\log\frac{\text{LPE}}{\text{TPE}} - \underset{(5.36)}{1.01}\,\frac{\text{IVA}_{\text{nc}}}{\text{IVA}_{\text{s}}} \tag{2}$$

$\bar{R}^2 = 0.87$
$F = 71.43$
$\text{DW} = 1.30$

$$\frac{\text{TPE}}{\text{GDP}} = \underset{(1.76)}{21.04} - \underset{(4.01)}{5.46}\,\frac{\text{IVA}_{\text{nc}}}{\text{IVA}_{\text{s}}} = \underset{(6.52)}{1.17}\,\frac{\text{LFC}}{\text{TFC}} \tag{3}$$

$\bar{R}^2 = 0.90$
$F = 99.83$
$DW = 1.47$

$$\log \frac{TPE}{GDP} = \underset{(1.70)}{1.48} - \underset{(4.72)}{0.84} \log \frac{IVA_{nc}}{IVA_s} + \underset{(5.31)}{0.96} \log \frac{LFC}{TFC} \quad (4)$$

$\bar{R}^2 = 0.90$
$F = 98.10$
$DW = 1.44$

The equations are apparently satisfactory, both statistically and theoretically. All of the parameter estimates have the correct sign and are statistically significant at the 1 per cent level.

The adjusted correlation coefficients are high and they suggest a good predictive power. The high values of F show that the relationships denoted by the regression are highly significant. Comparing equations (1) and (3), the latter performs better because the indicator chosen to express decentralization – the ratio of local final consumption to public final consumption (LFC : TFC) – gives a better representation of the content of decentralization as occurred in the period under observation, mainly regarding public services. The low Durbin–Watson values are unsatisfactory because they fall in the inconclusive range. This would suggest the possibility of autocorrelation, which is not unusual in time-series data where time trends can be expected to play an important role. This seems to be the case in the relationship under observation. In fact, by explicitly introducing time as a variable in the function (measured by the number of observation periods from a starting year onwards), the explanatory power of the equation was improved and the coefficient of disparities lost its significance (whereas the decentralization coefficient maintained its significance). The different impact exerted on these two variables by introducing time may be explained by the fact that the narrowing of disparities represents a strong time-trend phenomenon. On the other hand, decentralization is a phenomenon which has occurred because of institutional reasons at a specific point in time[22] and, although it may be influenced by other time-related economic factors, it seems to be less dependent on time trends.

In order to correct for possible autocorrelation, equation (3) has been estimated after transforming the original data using the Cochrane–Orcutt method. The results are as follows:

$$\frac{TPE}{GDP} = \underset{(1.60)}{17.61} - \underset{(2.83)}{5.56} \frac{IVA_{nc}}{IVA_s} + \underset{(4.69)}{1.06} \frac{LFC}{TFC} \quad (5)$$

$\bar{R}^2 = 0.82$
$F = 47.95$
$DW = 1.84$

As may be seen, results seem to be satisfactory; the parameters have the correct sign and the result is significant at the 5 per cent level. The Durbin–Watson value is such that the null hypothesis of no autocorrelation may be accepted.

The equations presented above, as in most empirical testing, may embody specification problems. First of all, there may be simultaneity problems, because the narrowing of regional disparities is likely to be a function of the growth of government. Moreover, slight problems of simultaneity might derive from the indicator chosen to represent decentralization; in fact local expenditure is a component of both dependent and independent variables. This problem may be overcome by choosing a different indicator to represent decentralization. On this question, some comments are in order.

In general, the choice of suitable indicators to represent variables is arbitrary and, moreover, this problem is a particularly difficult one to solve in the case of decentralization. In fact, as Oates (1978) has pointed out, there are no unambiguous, non-arbitrary measures of the extent of decentralization.[23] Even if we are not concerned with the difficult question of measuring the 'quantity' of decision-making power, according to its spread among different levels of sub-central governments, we nevertheless, need to measure how expenditure decision-making is divided between central and sub-central levels of government, and therefore how such expenditure is financed. The *decentralization ratio* LPE : TPE does not represent this phenomenon in a completely satisfactory way, because it does not take into account how expenditure is financed. This problem may not be overcome by including in the equation an indicator describing local expenditure financing such as, for instance, the share of total local expenditure financed by locally raised tax revenue, given by the ratio LTR : LPE, because of the likely strong correlation existing between this latter variable and the ratio LPE : TPE. In fact, supported by previous analytical considerations, the strength of the relationship between decentralization and the growth of government is affected by the degree of fiscal dependence of local authorities on central government. Therefore, in this way, the local financing system itself affects the growth of government.[24]

In order to solve this specification problem, a fruitful avenue of inquiry might be to look for a new indicator to represent decentralization: for instance, some sort of 'physical' indicator based on the number of decentralized functions, rather than on the amount of resources locally administered. The use of such an indicator would be compatible with the other one, representing local expenditure financing.

Lastly, let us consider regional disparities. Among all the indicators listed above to represent this phenomenon, we have chosen the ratio $IVA_{nc} : IVA_s$, because it seems to be the most satisfactory. In fact, although all the other indicators were also significant, the explanatory power of the equations was reduced when the ratio $IVA_{nc} : IVA_s$ was replaced by them.

The above-mentioned reservations are intended to advise caution in evaluating the results. However, the econometric findings emerging from this chapter seem to be interesting: Italian evidence for the period 1960–81 is not incompatible with the hypothesis of a 'decentralization effect'[25] nor with an interregional disparities effect.[26]

CONCLUSIONS

The results of this essay are at least suggestive, and perhaps interesting as well. First, it has been shown that there has been a positive effect of decentralization in expenditure, coupled with a decline of fiscal responsibilities of local administrators. This would tend to stress the relevance of the local-level 'institutional' factors in explaining the growth of government. Indeed, other features of decentralization such as the degree of fragmentation of the structure, or the extent of interdependence between different levels of government may be influential. Such possible effects have not been adequately explored to date.

The second fruitful area of inquiry is to study the impact of the narrowing of regional disparities on the growth of public expenditure. This chapter, using a crude measure of interregional inequalities, shows that there exists a relationship; it might be interesting to investigate such a relationship using less aggregative indicators, allowing for the existence of relevant differences within the major statistical regions.

Finally, the chapter implies that future control of public expenditure requires investigation of the effect of increasing the fiscal independence of sub-central authorities, for instance through other forms of fiscal federalism and by allowing for the fiscal autonomy of local units.

NOTES

I wish to acknowledge support of the National Research Council (CNR) under the NATO Junior Fellowship programme. I am especially indebted to Alan Peacock for his invaluable suggestions, advice and encouragement. I also wish to acknowledge discussions on an earlier draft of this chapter with R. Battiato, M. Ricketts and G. K. Shaw, helpful econometric suggestions by D. Greenaway, and useful comments by Professors E. Giardina and L. Weber, and all the participants of the conference. My thanks are also due to M. A. Greco for his assistance in collating the data.

1 Following many studies in the field see, for instance, Reviglio (1981) and Fossati (1981). We define the public sector as *public administration*, including central government, local authorities and social insurance bodies.

2 For the purposes of this research, it seems more convenient to consider total expenditure as a measure of public sector, instead of considering only public final consumption. In fact, a ratio omitting transfers would be without any general

significance as a broad indicator of changes in the government's overall influence in the community over time.

3 The main issue underlying the choice of an appropriate deflator has been discussed by Heller (1981) and Beck (1981).

4 Such an aggregate includes regions, provinces, communes, local health and welfare units, and other local bodies such as universities, provincial tourism bodies and chambers of commerce.

5 Although in the period 1960–81 relevant changes have occurred in national accounts methodology (the effects of health reform, the introduction of SEC system), expenditure data presented in table 4.1 are homogeneous. The Central Institute of Statistics has published 'adjusted' public administration expenditure data (1960–81) and local authorities' expenditure data (1970–81). For the period 1960–9 we have recalculated local authorities' expenditure to make it consistent with the series published by the Central Institute of Statistics.

6 In the literature it has been pointed out (see Davies, 1970) that the degree of centralization (and therefore of decentralization) varies if we consider the revenue system instead of expenditure system. Moreover, Musgrave (1971) notes that the latter is usually less centralized than the former. The idea is relevant in the Italian case, where decentralization in expenditure is coupled with the increasing centralization in revenue as table 4.2 shows.

7 Note that the ratio of LPE : TPE compares two aggregates which are not homogeneous. TPE, being the consolidation of expenditure of central, local and social security bodies, does not include financial operations such as transfers to other public institutions, which are included in LPE. The problem might be solved by adjusting the numerator, but this solution does not seem satisfactory with respect to the scope of our analysis, which is aimed at explaining the growth of government looking at local expenditure. Therefore, the econometric testing (see below) has been done with an unadjusted ratio; this choice, however, has been supported by the fact that, even using an adjusted ratio, results were fairly similar.

8 Total local receipts figures have also been recalculated for the period 1960–9 to make them consistent with data published by the Central Institute of Statistics for the following period (1970–81).

9 The pattern of this growth is rather uneven; in fact, 29.8 percentage points are concentrated in the period 1977–8, probably because of the fact that in 1977 communal debts have been balanced by central government grants.

10 Historically, Italy has been characterized by a strong 'dualism' between north and south. Today, however, such a clear-cut distinction is considered not completely satisfactory (see, Becattini and Bianchi, 1982), because of relevant economic and structural differences emerging within the traditional major statistical regions. For instance, the north–central eastern regions have moved away from such a dualistic scheme.

11 Even since Adolph Wagner expounded his law of 'expanding scale of state activity', attempts to explain the secular increase in government spending have usually emphasized demand factors such as population and income growth, urbanization and industrialization, technological change, social and cultural changes. For a survey, see T. E. Borcherding (1977).

12 A politically 'dominant' policy is that which maximizes the difference between the number of beneficiaries perceiving the policy as the best 'deal' and losers

perceiving it as the worst. Assuming that political preferences are motivated only by self-interest, it is likely that political competition leads actual policy to converge on the dominant policy.

13 The role of income distribution has been stressed by Meltzer and Richard (1981), who consider the growth of government as essentially depending on the demand for redistribution.

14 The relationship between politicians and bureaucrats is more complex. Following Niskanen (1971), bureaucrats are simply monopolists who are able to impose their own preferences on the governing political party. In contrast with this thesis, Breton and Wintrobe (1975) support the idea that politicians are able to enforce their own preferences by the use of control devices over bureaucrats' over-production and cross-inefficiency.

15 A different idea has been supported by Nellor (1984), suggesting that the larger the jurisdiction, the more effectively budget-maximization will be pursued.

16 The thesis that fiscal illusion produces an underestimation of the tax price of public expenditure, and therefore results in voting behaviour favouring large public sectors, has been supported by Buchanan and Wagner (1977). In contrast with this view, Downs (1960) reached the opposite conclusion, that the actual budget is smaller than the correct budget, because taxpayers perceive expenditure tax prices more clearly than expenditure benefits.

17 See Peacock and Wiseman (1967). As is well known, they argue that the concentration process may be considered loosely associated with the displacement effect. The former can occur independently of the latter, but we should expect to find some relation. In fact, during periods of social upheaval the pressures for concentration are not weakened by the political opposition to change. At the same time, events such as wars imply a faster growth of central functions; in this situation, the needs of war are expected to become more important than issues such as local autonomy.

18 There are several ways in which the interaction of local governments can influence the level of expenditure. There is wide consensus that local governments do or should take into account the competition from other jurisdictions in determining their tax-expenditure package and that, the competition on the tax side would lead to a reduction in the level of local expenditure. However, it should be taken into account that competition is likely to exist also in terms of expenditure; in such a case a possible effect would be to expand the budget.

19 Under these conditions, expanding local expenditure requires that politicians at central level support increasing grants to local levels of government. They might do so because, given the institutions and the rules governing the decision-making process, being generous in increasing grants can become profitable within the local political market.

20 In 1970, regional governments were created and, since then, they have been progressively endowed with relevant functions in various fields such as environment, education, health, agriculture, planning and so on. At the same time, correspondingly important functions have been assigned to communes. Broadly speaking, the state–region–commune line represents the main hierarchy. In addition to these basic structures, there are provinces and other units, such as *comprensori* (groups of communes) and *circoscrizioni* (communal sub-units) and some other 'intermediate units', above commune and below region. The

existing structure therefore is characterized by a high degree of fragmentation and overlapping of territorial units.

21 With reference to communal experience, see Martinotti (1981); Brosio, Nyman and Santagata (1980).

22 In order to exploit further the role of institutional changes, dummy variables, representing institutional changes that occurred in the early, 1970s, after the tax reform, were introduced. The results were as follows:

$$\frac{\text{TPE}}{\text{GDP}} = \underset{(2.42)}{32.76} - \underset{(3.74)}{5.21}\frac{\text{IVA}_{nc}}{\text{IVA}_{s}} + \underset{(2.97)}{0.79}\frac{\text{LFC}}{\text{LTC}} + \underset{(1.99)}{3.15}\,\text{D}_0 \qquad (6)$$

$\bar{R}^2 = 0.91$
$F = 69.49$
DW $= 1.44$

$$\frac{\text{TPE}}{\text{GDP}} = \underset{(2.63)}{36.24} - \underset{(3.86)}{5.27}\frac{\text{IVA}_{nc}}{\text{IVA}_{s}} + \underset{(2.47)}{0.69}\frac{\text{LFC}}{\text{LTC}} + \underset{(2.20)}{0.094}\,\text{D}_1\frac{\text{LFC}}{\text{LTC}} \qquad (7)$$

$\bar{R}^2 = 0.92$
$F = 72.76$
DW $= 1.46$

where D_0 and D_1 are dummy variables, respectively, used to measure the changes of the intercept and the slope parameters as a consequence of the mentioned institutional changes. As expected, both have positive signs, indicating that after such institutional reform an upward shift occurred in the function, representing the growth of government as dependent on decentralization and that the slope was positively affected as well. Indeed, the latter effect would seem to be stronger than the former. Apart from the fact that equation (7) performs slightly better than equation (6), this argument is supported on the grounds that including both variables in the same equation, the D_0 coefficient changed sign and its significance was slightly reduced. Moreover, both equations are statistically significant. The low Durbin–Watson value falling in the inconclusive region would suggest the possibility of autocorrelation; however, after transforming the original data using the Cochrane–Orcutt method, the equations were still statistically and theoretically significant, with no autocorrelation.

23 Oate's argument refers to centralization; however, it also holds for decentralization. On this issue, see also Ashford (1979).

24 We tested this hypothesis, that is, that increasing fiscal dependence may enhance the growth of government. After transforming the original data, using the Cochrane - Orcutt method, the results were as follows:

$$\frac{\text{TPE}}{\text{GDP}} = \underset{(7.72)}{47.12} - \underset{(4.43)}{0.32}\frac{\text{LTR}}{\text{LPE}} - \underset{(2.28)}{4.92}\frac{\text{IVA}_{nc}}{\text{IVA}_{s}} \qquad (8)$$

$\bar{R}^2 = 0.81$
$F = 44.66$
DW $= 1.21$

Parameter estimates are both statistically and theoretically significant and the explanatory power is satisfactory as well, as may be seen from the high values of R and F. Such results seem to indicate the existence of a positive effect of local financial dependence (increasing when the ratio of LTR : LPE decreases) on the growth of expenditure. However, the low Durbin–Watson value falling in the inconclusive range suggests the possibility of autocorrelation and therefore some reservations have to be made on the above estimates. It must be pointed out that the result shown in equation (8) cannot be generalized, because it is likely to hold only if specific conditions are fulfilled, for instance the lack of central control over local expenditures, which has characterized the Italian decentralization process in the 1970s. Using different indicators and referring to other countries, Gould (1983) reaches different conclusions.

25 The decentralization hypothesis seems to be confirmed – although to a lesser extent than in the Italian case – by a regression run for the UK for the period 1961–82. The different strength of the relationship between decentralization and the growth of government in the two countries gives some useful insights into policy implications. Central control, coupled with a certain degree of fiscal independence, characterizing the UK situation, are relevant institutional factors which are likely to reduce the influence of the decentralization effect.

26 With reference to the Italian case, other hypotheses on the causes of the growth of government have been tested by Giannone (1983) and Fratianai-Spinelli (1982).

REFERENCES

Ashford, D. E. (1979), 'Territorial politics and equality: decentralisation in the modern state', *Political Studies*.

Baumol, W. J. (1967), 'The macroeconomics of unbalanced growth: the anatomy of urban crisis', *American Economic Review*, vol. 57, pp. 415–26.

Becattini, C. and Bianchi, G. (1982), 'Sulla multiregionalita dello sviluppo economico italiano', *Note Economiche*, pp. 19–37.

Beck, M. (1981), 'On measuring public sector shares', *National Tax Journal*, pp. 487–8.

Borcherding, T. E. (1977), 'The sources of growth of public expenditures in the United States, 1902–1970', in T. E. Borcherding (ed.), *Budgets and Bureaucrats the Sources of Government Growth*. Durham: Duke University Press.

Breton, A. and Wintrobe, R. (1975), 'The equilibrium size of a budget maximising bureau: a note on Niskanen's theory of bureaucracy', *Journal of Political Economy*, pp. 195–207.

Brosio, G., Nyman, D. N. and Santagata, W. (1980), 'Revenue sharing and local public spending: the Italian experience', *Public Choice*, vol. 35, no. 1, pp. 3–15.

Buchanan, J. and Wagner, R. (1977), *Democracy in Deficit: The Political Legacy of Lord Keynes*, New York: Academic Press.

Davies, G. D. (1970), 'The concentration process and the growing importance of non-central government in federal states', *Public Policy*, pp. 649–57.

Downs, A. (1960), 'Why the government budget is too small in a democracy', *World Politics*, July, pp. 541–63.

Fiorina, M. and Noll, R. P. (1978), 'Voters, bureaucrats and legislators', *Journal of Public Economics*, vol. 9, pp. 239–54.

Fossati, A. (1981), 'La spesa pubblica in Italia del 1951 al 1980', *Riviata di diritto finanziario e scienza delle finanze*, pp. 322–75.
Fratianni, M. and Spinelli, F. (1982), 'The growth of government in Italy: Evidence from 1861 to 1979, *Public Choice*, vol. 39, pp. 221–43.
Giannone, A. (1983), 'Spesa pubblica e sviluppo economico in Italia nel periodo 1960–1981', *Note Economiche*, pp. 5–39.
Gould, F. (1983), 'The development of public expenditure in western industrialised countries; a comparative analysis', *Public Finance*, vol. 38, no. 1, pp. 38–69.
Heller, P. (1981), 'Diverging trends in the shares of nominal and real government in GDP: implications for policies', *National Tax Journal*, vol. 34, no. 1, pp. 61–74.
Martinotti, G. (1981), 'The illusive autonomy: central control and decentralisation in the Italian local financial system', in L. J. Sharpe (ed.), *The Local Fiscal Crisis in Western Europe, Myth and Realities*, New York: Sage Publications.
Meltzer, A. and Richard, S. F. (1981), 'A rational theory of the size of government', *Journal of Political Economy*, vol. 89, no. 5, pp. 914–27.
Musgrave, R. (1971), *Fiscal Systems,* New Haven, Conn: Yale University Press.
Nellor, D. L. (1984), 'Public bureaus, budgets and jurisdiction size: an empirical note', *Public Choice*, vol. 42, pp. 175–85.
Niskanen, A. (1971), *Bureaucracy and Representative Government*, Chicago: Aldine-Atherton.
Oates, W. E. (1978), 'The changing structure of intergovernmental fiscal relations', in H. C. Recktenwald (ed.), *Secular Trends of the Public Sector.* Editions Cujas.
Peacock, A. T. and Wiseman, J. (1967), *The Growth of Public Expenditure in the United Kingdom, 1890–1955*, rev. edn. London: George Allen and Unwin.
Peacock, A. T. and Wiseman, J. (1979), 'Approaches to the analysis of government expenditure growth', *Public Finance Quarterly*, pp. 3–23.
Peltzman, S. (1980), 'The growth of government', *Journal of Law and Economics*, vol. 1, no. 2, pp. 209–87.
Reviglio, F. (1981), 'Il "controllo" della spesa pubblica negli anni '80', *Rivista di Politica Economica*, pp. 1237–68.
Wagner, A. (1967). 'The nature of fiscal economy', in R. A. Musgrave, A. T. Peacock (eds), *Classics in the Theory of Public Finance.* London: Macmillan, and New York: St. Martin's Press.

5

Collective Choice, Social Welfare and Economic Growth

Gianni Zandano

INTRODUCTION

In the last few decades, research on public-expenditure growth has undergone truly remarkable changes, and equally remarkable progress. A few studies devoted to the long-term growth of public expenditure in the United States, in the early and mid-1950s, marked the beginning of a new interest for this subject, which, at least as far as economic research is concerned, had been neglected for a long period.[1] Since then this interest has greatly strengthened, with the appearance of an increasing number of studies devoted to many countries, and now a vast body of literature is available. Also, this quantitative development of studies has been accompanied by qualitative improvement, as description of facts gave way to analysis, and intuitive reasoning to more carefully formulated hypotheses. Nevertheless, it is difficult to escape the feeling that progress has been less than could have been expected (or hoped).

The present situation, indeed, is one where many findings and hypotheses have accumulated, but no unifying theory has emerged. Similar remarks have been put forward repeatedly, and have inspired a number of attempts to survey and discuss the existing literature, to sort out the main difficulties and the possibilities for overcoming them.[2]

The aim of this chapter is to contribute further to this effort. I will not try to give an extensive survey of the literature; instead, I would like to concentrate on what are, in my opinion, the main issues. I shall briefly start with a conceptual discussion required for empirical analysis; then I will proceed to consider the problem of theory building, focusing on the link between the working of political processes and public-expenditure growth; finally, I will try to probe the possibility of forming an understanding for the judgement of public expenditure – that is, to answer the question of whether, as it has often been said, this growth has been excessive.

THE MEASUREMENT PROBLEM

In the field of empirical analysis, two main questions have received most of the attention: the question of the time pattern of public-expenditure growth, and the question of the divergence between nominal and real growth.

The first question has given rise to a prolonged and, on occasion, lively debate, between those maintaining that the growth of public expenditure (relative to national income) has been an essentially continuous process (conforming therefore to Wagner's law), and those maintaining, on the contrary, that it has been marked by severe discontinuities or displacement effects, following the treminology originally introduced by Peacock and Wiseman (1967). This debate has not definitely produced winners and losers and, moreover, it seems to have subsided in the last few years. This can be explained in a number of ways.

The available data are never, as is well known, completely reliable; furthermore, they vary greatly from country to country and, as far as single countries are concerned, from period to period. But this is a situation that individual researchers must take as given (and, by the way, no decisive improvement can be anticipated for the short term). By contrast, the individual researcher's judgement enters, and has a substantial role, in the selection of data and the choice of econometric techniques. In both these respects, widely differing decisions have been taken, resulting, quite obviously, in differing answers to the question of continuity *vis-à-vis* discontinuity in the growth of public expenditure.

Specifically, in recent years, it has been found that the concepts of continuity and discontinuity, which have been empirically tested, are not mutually exclusive, but overlap. When it was maintained that following the two world wars and the Great Depression a displacement effect had occurred in the United Kingdom, reference was made to every kind of modification in the trend of public-expenditure growth, as reflected in changes in the values of the coefficients of the estimated equation.[3] Instead, when it was maintained that Wagner's law was verified (and no displacement effect had occurred), reference was made to a narrower concept of discontinuity, one including only the shifts of the trend, and, accordingly, to a larger concept of continuity, embracing all phenomena of continuous growth of public expenditure, even if characteristically different from period to period (Henning and Tussing, 1974; Ganti and Kolluri, 1979). Now it is fairly obvious that all modifications in the trends of public-expenditure growth are discontinuities, as indeed they reflect changes in the causal relationships governing the process of growth. Nevertheless, it is important to distinguish among different types of discontinuities: if a given trend is simply shifted; if its slope has changed; or if both these changes have occurred together.

If these distinctions are made, it will be difficult to stick to simple generalizations of empirical behaviour based on the two concepts of continuity and discontinuity, and it will be necessary to admit that things are more complicated (and mixed). This, however, would be surely preferable to the present state of very limited knowledge, in which the only reliable fact is evidence of growth of public expenditure, that is, the finding already offered in the earliest studies.

Problems of a different nature and importance exist also with the second main question, which has been subjected to deeper empirical research, that of the divergence between nominal and real growth of public expenditure. There seems to be no doubt on the existence of such a divergence, as well as its considerable width. The reasons are now well known, and were put forward by Baumol (1967): productivity growth has been slower in the public sector than in the private sector, because of the inherently labour-intensive nature of most public services (and also, many would add, because of the tendency of the public sector to inefficiency and waste); but labour costs have tended to rise together – at least approximately – in the two sectors, and this has caused the costs of public services to go up faster than the costs and prices of goods and services produced in the private sector.

What is to be doubted is the reliability of the available quantitative measures of the escalation of costs in the public sector – that is, of the official estimates of the price deflators for this sector. The attempt to disentangle real from nominal growth of public expenditure, due above all to Beck (1976, 1979 and 1981), has understandably relied on these official estimates; therefore, the results obtained, however interesting they are, should be taken with extreme care. Future research should tackle, first of all, the problem of the meaning and limitations of the data.[4]

THE TASK OF MODEL BUILDING

The attempt to build a theory of public-expenditure growth has taken a clearly discernible path towards a fuller and more explicit treatment of the working of political processes. It is no longer possible to be content with the structure of reasoning typical of early studies, where the growth of public expenditure was linked to some contemporary economic, social or demographic transformation, and no illustration was given – indeed no mention was made – of the nature and the working of the links themselves. These links are quite obviously political links – that is, pertaining to political representation and decision-making – and their consideration fills a gap in the analysis and was much needed.

However, I am not sure that the attempt to warrant this consideration has taken the most direct and promising route. What has been offered is one version or another of theories that can be labelled, for short, economic theories of the political processes: theories, that is, representing those political processes fundamentally as electoral processes, where rational economically motivated individuals vote directly on competing programmes of public expenditure and taxation, proposed by politicians or parties.[5] In more elaborate versions, theories that modify this basic framework allow a role for another group of individual agents, the public bureaucrats.[6]

I cannot enter here into a discussion of the merits and weaknesses of these theories. I will simply remark that, from the point of view of the explanation of public-expenditure growth, they have singled out two main causes of growth: the ability of low- and average-income groups (being the majority) to obtain control of government activity at the expense of high-income groups, and to use this control to expand redistributive public expenditure and taxation (see Brunner, 1978; Meltzer and Richard, 1975 and 1981; Peltzman, 1980); and the ability of public bureaucracies to propel the expenditure expansion they are interested in, because of the strategic position they occupy in the operation of government activity and because of their weight as voters (see Bush and Denzau, 1977, pp. 90–9; Courant, Gramlich and Rubinfeld, 1979).

EXPENDITURE ON WHAT

A question that has received only scanty attention in empirical analysis, but that is worth mentioning because of its importance, is that of the disaggregate behaviour of public expenditure.[7] Most of the literature on public-expenditure growth can best be assessed by examining the actual data available for the major industrial countries (table 5.1).

Assembling the different types of expenditure according to functions, it is possible to see that the traditional activity of government in supplying public goods (defence and general government expenses) has decreased in most countries over the last thirty years. Expenditure on defence and general administration is not linked in any direct way to the national income. The fall of these shares as a percentage of GDP since the mid-1950, mainly due to the steady fall in defence expenditure, seems to supply an indirect support to the Wagner law. However, it is well known that correlation does not imply causation. Moreover, attempts to test the supposed relationship between government expenditure, as a ratio of GDP, and per-capita income have failed to establish any substantial evidence (Denison, 1979). For that matter, none of the political decision-making theories (OECD, 1983a) that have been put forward in recent years have received any statistical evidence. Typically equations have been estimated by using government expenditure as a dependent variable and GDP as one of the explanatory variables. This, it will be noted, is precisely the reverse-order causation relationship of the common Keynesian income–expenditure system. The simultaneous approach would be needed, and consequently the econometric problem would increase a great deal. In defence of the political decision-making models, it has to be said that statistics is not the main ground on which they are supposed to be judged.

Table 5.1 *Index numbers of public expenditure to GDP ratio (1954 = 100)*

	France (1979)	*Federal Republic of Germany (1979)*	*Italy (1980)*	*Japan (1980)*	*United Kingdom (1979)*	*United States (1979)*
Total expenditure	129.5	152.4	159.6	142.2	122.6	121.6
Public goods	64.3	83.3	n.a.	73.7	60.3	52.9
Defence	56.7	76.3	n.a.	42.9	55.3	40.7
Administrative costs	73.1	87.5	n.a.	91.7	67.9	84.1
Merit goods	180.2	185.3	261.2	431.0	163.5	234.2
Education	158.3	141.7	196.4	263.2	138.5	186.7
Health	260.9	260.0	421.4	470.0	162.1	312.5
Income maintenance	159.8	165.2	152.4	251.7	182.8	239.0
Pensions	246.0	180.5	286.3	500.0	206.3	261.5
Unemployment compensation	120.0	81.8	75.0	100.0	700.0	66.7
Family allowances	50.0	550.0	42.0	160.0	233.3	250.0
Others	115.0	133.3	51.0	600.0	144.4	300.0
Other Services	129.0	278.9	n.a.	52.3	272.7	166.7
Interest on public debt	115.4	237.5	281.8	533.3	117.9	180.0

n.a. Data not available for 1954.
Source: OECD Observer, March 1983, n. 121.

Table 5.2 *Total public outlay/GDP and social expenditure/total public outlay percentage shares at current and constant prices in 1960 and 1981*

Countries	*1960*				*1981*			
	Total outlay/GDP		*Social outlay/total outlay*		*Total outlay/GDP*		*Social outlay/total outlay*	
	Current	*Constant*	*Current*	*Constant*	*Current*	*Constant*	*Current*	*Constant*
United States	28.1	30.9	38.7	36.4	35.9	34.3	58.5	59.5
Japan	17.0	22.8	47.1	44.8	30.7	23.1	57.0	59.1
Germany	31.4	33.5	65.3	60.9	47.7	42.6	66.0	68.5
France	33.8	37.6	39.7	35.6	48.7	44.9	48.9	54.6
Italy	29.9	34.7	55.2	50.8	45.4	38.7	64.1	67.7
United Kingdom	33.2	36.2	41.9	38.8	45.6	43.2	54.6	58.8

Source: OECD, 1983b.

Two points are worth stressing, if one looks at the recent trends of public expenditure.

1. In all industrial countries, the price deflators of current public expenditure on goods and services have risen much more than those for consumption. The suspicion of a lower or null increase in public servants' productivity is very old and has been variously explained (Godley and Taylor, 1977). However, there seems to be evidence to support the view that government management has been lax, because of the absence of market constraints and available alternatives to consumers.[8]
2. In addition to the already large increase, as a share of GDP, of total government outlay in the period 1960–81, social expenditure (as defined by the set of expenditures on merit goods and income-maintenance programmes) has increased even more sharply (see table 5.2).

Public expenditure, therefore, in addition to its growth (well above the improvement of the underlying economic condition), has changed its composition towards more social objectives. The reasons behind such a change are both political and economic. Expenditure on health, education, old age pension and unemployment compensation has been justified by reference to the market's failures both to guarantee outcomes that meet society's equity objectives and to any of the possible causes of market inefficiency: imperfect competition; absence of future markets; structural unemployment; externalities; public and merit goods.

For instance, the cases of health and education can be taken as examples of possible failures of the market that might have supported public-expenditure growth. In health care, it is argued that society's objective is to guarantee equality of access, cost and outcome for those with equal need, while ensuring that the delivery system uses resources efficiently. Market provision most likely would not achieve either equity or efficiency. The best health care would go to those who could pay the most, and the poor might not be able to afford health care at all. Inefficiency would stem from the many externalities that characterize health care or from consumer ignorance and uncertainty.

In education, it is correspondingly argued that society's objective is to achieve equality of educational opportunities for those of equal ability, and an efficient allocation of resources. In this case also, market provision would be likely to result in lack of both efficiency and equity. Only the rich families could afford to send their children to school. Moreover, ignorance and uncertainty as to the return of education would make the market inefficient.

Similar arguments hold for the case of income-maintenance programmes, even though for unemployment compensation and family allowances the equity problem is felt much more than the efficiency conditions. The redistribution of income towards the disadvantaged member of the community has actually been the major objective of government since the early 1960s.

In their broad pursuit of these objectives, governments have had three main types of instruments available: control of individual activities by law, regulation and administrative controls; reallocation of private resources through changes in the structure of taxation; direct involvement in production and expenditure programmes. All these instruments have been applied more or less intensively across different countries in the last decades. Evaluating their impact on the private sector is a tough task, and it would not be surprising if it turned out that regulations, rather than direct expenditure by the government, have had a major impact on the distribution of resources. However, regulation of private activity, in contrast to direct government expenditure on entitlement programmes, is characterized by the flexibility of coming to an end when the private sector does not produce any more net wealth!

Public-expenditure programmes that are not (or are inversely) related to the level of private activity pose the problem of aggregate compatibility, owing to the financing requirements. This has become a problem only in recent years, due to the financing constraints imposed by the anti-inflationary monetary policy. The major strain on the financing constraints of public-sector expenditure and deficit has been set against the relatively small success gained by monetary policy in curbing inflation and price expectations. It has been argued (Boltho, 1983) that, given the actual structure of monetary policy, fiscal policy might have a major impact on the price expectations held by the public. Therefore some of the worries about the long-run tendency of public expenditure seem to be justified, for there is the question of whether the economy could continue to supply social services and welfare payments at the long-experienced level and rate of growth. In addition, there are well-grounded doubts as to whether the composition and the operating system of the welfare state actually meet, with a sufficient degree of confidence, the intended objectives. I believe that these two questions are the proper economic criteria to judge the present state of public expenditure.

PUBLIC EXPENDITURE AND ECONOMIC PERFORMANCE

By taking an economic point of view, I do not mean to dismiss all at once the relevance of the decision-making process that remains the main problem. However, as argued above, decision-making literature is too abstract to shed much light on the reasons for the expansion of the government's role. The decision-making theorists have contributed more in reshaping the approach to state intervention in the economy than in explaining past trends and objectives. From an economic point of view, therefore, the central problem, as far as public expenditure is concerned, is not its level or rate of growth, but rather its effects on the potential rate of growth of the economy. Instead, from a collective-choice point of view, the problem is to assess public-expenditure performance in fulfilling equity objectives. In these respects, the crisis of the welfare state is economic and not political,[9] which is to say that concern about the government's role comes from a relatively poor (less than expected) performance of state intervention both in fostering economic growth and improving equity. On the one hand, good economic performance may be inconsistent with high and prolonged redistribution of resources. On the other hand, inefficiency in income redistribution is inconsistent with high levels of taxation and public expenditure. Politicians, vested-interest groups and bureaucrats may well wish to continue expanding public expenditure even beyond any reasonable economic limit, but this would only give rise to a vicious circle in the hopeless attempt, by different social categories, to get hold of an extra non-existing share of the cake. Pointing out (Klein, 1984, p. 13) that the crisis of the welfare state has been first perceived in countries like Britain and the United States, where the levels of public expenditure on welfare are among the lowest in the industrial countries, rather than supporting a non-correlation between the size of public expenditure and economic performance, may not tell us very much about the capability of politicians in the other industrial countries in managing the economy. Such a view gains momentum when related to the use that has been made of public spending in achieving social consensus. Also counter-cyclical policy has been affected by such a distorted way of managing public resources. In fact, even when the economy is out of the slump, public expenditure remains at that level until one other 'displacement' effect occurs to give place to a further increase.[10]

An 'excessively' large public-sector share of GDP will ultimately be reflected in a decline of the rate of economic growth. This may result both from a reduction of factor supply following increases in taxation and in unemployment and social security benefits, and from the crowding-out effect of government deficits. Econometric testing of the contribution of public expenditure to economic growth often fails to identify a specific way through which government activity influences the economy (see Denison, 1979; OECD, 1983a, p. 12. For this reason only speculations can be made. A better insight into the working of the public and private sector can be given by the criterion of separating sectors according to whether their output is marketed or not (Bacon and Eltis, 1975 and 1978). The rationale behind this approach is that the market sector, since it produces all output sold both at home and abroad, must meet all consumption, investment and export demands. Therefore, if the non-market sector is to absorb an increasing share of marketed output, this implies that the share left for market consumption, investment and net export must decrease.

A more fundamental question arises from the crowding-out argument. The growth of public expenditure and its method of financing would displace an equal amount of private investment, and in the long run could also reduce the growth capacity of the economy (see Friedman, 1978). Econometric research using cross-section data on OECD countries for the period 1961–72 shows a 'significant inverse' relationship between the ratio of government

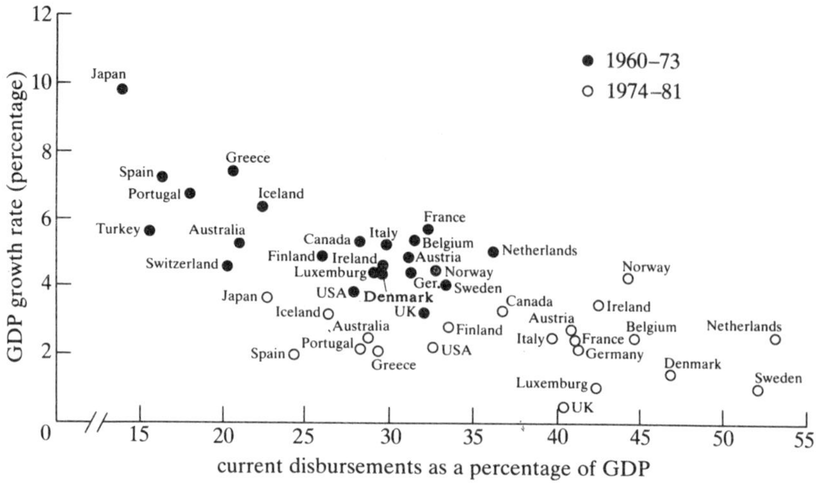

Figure 5.1 Public expenditure and GDP growth rate (annual averages).

final consumption of gross investment to national disposable income (OECD, 1983a). An observed positive relationship between investment and economic growth, the inverse relationship between public-sector size and economic growth is therefore easily established. As a rule of thumb, it has been suggested that an increase of 5 per cent in the share of public expenditure to national disposable income curtails GDP growth by 1 per cent. However, the result is very sensitive to the way the public sector is defined, and varies across the countries.

Figure 5.1 supplies a statistical background to a possible negative relationship between public expenditure and growth of GDP. Appropriate statistical tests show that the long-term relationship between growth of GDP and the share of public expenditure breaks into two different parts for the sub-periods 1960–73 and 1974–81. On the one hand, such a result suggests a possible negative effect of public expenditure on GDP growth. On the other hand, however; it largely misses one important feature of recent problems with public expenditure. In fact, given the way in which public expenditure is included in the national accounts a bias towards a positive relationship is to be expected. A more accurate procedure would be that of testing the correlation between growth of GDP and budget deficit, the underlying assumption being that excessive public expenditure can only show its negative effects not through a reduction of effective demand (tax financing), but rather through a reduction of private investment and production brought about by the crowding-out effect of debt financing. Such a hypothesis can be tested by regressing on GDP both public expenditure and the non-monetized part of the budget deficit. In the case of Italy, the estimated regression produces the following result:

$$D_{\mathrm{GDP}} = 7.542 + 0.440\, D_{\mathrm{EXP}} - 0.084\, D_{\mathrm{DEF}}$$
$$(5.471)\ (5.236)\qquad (-2.817)$$

$$\mathrm{corr.}R^2 = 0.464$$
$$\mathrm{DW} = 1.662$$

where D represents percentage change, EXP public expenditure including capital transfers, and DEF the bond finance part of the total budget deficit (t-ratios are given in parentheses).

Similar attempts have been made for other major countries, obtaining largely satisfactory results even at this highly aggregative level. The basic idea behind such a way of reasoning is not new (see Friedman, 1978; also Blinder and Salen, 1973; Tobin and Buiter, 1976, pp. 273–309). The better results that seem to characterize recent years directly follow from both the relative decrease in the level of money financing and from the small wealth effect attached to the increased holding of bonds in the public portfolio.[11]. The theory of non-clearing markets (Muellbaner and Portes, 1978) and the increasing evidence (Sinclair, 1983, ch. 7) that the economy may easily shift more than once within the same cycle back and forth, from Keynesian to classical unemployment in the labour market and from repressed inflation to underconsumption in the goods market, should cast many doubts on the traditional stabilization policy and, above all, on the expansionary effects of deficit spending. More accurate research is needed to assess the long-term relationship between the growth of public debt and that of GDP. The little evidence available and common sense would suggest a negative sign.

PUBLIC EXPENDITURE: EQUITY AND EFFICIENCY

Translating the previous economic arguments into social behaviour means arguing that modern societies hold implicit acceptable limits of public expenditure which they are prepared to finance out of disposable income (taxes and regulations). Once the limit has been reached, further growth of public expenditure has to be financed by deficits, thus causing a reduction of potential growth. Equity and efficiency, in such a framework, might be divergent goals. More equity will have to be traded off with less efficiency and ultimately with less social welfare. This is why, in a context of scarce resources, efficiency in public-sector resources allocation has to have first priority. Unless efficiency can be granted in pursuing welfare-state objectives, the implicit limit of public willingness to contribute to its maintenance will be more binding. Inefficiency would then present the decision-making politicians with the alternative of either reducing public commitments or keeping them at the expense of economic growth. This may well constitute the description of a negative-sum non-cooperative game of the 'prisoner's dilemma' type.[12] On the one hand, the political decision-making process (variously explained by theories) in general leads to increasing levels of public expenditure. On the other hand, individual choices are aimed at decreasing the tax burden, and yet at increasing provision of public goods and services (or, more directly, cash transfers) to compensate for redistributive inefficiency and the increasing social costs arising from higher standards of living. Higher standards come to depend more and more on social costs and benefits than was the case in early industrial societies.[13] Pollution, traffic, poverty, health, education and so on are more and more regarded as social needs with a heavy externality component in consumption. Public provision might be justified, but resources could simply not be available, if long-lasting inefficiency in public spending is not removed.

The situation in the mid-1980s is the opposite of that of the early 1950s and 1960s when 'The Welfare State flourished because the Growth State prospered' (Klein, 1975, p. 1). The belief that exogenous economic growth would finance any public expenditure commitment and that the *ex-post* distribution of resources had nothing or little to do with economic performance has made it possible for the welfare state to absorb resources to finance programmes well beyond its objectives. The systems of health care, education and pensions, for instance, were originally conceived as a means of public protection and insurance against circumstances for which the individual could not easily make adequate provision. Instead, these systems have become ever-growing items of personal consumption, because they appeared costless and in unlimited supply to the potential consumers. As far as the redistributive aspects of the systems are concerned, it is becoming more and more apparent that, in order to re-channel resources towards the lower-income groups, the generality of most of the public services and subsidies means that a large proportion of social expenditure must return in cash or in kind to the original taxpayers and contributors. Whereas the basic objective of the welfare state is to support minorities, weak and unfortunate people, the circularity of the tax-benefit system applies to the large majority, although it was intended only for selected categories of citizen.

CONCLUDING COMMENTS

A number of observations can be drawn from the preceding two sections. The contribution to economic performance of public expenditure, inasmuch as it is financed by deficits, is at least low and it might well be negative.

The contrasting interest between the public as a whole (as it is represented by politicians' vested interests, trade unions, etc.), aiming at further expansion of the share of resources it controls, and each individual, seeking his or her own welfare, which would lead to the growth of privately owned resources (though at the expense of rising social costs), can be thought of as a game such as the prisoner's dilemma, which could end in the same way, if the required political and economic adjustments are not made.

Possible policy alternatives have to be devised in order to rescue the economy from self-destruction. Broadly speaking, reconciliation of public and private sector of the economy has to start off from a 'well-known fact': present expectations for social expenditure programmes, though already embodied in people's behaviour (saving, work effort, standard of living) are not consistent with the expected rate of growth of the economy as a whole. Moreover, on theoretical grounds, I feel a more general question has still to be answered. The long-accepted criterion, calling for public intervention whenever the market performance or outcome are not optimal, has to be revised because its application can be compared 'to that of the emperor judging a musical competition between two players, who gave the prize to the second having heard only the first' (Atkinson and Stiglitz, 1980, p. 10). The same has been applied to public intervention that has been implemented whenever the market failed to achieve the first optimum conditions. Instead, the choice between public or private provision should be made on the basis of a detailed cost-benefit analysis for each decision. Moreover, from my own point of view of the social system, it would be of importance, in setting up the framework for social choice, for public intervention to be given a negative social utility, as it restrains private choices and opportunities.[14]

In tackling the short-term problems of the welfare state, it would be appropriate to redefine its limits by considering that its first objective is to provide a minimum standard of living to those unable to gain it from the market. This is the complete opposite of the present situation whereby 'everything is granted to everybody'. Therefore the task of controlling public expenditure while maintaining a satisfactory level of welfare can best be achieved by more selective control of entitlement programmes.

NOTES

1 It is well known that to find a sustained interest for public-expenditure growth it is necessary to go back to the second half of the last and the beginning of the present century, and above all to Adolph Wagner's work. The American studies referred to in the text are by Fabricant (1952); Musgrave and Culberston (1953); Kendrick (1955).

2 The widest and most complete survey to date is Larkey, Stolp and Winer (1981). An earlier, still useful attempt to survey the literature is by Tarschys (1975). Discussion of the literature plays an important part in Brunner (1978); Peaçock (1979, pp. 80–95); Aranson and Ordeshook (1981, pp. 143–76); Beck (1982).

3 The bases for this conceptualization of the displacement effect are laid out in Wiseman and Diamond (1975); the actual test is performed in Diamond (1977).

4 An important step in this direction is Heller (1981).

5 The foundations of these theories were laid out by Downs (1957) and Black (1958). See also Davis, Hinich and Ordeshook (1970); Comanor (1976).

6 I refer here to the theories originated in the book by Niskanen (1971). See Breton (1974); Fiorina and Noll (1978).
7 Lack of analysis in this respect has often been complained of, for instance, by Pryor (1967); Bird (1970); Pedone (1982, pp. 340–409).
8 The argument put forward by Bacom and Eltis (1978) still holds.
9 With great respect to Klein (1984).
10 'Displacement effects' have usually been associated with major social and economic changes (see Peacock and Wiseman, 1967). However, in recent years relatively minor changes may have accounted for rather important displacements.
11 Providing an answer to Barro (1974).
12 For an interesting use of game theory in economics, with special reference to the implications of the 'prisoner's dilemma', see Bacharach (1976).
13 Such a point has already been maintained by Titmuss (1968).
14 This point of view has already been clearly expressed by Rowley and Peacock (1975, p. 103).

REFERENCES

Aranson, P. H. and Ordeshook, P. C. (1981), 'Alternative theories of the growth of government and their implications for constitutional tax and spending limits, in H. F. Ladd and N. T. Tideman (eds), *Tax and Expenditure Limitations.* Washington, DC: Urban Institute.

Atkinson, A. B. and Stiglitz, J. E. (1980), *Lectures on Public Economics.* Maidenhead, Berks: McGraw-Hill.

Bacharach, M. (1976), *Economics and the Theory of Games.* London.

Bacon, R. and Eltis, W. (1975), 'The implication for inflation, employment and growth of a fall in the share of output that is marketed', *Oxford Bulletin of Economics and Statistics*, vol. 37, pp. 269–95.

Bacon, R. and Eltis, W. (1978), *Britain's Economic Problem: Too Few Producers.* London. Macmillan.

Barro, R. J. (1974), 'Are government bonds net wealth?', *Journal of Political Economy*, vol. 82, pp. 1095–117.

Baumol, W. J. (1967), 'Macroeconomics of unbalanced growth: the anatomy of urban crisis', *American Economic Review*, vol. 57, pp. 415–26.

Beck, M. (1976), 'The expanding public sector: some contrary evidence', *National Tax Journal*, vol. 29, pp. 15–21.

Beck, M. (1979), 'Public sector growth: a real perspective', *Public Finance*, vol. 34, no. 3, pp. 313–56.

Beck, M. (1981), *Government Spending: Trends and Issues.* New York: Praeger.

Beck, M. (1982), 'Towards a theory of public sector growth', *Public Finance*, vol. 37, no. 2, pp. 163–77.

Bird, R. M. (1970), *The Growth of Government Spending in Canada.* Toronto: Canadian Tax Foundation.

Black, D. (1958), *The Theory of Committees and Elections.* Cambridge: Cambridge University Press.

Blinder, A. S. and Salon, M. R. (1973), 'Does fiscal policy matter?', *Journal of Public Economics*, vol. 2, pp. 319–37.

Boltho, A. (1983), 'Is Western Europe caught in an expectation trap?', *Lloyds Bank Review*, vol. 143, pp. 1–13.

Breton, A. (1974), *The Economic Theory of Representative Government*. Chicago: Aldine.

Brunner, K. (1978), 'Reflections on the political economy of government: the persistent growth of government', *Schweizerische Zeitschrift für Volkswirtschaft unf Statistik*, vol. 114, pp. 649–80.

Bush, W. C. and Denzau, A. T. (1977), 'The voting behavior of bureaucrats and public sector growth', in T. E. Borcherding (ed.), *Budgets and Bureaucrats: The Sources of Government Growth*. Durham, NC: Duke University Press.

Comanor, W. S. (1976), 'The median voter rule and the theory of political choice', Journal of Public Economics, vol. 5, pp. 169–77.

Courant, P. N., Gramlich, E. M. and Rubinfeld, D. L. (1979), 'Public employee market power and the level of government spending', *American Economic Review*, vol. 69, pp. 806–17.

Davis, O. A., Hinich, M. J. and Ordeshook, P. C. (1970), 'An expository development of a mathematical model of the electoral process', *American Political Science Review*, vol. 64, pp. 426–48.

Denison, E. F. (1979), *Accounting for Slower Economic Growth. The United States in the 1970s*. Washington, DC: Brookings Institution.

Diamond, J. (1977), 'Econometric testing of the displacement effect: a reconsideration', *Finanzarchiv*, NF, vol. 35, no. 3, pp. 387–404.

Downs, A. (1957), *An Economic Theory of Democracy*. New York: Harper and Row.

Fabricant, S. assisted by Lipsey, R. E. (1952), *The Trend of Government Activity in the United States since 1900*. New York: National Bureau of Economic Research.

Fiorina, M. P. and Noll, R. G. (1978), 'Voters, bureaucrats and legislators: a rational choice perspective on the growth of bureaucracy', *Journal of Public Economics*, vol. 9, pp. 239–54.

Friedman, B. M. (1978), 'Crowding out or crowding in? Economic consequences of financing government deficits', *Brooking Papers on Economic Activity*, vol. 3, pp. 593–654.

Ganti, S. and Kolluri, B. R. (1979), 'Wagner's law of public expenditures: some efficient results for the United States', *Public Finance*, vol. 34, no. 2, pp. 225–33.

Godley, W. and Taylor, C. (1977), 'Measuring the effect of public expenditure', in M. W. Posner (ed.), *Public Expenditure*. Cambridge: Cambridge University Press.

Heller, P. S. (1982), 'Diverging trends in the shares of nominal and real government expenditure in GDP: implications for policy', *National Tax Journal*, vol. 34, no. 1, pp. 61–74.

Henning, J. A. and Tussing, D. A. (1974), 'Income elasticity of the demand for public expenditures in the United States', *Public Finance*, vol. 29, no. 3–4, pp. 325–41.

Kendrick, M. S. (1955), *A Century and a Half of Federal Expenditures*. New York: National Bureau of Economic Research.

Klein, R. (1975), *Inflation and Priorities*. London.

Klein, R. (1984), 'Privatization and the welfare state', *Lloyds Bank Review*, vol. 151, pp. 12–29.

Larkey, P. D., Stolp, C. and Winer, M. (1981), 'Theorizing about the growth of government: a research assessment', *Journal of Public Policy*, vol. 1, pp. 157–220.

Meltzer, A. H. and Richard, S. F. (1978), 'Why government grows (and grows) in a democracy', *Public Interest*, vol. 52, pp. 111–18.

Meltzer, A. H. and Richard, S. F. (1981), 'A rational theory of the size of government', *Journal of Political Economy*, vol. 89, no. 5, pp. 914–27.

Muellbauer, J. and Portes, R. (1978), 'Macroeconomic models with quantity rationing', *Economic Journal*, vol. 88, pp. 788–821.
Musgrave, R. A. and Culberston, J. M. (1953), 'The growth of public expenditures in the United States', *National Tax Journal*, vol. 6, pp. 97–115.
Niskanen, W. A., Jr (1971), *Bureaucracy and Representative Government*. Chicago: Aldine-Atherton.
OECD (1983a), 'Consequences of public sector size and growth', mimeo.
OECD (1983b), 'The growth of social expenditure', mimeo. Paris.
Peacock, A. T. (1979), 'Public expenditure growth in post-industrial society', in B. Gustaffsohn (ed.), *Post-Industrial Society*. London: Croom Helm.
Peacock, A. T. and Wiseman, J. (1967), *The Growth of Public Expenditure in the United Kingdom*, rev. edn. London: Allen and Unwin.
Pedone, A. (1982), 'Public expenditure', in a Boltho (ed.), *The European Economy: Growth and Crises*. Oxford: Oxford University Press.
Peltzman, S. (1980), 'The growth of government', *Journal of Law and Economics*, vol. 23, no. 2, pp. 209–87.
Pryor, F. L. (1967), 'Elements of a positive theory of public expenditures', *Finanzarchiv*, NF, vol. 26, pp. 406–30.
Rowley, C. K. and Peacock, A. T. (1975), *Welfare Economics – A Liberal Restatement*. London: Martin Robertson.
Sinclair, P. J. N. (1983), *The Foundation of Macroeconomic and Monetary Theory*. Oxford: Oxford University Press.
Tarschys, D. (1975), 'The growth of public expenditures: nine models of explanation', *Scandinavian Political Studies*, vol. 10, pp. 9–31.
Titmuss, R. M. (1968), *Commitment to Welfare*. London: George Allen and Unwin.
Tobin, J. and Buiter, W. (1976), 'Long run effects of fiscal and monetary policy on aggregate demand', in J. Stein (ed.), *Monetarism*. Amsterdam.
Wiseman, J. and Diamond, J. (1975), 'Comment: on long-run growth of nondefense government expenditures in the United States', *Public Finance Quarterly*, vol. 3, pp. 411–14.

Part II
Public Choice and the Control of Public-Sector Growth

6

Are there Natural Limits to the Growth of Government?

Bruno Frey

NATURAL AND CONSTITUTIONAL LIMITS TO GOVERNMENT: A SURVEY

Two kinds of limits on government activity may be distinguished:

1. Natural limits, which appear endogenously within a given institutional structure of society, particularly given the economic institutions;
2. Constitutional limits, which are imposed exogenously by the consensus reached among individuals behind the veil of uncertainty (see Buchanan and Tullock, 1962; Buchanan, 1977; Frey, 1983).

Government activity takes place in three different forms:

1. taxation;
2. public expenditure;
3. regulation.

The three forms of activity can be combined with the two kinds of limits as is shown in table 6.1. This table indicates the amount of knowledge about governmental limits, and hints at the scientific contributions dealing with these limits.

This section looks briefly at the state of our knowledge about the limits to government, proceeding from taxation, to public expenditure, to regulation. The next section aims at making a contribution about that area of government activity whose limits are least known: regulation. A politico-economic model is presented that establishes natural limits to government regulations. The third section shows that testable propositions can be derived, and the final section presents a summary.

Table 6.1 *Knowledge about forms of, and types of limits to, government activity*

	Forms of government activity		
Limits	*Taxation*	*Public expenditure*	*Regulation*
Natural limits	Much knowledge: Laffer curve and shadow economy	Considerable knowledge: traditional economics	Very little knowledge
Constitutional limits	Much knowledge: Brennan–Buchanan type of rules	Some knowledge: Institutional public-choice	Little knowledge

Taxation

Natural limits

The Laffer curve (as it is now called) is a generally known representation of the limits to taxation which arise endogenously, given the institutions of society: a too large increase in the tax rate does not raise tax revenues, but diminishes them after some time, because individuals and firms reduce the input of labour and capital. Of even greater importance than increased leisure is the switch to the shadow economy, where economic activity is not taxed.[1] According to Tanzi's (1980), Feige's (1982) and Frey and Weck's (1984) empirical estimates, increasing tax rates lead to an increase in the size of the untaxed shadow economy. As Peacock and Shaw (1982) have shown, this does not result in a corresponding decrease of tax revenues, because disposable income is higher and part of it is spent on goods produced and sold in the official (taxed) economy. Nevertheless, under most conditions, the switch to the shadow economy is likely to reduce tax revenue.

An important contribution to the Laffer curve and the limits of taxation has been made by Buchanan and Lee (1982), who distinguish two time periods. In the short term, defined by the time horizon of the government,[2] the individuals (and firms) have little possibility in adjusting to an increase in the tax rate. This short-run Laffer curve shifts downwards over time, as shown in figure 6.1. The long run is that time period within which all the adjustments (reductions in work time, switch to the shadow economy, etc.) have been completed. This yields the long-run Laffer curve, also shown in figure 6.1. Assuming that the government maximizes tax revenue, an equilibrium (stable) tax rate τ^{**} exists where the maximum on a short-run Laffer curve cuts the long-run Laffer curve in figure 6.1, $SRLC_2$. There is no incentive to change this tax rate: the individuals have completed their

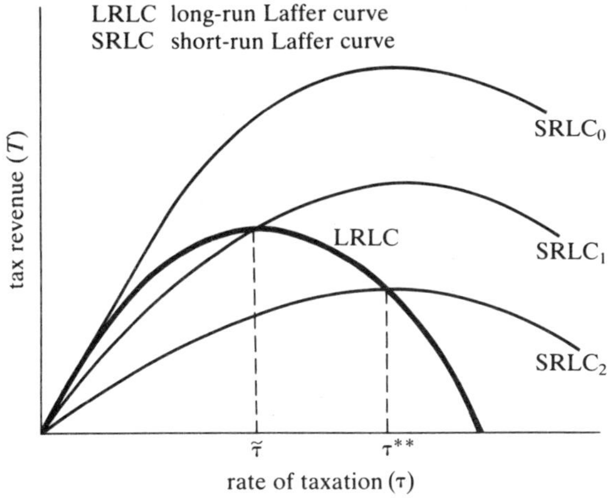

Figure 6.1 Short-run and long-run Laffer curves, the equilibrium rate of taxation (τ^{**}) and the long-run revenue-maximizing rate of taxation ($\tilde{\tau}$).

adjustments (they are on the long-run Laffer curve), and the government maximizes its revenue. A tax rate lower or higher than τ^{**} would reduce tax revenues within the relevant political time horizon, as indicated by the short-run Laffer curve $SRLC_2$. As may be seen from the figure, this equilibrium tax rate τ^{**} is *finite*, but is larger than the tax rate $\tilde{\tau}$, which maximizes tax revenues in the long run. The politico-economic analysis of the Laffer curve thus indicates that there are endogenous limits to taxation.

Constitutional limits to taxation

The tax burden imposed on the population may be *directly* limited by establishing constitutional limits to the maximum share of GNP that may be taxed. Efforts have been made in the United States to bring about such rules, and referenda have been carried out to prevent state governments from exceeding certain limits, or to raise certain taxes (see, for example, Ladd and Tideman, 1981). More *indirect* constitutional limits on taxation have been propounded, especially by Brennan and Buchanan in their book, *Power to Tax* (1980). These rules – for example, restricting the tax base or prohibiting regressive tax rates – need not be repeated here. A more general way of looking at these indirect rules would be that they serve to encourage tax avoidance by either increasing the *range* of economic activities that remain untaxed (for example facilitate the exit to all kinds of 'unofficial' economies, or to lower-taxed regions and countries), or by increasing the *incentives* to leave the (more highly) taxed sector (for example, by regulating the admissible tax schedules or by reducing expected punishment for tax fraud).

The literature on the constitutional limits to taxation offers a rich menu of possibilities, and the theoretical and empirical research in the area is rapidly progressing. The tax-limitation proposals, however, are not without problems and the government may resort for finance to all sorts of para-fiscal bodies such as public enterprises, for which a monopoly position is provided. Such manoeuvres are difficult, and sometimes impossible, to prevent on the basis of simple constitutional provisions. This means that the constitutional approach to tax limitations may result in a game between the providers of constitutional rules and governments which constantly seek new ways to raise finance. History teaches us that although governments are not usually known as great inventors, they show a remarkable ability in finding new ways of finance (see chapter 9 below).

Public expenditure

Natural limits

The basic problem of limiting public expenditure (compared to limiting taxation) is that the *benefits* of such activity are separated from the *cost* of financing, be it by taxation, credit or money-printing. This separation occurs over time, because the cost of financing – for example, by debt issue (the induced rise in the rate of interest and crowding out of private investment – is not immediately felt, and it occurs between groups, because those who benefit from public expenditure are not usually those who have to carry the respective burden of financing them. These relationships are the object of traditional economics, which has studied the effect taxes, bond issues to the public and money-printing have on economic activity (especially GNP), and how this in turn influences the future possibilities for financing government expenditure. The conditions (for example, open or closed economies, fixed or flexible exchange rates) influencing these interactions between the benefit and cost side of public expenditure, and therewith the endogenous limits to such public activity, are reasonably well known.

Constitutional limits

The *direct* approach to limiting public expenditure is, as in the case of taxation, to set a maximum share of GNP which may not be surpassed, or to require budget balance (in the strict sense). Such efforts have again been made in the United States. A more *indirect* approach is to strengthen the relationship between *benefit* and *costs*. One possibility is to reduce 'fiscal illusion'; another is to weaken the position of those political actors (such as public bureaucracy) who have an interest in maintaining and expanding the separation between benefits and costs of government expenditure. This can be reached by many different institutional provisions, such as the creation of small governmental units (which result in better information and a stronger participation of the population in public decisions), or increased formal possibilities for political participation by the population, such as referenda. The latter has been empirically shown (Pommerehne and Frey, 1978) to weaken the government's and bureaucracy's power to expand expenditures. Although there exists considerable theoretical knowledge of how to limit the government's expansion of its expenditures, on the whole there is relatively little empirical evidence on how effective such institutional provisions are. Moreover, there may be great political resistance to the introduction of such constitutional rules.

Governmental regulations

Direct, non-monetary interventions of the government in economic activities are of great and increasing importance in modern industrial societies. The costs imposed thereby on individuals and firms seem to be quite substantial, if we can trust the estimates by Weidenbaum (1979), who calculates that these costs in the United States amounted to 4.3 per cent of GNP in 1979,[3] or by Downing and Lawson (1979), who calculate them for the same country to be 9.4 per cent of GNP in 1976. The increasing importance of this type of government activity – at least in the United States – is also noted by authors such as Christainsen and Haveman (1981): setting the index base at 100 in 1947, the cumulative number of 'major' pieces of regulatory legislation has grown to 402 in 1977, the volume of federal expenditure on regulatory activities to 1004, and the number of full-time federal personnel engaged in regulatory activities to 668. A surge in governmental regulations must be expected to occur to the extent that the limits on taxes and public expenditure are effective: governments then have an increased incentive to resort to this instrument for wielding power, as has been noted, among others, by Aranson and Ordeshook (1981). Consequently, it is of great importance to study the endogenous and exogenous limits to public regulations.

Practically nothing is said or known in the literature about possible endogenous forces or exogenous limits which might limit the growth of governmental regulations.[4] In their book *Power to Tax*, Brennan and Buchanan fully accept the (potential) importance of regulations by stating: 'A government subjected to tax-limit pressures will surely be predicted to exert more efforts through the legal process towards opening up direct regulatory channels', but immediately admit: 'There is little that we can do here than to acknowledge the "limits of tax limits" in this respect' (1980, p. 166). Indeed, the topic is not treated elsewhere in the book, nor is it in other specialized treatises on the subject such as Ladd and Tideman (1981) or Folkers (1983).

While the scientific literature is silent on the issue, in practical politics types of 'constitutional' limits that may serve to restrict public regulations have been discussed and actually applied. In Switzerland, for instance, the number of public employees on the federal level has been strictly limited for several years. This of course restricts the number of regulations issued only if the 'productivity' of public bureaucrats with respect to issuing regulations is constant, an assumption for which there is no basis. It has also been suggested that the number of laws issued by parliament should be restricted constitutionally. Again, the purpose is only served if it may be assumed that the 'quality' or content of the laws remains unchanged, which is unlikely to be the case.

The lack of ideas on how to limit effectively the *effects* of regulations by *constitutional* rules is due to the difficulty or impossibility of measuring the 'output' for this kind of public activity. This constitutes a major difference to both taxation and to public expenditure, which due to their monetary form are, at least in principle, amenable to measurement. Due to the inherent difficulty of measuring the output of the government's regulatory activity, there does not seem to be any possibility to restrict the growth of public regulations by any kind of direct constitutional rule.

Evaluation of the limits to government

Our discussion suggests that there is a relatively large amount of knowledge about the natural and constitutional limits to taxation. Less is known about how to limit public expenditure effectively, but the real problem lies with the growth in government *regulations.* This fact is not the result of chance. In a period in which the public and the politicians become increasingly aware that an extension of government activity does not in general solve social problems (and sometimes may even worsen them), and political pressure mounts to put limits on the state, the government and its bureaucracy have an incentive to become more active in the regulatory area, which by its very nature is difficult or even impossible to control by direct constitutional limitations. There is thus an urgent need to find out whether *natural limits to the growth in regulations* exist, whose workings may then be supported by appropriate (indirect) constitutional rules. In order to find such rules, it is necessary to know the characteristics of such endogenous processes restricting public regulations. More research is needed, and with this demand the paper might end. Instead, an attempt is made to analyse *one* specific process which is conceived to limit the growth of public regulations. The analytical model constructed concentrates on the possibility to *exit*, that is, to evade regulations by moving to an unregulated (or less regulated) sector. For this reason, *voice* in the form of reactions by the (over)-regulated voters and interest groups via the political process is disregarded here.

NATURAL LIMITS TO REGULATIONS

Intensity and range of regulations

It is essential to distinguish clearly two concepts: the *intensity* with which a given sector of economic and social activities is regulated and the range of the regulations. An example of the former can be taken from the building industry. The construction of private residences may be controlled by dozens, hundreds or even thousands of public regulations which restrict the freedom with respect to *how* the building activity is to be undertaken: for instance, concerning the noise and pollution emission, the composition of the workforce (no children, certain shares of minorities), the condition of the work (health and security standards, etc.), the suppliers (a certain share of local firms), etc. The regulations on the construction of private residences also refer to how the *final product* has to look: for instance, concerning the type, shape, size and height of the building, the colour, the size of the surrounding garden, etc. What is relevant is the *actual* application of the regulations, and not how they should be applied according to the statute of the law. Many regulations formally exist, but are never applied, others are applied leniently, and yet others are applied strictly. This unequal degree of application is reflected in the punishment an individual or firm subjectively expects when disregarding regulations. A highly expected punishment *ceteris paribus* points to a high degree of strictness of application, and the reverse. The striking impression is that the intensity with which economic production (and consumption) activities are regulated *varies* greatly *between sectors*. The *intensity* with which a sector is publicly regulated is an operational and empirically measurable concept.

The *range* of regulation states how large the area of economic and social activities is in which the regulations are applied. Some of the regulations apply to all kinds of economic activities (for example, the health and security requirements, the prohibition of child labour).[5] Other regulations extend to a limited economic sector only. For instance, certain hygienic regulations apply to the restaurant business, but not to other areas. Similarly, the absolute prohibition of alcohol applies to certain activities (especially to professional driving), but not to others. One area in which (almost by definition) no public regulations apply is the shadow or underground economy, and in a more limited way also the various kinds of 'grey' activities in the rapidly growing 'informal' sector.[6] The *range* of regulations is an operational concept, in principle accessible to measurement.

There is a crucial difference between the intensity and the range of regulation with respect to economic policy. The intensity is an *instrument* in the hands of the government (and its bureaucracy). Within its political possibilities it can issue the number of regulations formally applying to a particular economic sector, and it can (to a large extent) control the *actual* degree of application by allocating resources to discovering and punishing those disregarding the regulation. The range in which the regulations apply, on the other hand is *not* an instrument of the government. The range of application is rather controlled by the individuals and firms, who can choose whether they observe the regulations and stay in the official economy, or whether they undertake the same activity in the unregulated (or unofficial) economy, and risk punishment. If they choose to move into the unofficial economy, the range in which the regulations apply shrinks.

The '*total amount*' *of regulation* R is a function of both the intensity ϱ and the range B^R of regulation. When either the intensity of application is zero, *or* the range of application is zero (that is, all activity takes place in the unofficial economy), regulation is defined to be non-existent, which means that the functional relationship is multiplicative. The simplest formulation is:

$$R = \varrho B^R \tag{1}$$

but one could also think of:

$$R = \varrho^{\alpha}(B^R)^{\beta} \qquad \alpha,\beta > 0 \tag{1a}$$

which allows us to give relatively more weight to the intensity or to the range of regulation.

The analogy to taxation is obvious: regulatory intensity corresponds to the tax rate τ, the range of regulation to the tax base B^T, and the amount of regulation to tax revenue T:

$$T \equiv \tau B^T \tag{2}$$

Equations (1) and (2), however, are not identical, because the tax revenue is *independently observable* from τ and B^T, whereas the amount of regulation R is not. It is only measurable once ϱ and B^R (and in the case of equation (1a) α and β) are known.

A politico-economic model of regulation

A simple model is constructed consisting of two sets of decision-makers, the government and the individuals/firms. It will be shown that their interaction produces an *endogenous limit* to *regulation* as well as to *taxation*. The formal model closely follows parts of Frey and Ramser (1983).

Government

For our purpose the government is taken as a homogenous unit, including the public bureaucracy. It maximizes its own utility subject to the constraints imposed from outside. Its time horizon is limited, it maximizes myopicly over a time period which depends on the exogenously given election period. The government derives utility from the amount of regulation R which it can impose on the private economy: its influence over the private economy (and society) rises when the intensity of regulation, as well as when the range over which its 'commands' are observed, are increased. Government and its bureaucracy enjoy wielding this power. In some cases, especially in developing countries, an increase in regulations also means that its monetary income rises, because the individuals and firms active in the private (official) sector resort to corrupting politicians and public officials in order to reach their goals more effectively and more quickly. The government's utility is also positively related to the size of tax revenues T: this command over resources can be used for private purposes or to wield power by spending it in a politically appropriate way. As usual, there are diminishing returns:

$$U = U(R, T)$$
$$U_R, U_T > 0;\ U_{RT} \leq 0;\ U_{RR},\ U_{TT} < 0 \qquad (3)$$

The government simultaneously uses the two instruments at its disposal, the intensity of regulation ϱ and the tax rate τ, to maximize its utility subject to the constraints imposed by equations (1) and (2):

$$\max_{\varrho,\tau}\ U(R, T) \qquad (4)$$

subject to:

$$R = \varrho B^R \qquad (1)$$
$$T = \tau B^T \qquad (2)$$

Private sector

The individuals and the firms in the private sector have an incentive to evade the official economy, when the burden imposed on them by the government rises. When the intensity of regulation ϱ is raised, individuals and firms will increasingly move to the unregulated unofficial economy, that is, the range of regulation B^R falls. The 'regulation-evasion function' reads:

$$B^R = B^R(\varrho) \qquad \delta B^R/\delta\varrho \equiv B^R_\varrho > 0 \qquad (5)$$

Similarly, when the tax rate τ is raised, individuals and firms have an incentive to move into the untaxed unofficial economy, that is, the tax base B^T falls. The 'tax-evasion function' reads:

$$B^T = B^T(\tau) \qquad \delta B^T/\delta\tau \equiv B^T_\tau < 0 \qquad (6)$$

For simplicity, the unregulated and the untaxed unofficial economy will be identified so that there is only one range B over which both tax rates and regulation intensity apply:

$$B = B^R = B^T \tag{7}$$

The range of regulation and taxation B according to equations (5) and (6) depends on the intensities of regulation ϱ and of taxation τ:

$$B = B(\varrho,\tau) \tag{8}$$

Individuals and firms, however, are not able to adjust to a new intensity of regulation and taxation immediately. They have organized their economic production activity and their consumption life-style on the basis of a historically given regulatory intensity ϱ_0 and tax rate τ_0. They can be thought of as the traditional or expected burden to which the individuals and firms are accustomed. The effect of raising these two intensities on the range has a short-run component depending on the differences $(\varrho - \varrho_0)$ and $(\tau - \tau_0)$ and a long-run component depending on ϱ and τ. For simplicity, it is assumed that these effects are additively separable:

$$\begin{aligned} B &= B(\varrho,\tau,\varrho_0,\tau_0) \\ &= B^{s}(\varrho - \varrho_0,\tau - \tau_0) + B^{l}(\varrho,\tau) \end{aligned} \tag{9}$$

Taking account of (1), the amount of regulation is also composed of a short-run R^s and a long-run R^l component:

$$R = R^{s}(\varrho,\tau,\varrho - \varrho_0,\tau - \tau_0) + R^{l}(\varrho,\tau) \tag{10}$$

Accordingly, taking account of equation (2), the short-run T^s and long-run T^l components of tax revenue are:

$$T = T^{s}(\varrho,\tau,\varrho - \varrho_0,\tau - \tau_0) + T^{l}(\varrho,\tau) \tag{11}$$

Interaction between government and private sector

The behaviour of individuals and firms reacting to regulation and taxation, and the behaviour of the government which pursues its own utility, produces an internal optimum for the government's short-run maximization problem[7] given by $(\varrho^*,\tau^*)>0$ (with ϱ_0 and τ_0 kept constant). The necessary and sufficient conditions for the optimal instrument use is:

$$R_i^{l}(\varrho^*,\tau^*) + \gamma T_i^{l}(\varrho^*,\tau^*) = [R_i^{s}(\varrho^*,\varrho^* - \varrho_0,\tau^* - \tau_0) + \gamma T_i^{s}(\tau^*,\varrho^* - \varrho_0,\tau^* - \tau_0)] < 0$$

with

$$\gamma \equiv U_T/U_R > 0 \qquad i = \varrho,\tau \tag{12}$$

This equation shows that a utility-maximizing government sets its instruments ϱ and τ higher than would in the long run maximize the sum of the (utility-weighted) power of regulation and taxation ($R_i^1+\gamma T_i^1<0$). Compared to this long-run maximum (when $R_i^1+\gamma T_i^1=0$), the government, which is only interested in the short-run election period, in general both 'over-regulates' and 'overtaxes'. However, there is an endogenous finite limit to both *regulation* and *taxation*, as there exists a unique internal optimum given by (ϱ^*,τ^*): the government has no incentive to extend the intensity of regulation and taxation too far, because the individuals and firms react by moving into the unofficial economy. There is no point in the government pushing through high intensities of regulation and taxation, if the range over which they are applied shrinks more and more. This is, of course, a variant of the old principle that it is irrational to kill the goose that lays the golden egg.

In the long run, the initial intensities of regulation and taxation (ϱ_0,τ_0) to which the individuals and firms are accustomed are gradually adjusted to the current levels. This adjustment creates cost: the individuals and firms have to search for new ways to get around regulations and to evade taxes. They have, for instance, to hire tax consultants to find out ways to save taxes when the government imposes higher tax rates. It is reasonable to assume that there are increasing marginal costs of adjustment, because it becomes more and more difficult to find ways to evade taxation and regulation. The adjustment cost function is:

$$C=C(\dot{\varrho}_0,\dot{\tau}_0) \tag{13}$$

with

$$C_{\dot{\varrho}_0}>0,\ C_{\dot{\tau}_0}>0,\ C_{\dot{\varrho}_0\dot{\varrho}_0}>0,\ C_{\dot{\tau}_0\dot{\tau}_0}>0$$

For simplicity, it is assumed that the cost of adjusting to regulation is independent of the cost of adjusting to taxation, that is, the cost function is taken to be additively separable:

$$C(\dot{\varrho}_0,\dot{\tau}_0)=C^{\varrho}(\dot{\varrho}_0)+C^{\tau}(\dot{\tau}_0) \tag{14}$$

It follows that the adjustment process can be described by an adaptive formulation:

$$\dot{\varrho}_0=\delta^{\varrho}(\varrho-\varrho_0) \tag{15}$$

$$\dot{\tau}_0=\delta^{\tau}(\tau-\tau_0) \tag{16}$$

with

$$\delta^{\varrho},\delta^{\tau}\ \text{constant}\ 0$$

Using the short-run optimal values of the instruments:

$$\varrho=\varrho^*=\psi^{\varrho}(\varrho_0,\tau_0) \tag{17}$$

$$\tau=\tau^*=\psi^{\tau}(\varrho_0,\tau_0) \tag{18}$$

it follows that:

$$\lim_{t\to\infty} \dot{\varrho}_0 = \lim_{t\to\infty} \dot{\tau}_0 = 0$$
$$\lim_{t\to\infty} (\varrho^*, \tau^*) = (\varrho^{**}, \tau^{**}) \quad (19)$$

where $(\varrho^{**}, \tau^{**})$ are the *long-run* optimal intensities of regulation and taxation. They are the solution of:

$$R_i^1(\varrho^*, \tau^*) + \gamma T_i^1(\varrho^*, \tau^*) = -\left[R_i^s(\varrho^*, 0, 0) + \gamma T_i^s(\tau^*, 0, 0)\right] < 0$$
$$i = \varrho, \tau \quad (20)$$

Equation (19) tells us that the short-run optimal intensities (ϱ^*, τ^*) converge to the long-run optimal intensities $(\varrho^{**}, \tau^{**})$. Equation (20) tells us that in the long run (that is, when the individuals and firms have adjusted their customary notion of the 'normal' intensity of regulation and taxation to the actual intensity), there is – as is also in the short run – both 'over-regulation' and 'overtaxation'. However, there is again an *endogenous finite limit* to regulation and taxation.

TOWARDS TESTABLE PROPOSITIONS

The relationships established

Given the assumptions of the model constructed, in particular that the government maximizes its utility depending on the amount of regulation and tax revenue, that it acts myopicly and that the cost of adjustment of individuals and firms to new intensities of regulation and taxation can be described by an adaptive process, it has been shown that the amount of 'over-regulation' $(\varrho^{**} - \tilde{\varrho})$ and of 'overtaxation' $(\tau^{**} - \tilde{\tau})$ depends on the relationship between the *range* and the *intensity* of the burdens imposed by the government:

$$B = B(\varrho, \tau, \varrho_0, \tau_0) \quad (9)$$

Of special interest are the derivatives of this function, especially B_ϱ and B_τ. Once this function is empirically known, it is possible to calculate the amount of 'over-regulation' and 'overtaxation' from functions (12) and (20). The size of 'overburdening' can then be related to observable characteristics of the economy and society, and it can then be empirically tested whether these testable propositions can be maintained or are rejected by the empirical evidence.

Existing evidence

The range of function (9) has so far not been empirically established. There is some knowledge on the *partial* relationships:

$$B^R = B^R(\varrho) \quad (5)$$
$$B^T = B^T(\tau) \quad (6)$$

In the context of the Laffer curve, empirical tests have been undertaken to (indirectly) establish the *tax-range equation* (6), by estimating

$$T = T(\tau, \ldots\ldots.) \qquad (21)$$

Examples are provided, for instance, by Stuart (1981) or Fullerton (1981). Although it has been taken into account that the effect of the tax rate τ on tax revenue T depends on many factors (indicated by the points in equation (21), the (possible) interdependence with the intensity of regulation (as indicated in equation (9) has been neglected.

Very little is known about the *regulation-range equation* (5). In the data collected on regulation, insufficient attention has been paid to the crucial distinction between the intensity and the range of regulation. Some indicators, such as the number of regulatory legislations, can be interpreted to relate to regulation intensity, whereas other indicators, such as expenditure on regulatory activity and the number of public officials engaged in regulatory activity (see Christainsen and Haveman, 1981), rather stand for the total amount of regulation R. Both indicators may be expected to increase when either regulatory intensity ϱ and/or the range B^R increase.

The main shortcoming of the empirical research on regulation for the purpose at hand is that no effort has been made to determine to which range of economic activities such regulations apply. It clearly should make a difference if, for instance, a bureaucrat produces a certain amount of regulation R which relates intensively to a small area (large ϱ, small B^R) or slightly over the whole economy (small ϱ, large B^R). An important task for future empirical work is therefore to collect data on regulation, distinguishing between the intensity and the range of economic activities to which they apply.

Framework for data collection

In the model constructed, the simple case of an official economy with regulation and taxation, and an unregulated and untaxed unofficial economy

Table 6.2 *Regulation according to type and economic sector of application*

	Type of regulation				
Economic sectors	*Health*	*Environment*	*Work conditions*	*Etc.*	*Total regulation*
Agriculture					
Construction					
Services					
Etc.					
Whole economy					X

was considered. In empirical work it is necessary to distinguish according to the *type of regulation* (for example, for health, environment, on working conditions) and according to the *economic sector* (for example, agriculture, construction, services) to which they apply. This gives a matrix as shown in table 6.2. This matrix can be filled either by the intensity of regulation (ϱ_{sj}), where *s* represents the economic sector and *j* the types of regulation) or by the range, indicated for example by the size of the official to the unofficial economy (B_{sj}). The cell indicated by X then either shows the aggregate intensity ϱ or range *B* of regulation.

Estimating the regulatory-range function

The data collected in table 6.2 provide the basis for estimating the $B^R(\varrho)$ function, either by cross-section or time series. The parameters of the regulatory-range function can be determined by comparing the relationship of the size of the regulatory range and regulatory intensity *across economic sectors*, for a specific type of regulation or for overall regulation. If the data of the matrix are known for various years, it is possible to determine the dependence of the range of regulation on the intensity of regulation by running a regression *over time*, either for a specific type of regulation or for overall regulation. The time-series approach makes it possible to analyse the time structure of an increase in regulatory intensity on the range. The cross-section and time-series approaches can of course also be pooled. In each case, further variables influencing the size of the regulatory range, in particular the intensity of taxation (tax rates), must be taken into account in order not to mis-specify the estimation equation.

Such estimates are so far not possible because of the lack of data. Some preliminary attempts have been made in the context of the research on the shadow economy. In a pooled cross-section/time-series study of the relative size of the shadow economy in OECD countries, using the 'hidden variable' approach, Frey and Weck (1984) have found that both an increase in the intensity of regulation and taxation raise the size of the shadow economy in a statistically significant way. Using the (somewhat questionable) transaction approach (Feige, 1979) to measure the size of the shadow economy, Haveman *et al.* (1983) also find that the intensity of regulation and of taxation has a statistically significant influence. Both studies suggest[8] that the range of regulation and taxation (that is, the size of the official economy) is negatively related to the burden imposed on the individuals and firms by the government.

Testable propositions

Knowledge of the range of regulation and taxation function $B(\varrho, \tau, \ldots)$ allows one to calculate by how much the actual regulation intensity exceeds the long-run maximizing level ($\varrho^{**} - \sim\varrho$), and by how far actual tax rates exceed the long-run revenue-maximizing tax rates ($\tau^{**} - \tilde{\varrho}$), assuming that the politico-economic model constructed is constant with reality. Testable hypotheses can then be formulated which indicate on what *structural conditions* these deviations of actual from long-run maximizing intensities depend, or, in other words, on what point of the range in function (9) a specific country is expected to be at a particular point of time. In general, it can be expected that the negative effect of regulation and taxation on the size of the official economy (the range) will be stronger, the more *possibility* there is to exit to the unofficial economy. In particular, the deviations ($\varrho^{**} - \tilde{\varrho}$) and ($\tau^{**} - \tau$) will be smaller in the following sets of circumstances.

1. The *smaller* the units of government are to which a particular type of regulation and taxation applies. *Ceteris paribus*, in *federalist* countries, and in *small* countries, the intensity of regulation and taxation will be smaller than in unitary and large countries. To give an example, the regulations on sex and gambling which Switzerland imposes are relatively weak, because the Swiss can easily obtain the respective less regulated services just across the border in Lindau, Konstanz or Campione.
2. The *smaller* the *transaction costs* that are involved in switching to a less regulated and less taxed sector. In areas of economic activity in which *information* on similar or identical less regulated activities is easily available or is even advertised (as in the case of prostitution and gambling), and/or where the *transportation* costs of the switch are low, there will, *ceteris paribus*, be low regulation and taxation.
3. The *higher* the punishment is which the individuals and firms expect when they switch to the unofficial economy.

SUMMARY

Our discussion has led to the following conclusions:

1. There is much knowledge about the national and constitutional limits to *taxation*. There is considerable knowledge about the natural limits to *public expenditure*, and some knowledge about the constitutional limits to public expenditure.
2. Next to nothing is known about the limits to *regulation*. Regulation, however, is an important part of public activity, and will gain importance when, and in so far as, the limits to taxation and public expenditure become cffcctive.
3. *Natural* limits to *regulation* do exist. It is necessary to distinguish between the intensity and the range of regulations: a rise in intensity of regulation leads to a decrease in the range to which the regulations are applied. A utility-maximizing government will generally over-regulate compared to the intensity of regulation which maximizes the 'amount' of regulation,

but there is a definite endogenous limit to regulation intensity (and to the total 'amount' of regulation) above which the government would be irrational to go.

4. The intensity of regulation will be high in those areas where the elasticity of evasion is low, and it will be low where the elasticity is large.
5. Testable propositions about the limits of regulation are possible when the conditions determining the elasticity of the regulation evasion function are identified. Such conditions are the kind of government intervention, the alternatives for less regulated and unregulated activities, and the extent to which the formal regulations are in fact observed.

NOTES

I am grateful for discussions with my co-workers Heinz Buhofer, Reiner Eichenberger, Barbara Gorsler, Hannelore Weck-Hannemann, and to Werner W. Pommerehne. During the conference, I received particularly useful comments by Alan Peacock, Francesco Forte, Vito Tanzi, Dennis Mueller, Norman Barry and Peter Murrell.

1 In the last two years there has been much research on the shadow economy. See, for example, Tanzi (1982) and the survey by Frey and Pommerehne (1985).

2 Presumably, the government's time horizon equals the length of the election period (that is, around four years for a newly elected or re-elected government), an assumption also made in the literature on the political business cycle based on Nordhaus (1975). This assumption is, however, doubtful, because the government's time horizon certainly depends on how likely it evaluates its re-election prospects to be: if it is confident of winning the forthcoming election, its time horizon will at least extend over the following election period (that is, will be around eight years for a new government). For a formal presentation of this endogenous theory of the time horizon, see Frey and Ramser (1976).

3 Tabb (1980) has reminded us that government regulations not only impose costs, but may also provide benefits. Schwarz (1983) has shown that Weidenbaum's conclusions about the *increase* in the costs of regulations are deficient. If instead of an overall 'multiplier' (stating that the total cost of regulations are twenty times their administration cost) a sector-specific multiplier is used, no increase can be found because the sectors with highest multipliers grow less rapidly.

4 Very indirectly, the following limiting process could be constructed: when the number of public regulations increases, private-sector productivity falls, which reduces the government's ability to finance its expenditure. If this results in a reduction in the number of public employees, less public regulations per year will be issued. This construction is rather tenuous: although, there exists empirical evidence that rising public regulations lead to a decrease in private productivity (Christainsen and Haveman (1981) estimate, for instance, that federal regulations are responsible for between 12 and 21 per cent of the slowdown in the growth of labour productivity in US manufacturing during 1973–7 as compared to 1958–65; for environmental regulation see Gollup and Roberts (1983)), it is not

necessarily true at all that this results in a decrease in government expenditure and employees.

5 With the exception, of course, of professional sports such as ice skating, swimming or gymnastics, where child labour is extensively, if not exclusively, used.

6 For simplicity, in the following only two sectors are distinguished: one in which the regulations hold and another where they do not hold, which will be called 'official' and 'unofficial' sectors, respectively.

7 The algebraic model of the two (sets of) decision-makers and two time periods is similar to Buchanan and Lee's (1982) geometrical model. They use it to derive 'overtaxation', a position which is not generally true, as shown in Frey and Ramser (1983).

8 Because of the unsatisfactory measurement of regulation, the results should be accepted with caution.

REFERENCES

Aranson, P. H. and Ordeshook, P. C. (1981), 'Alternative theories of the growth of government and their implications for constitutional tax and spending limits', in H. F. Ladd and N. T. Tideman (eds), *Tax and Expenditure Limitations*, Washington: Urban Institute.

Brennan, G. and Buchanan, J. M. (1980), *The Power to Tax: Analytical Foundations of a Fiscal Constitution*. Cambridge: Cambridge University Press.

Buchanan, J. M. (1977), *Freedom in Constitutional Contract. Perspectives of a Political Economist*. College Station and London: Texas A & M University Press.

Buchanan, J. M. and Lee, D. R. (1982), 'Politics, time and the Laffer curve', *Journal of Political Economy*, vol. 90, pp. 816–19.

Buchanan, J. M. and Tullock, G. (1962), *The Calculus of Consent. Logical Foundations of Constitutional Democracy*. Ann Arbor, Mich: University of Michigan Press.

Christainsen, G. B. and Haveman, R. H. (1981), 'Public regulation and the slowdown in productivity growth', *American Economic Review, Papers and Proceedings*, vol. 71, pp. 320–5.

Conybeare, J. A. (1982), 'The rent seeking state and revenue diversification', *World Politics*, vol. 35, pp. 25–42.

Downing, P. B. and Lawson, A. (1979), 'Policy consequences of regulatory cost measurements', mimeo, Department of Economics, Virginia Polytechnic Institute and State University, Blacksburg, Virgina.

Feige, E. L. (1979), 'How big is the irregular economy?', *Challenge*, vol. 22, (November/December), pp. 5–13.

Feige, E. (1982), 'A new perspective on macroeconomic phenomena. The theory and measurement of the unobserved sector of the United States: causes, consequences, and implications', in M. Walker (ed.), *The International Burden of Government*, Vancouver.

Folkers, C. (1983), *Begrenzungen von Steuern und Staatsausgaben in den USA*. Baden-Baden: Nomos.

Frey, B. S. (1983), *Democratic Economic Policy. A Theoretical Approach*. Oxford: Martin Robertson and New York: St Martin's Press.

Frey, B. S. and Pommerehne, W. W. (1985), 'The hidden economy: state and prospects for measurement', *Review of Income and Wealth*, forthcoming.

Frey, B. S. and Ramser, H.-J. (1976), 'The political business cycle: comment', *Review of Economic Studies*, vol. 43, pp. 553–5.

Frey, B. S. and Ramser, H.-J. (1983), 'Where are the limits of regulation?' *Discussion Paper Series*, A–Nr.181, Faculty of Economics and Statistics, University of Konstanz, October.

Frey, B. S. and Weck, H. (1984), 'The hidden economy as an "unobserved variable"', *Discussion Paper Series*, Institute for Empirical Economic Research, University of Zurich.

Fullerton, D. (1982), 'On the possibility of an inverse relationship between tax rates and government revenue', *Journal of Public Economics*, vol. 19 (February), pp. 3–22.

Gollup, F. M. and Roberts, M. J. (1983), 'Environmental regulations and productivity growth: the case of fossil-fueled electric power generation', *Journal of Political Economy*, vol. 91, pp. 654–74.

Grossekettler, H. (1981), 'Der Brennan-Buchanan-Plan zur Eindaemmung der Staatstaetigkeit', *Finanzarchiv*, vol. 39, pp. 495–508.

Haveman, R. H., Pommerehne, W. W., Schneider, F. and Wolf, B. (1983), 'The decline of productivity growth and the rise of the shadow economy in the United States', mimeo, Department of Economics, University of Wisconsin, October.

Ladd, H. F. and Tideman, N. T. (1981), *Tax and Expenditure Limitations.* Washington: Urban Institute.

Nordhaus, W. D. (1975), 'The political business cycle', *Review of Economic Studies*, vol. 42, pp. 169–90.

Peacock, A. T. and Shaw, G. K. (1982), 'Tax evasion and tax revenue loss', *Public Finance*, vol. 37, pp. 269–78.

Pommerehne, W. W. and Frey, B. S. (1978), 'Bureaucratic behavior in democracy: a case study', *Public Finance*, vol. 33 (Fall), pp. 71–81.

Schwarz, J. E. (1983), 'The hidden truth about regulation', *Challenge*, vol. 26 (November/December), pp. 54–6.

Stuart, C. E. (1981), 'Swedish tax rates, labor supply, and tax revenues', *Journal of Political Economy*, vol. 89, pp. 1020–38.

Tabb, W. K. (1980), 'Government regulations: two sides to the story', *Challenge*, vol. 23 (November/December), pp. 40–8.

Tanzi, V. (1980), 'The underground economy in the United States: estimates and implications', *Banca Nazionale del Lavoro Quarterly Review*, vol. 135, pp. 427–53.

Tanzi, V. (ed.) (1982), *The Underground Economy in the United States and Abroad.* Lexington: Heath.

Weidenbaum, M. L. (1979), 'The high cost of government regulation', *Challenge*, vol. 22 (November/December), pp. 32–9.

7

Is there a Natural Limit to Public-Spending Growth? Or, the Spirit of the Age as a Determinant of the Development of Public Spending

Kurt Schmidt

The question I propose to consider in this chapter is related to the development of public expenditure during the prolonged period that followed the time when the 'displacement effect' was observed for the last time, that is, in the period after the Second World War.[1] This approach, however, must not be misunderstood as to mean comparative historiography; empirically, reference will be made only to the development in the Federal Republic of Germany, and I will confine myself to the expenditure of the federal government, of the *Länder* and of local governments (and will leave social insurance expenditure out of his account). The objective of my study is rather of an explanatory nature: I will attempt to find out which were the forces that determined the development of public expenditure during the period under consideration.

FORCES THAT DETERMINE PUBLIC SPENDING

Let us start by trying to find out which are the forces at work in respect of public spending. First of all, there is the people's desire and demand for public services – multifarious in kind and manifold in size. As most public services are provided free of charge and are, for a substantial part, consumed unconsciously, in respect of the public services people will prove to be not very service-conscious and still less cost-conscious. Cost-consciousness is awakened only indirectly, through taxation. The effect of taxes upon cost-consciousness, however, is imperfect, because in return for taxes (imposed on a compulsory basis) there are no concrete services. Tax payments are therefore said to be psychologically unmotivated payments. Not only is there no fiscal equivalence, in so far as for the individual the (actual or imagined) costs do not correspond to the (actual or imagined) benefits from public services, but, as passive consumers, most people are unaware of a major part of public services. It is therefore hardly surprising that, on the one hand, they call for more public services, but, on the other hand, they complain about the tax burden. This attitude – just on account of passive consumption – is more than mere 'free riding' in a big group and is also appositely described by Bastiat's sentence: 'L'État c'est la grande fiction à travers laquelle tout le mond s'éfforce de vivre aux dépens de tout le monde.'

In so far as public expenditure is financed by borrowing, citizens' cost-consciousness is even less awakened than if expenditure were to be covered by means of taxes. It cannot be surprising, therefore, that in times of a silent expansion of public borrowing, it is widely believed that the public sector is like a cow which is fed in the sky, but milked on earth. Nor is it surprising that in consequence people follow the maxim: 'When there is no charge, don't be mean'. However, when public debt increases spectacularly, the above attitude may change abruptly, notably when (for the purpose of reducing the negative effects of borrowing) a retrenchment of services and an increase of taxes is to be expected or when people even fear a monetary disaster. In such a situation, the service- and cost-consciousness of the public will be sharpened, eventually to such an extent as to engender a confidence crisis.

But people's attitude towards public economic activity is not only determined by their interests or by what they believe to be their interests. Ideas also play an important part, and here remarkable changes have occured. Fifteen years ago, 'market failure' and 'public squalor, private affluence' were popular topics and slogans in public discussion. In recent years, other subjects and slogans have become fashionable: 'government deficiencies' are causing concern and 'public wastefulness' is denounced. However, it should not be taken for granted that articulate public opinion must correspond to the silent opinion of the people, although both opinions certainly are not detached from each other. Therefore, it may be assumed that such changes in the public discussion on public economic activity are coupled with similar, though perhaps weaker, changes in the attitude of the people.

ROLE OF POLITICAL PARTIES AND PRESSURE GROUPS

Next, we should consider that in a representative democracy people only have an indirect influence on the development of public spending; their ideas and interests in regard of public economic activity will come into effect only when – encapsulated in currents of thought and group interests – they are given consideration in political decision-making. The 'transmission gear' to ensure this is provided by political parties and pressure groups. They actively and passively attend to the people's interests and ideas; passively, in so far as they take care that people with similar ideas and parallel interests are brought together; and actively, by making propaganda for their idealistic and material objectives. In this double sense, political parties and pressure groups not only channel the interests and ideas of the citizens; they also attend to the fact that these currents of thought and group interests become effective, that is, they represent them politically.

Nevertheless, there are differences between political parties and pressure groups. Pressure groups are primarily pursuing special economic interests (sometimes also non-material goals). Therefore, the individual with his manifold distinctive features and varying expressions of life can join different pressure groups at the same time. Political parties are struggling in many ways for the greatest possible share in power and, on account of this competing relationship, as a rule they preclude their members from adhering to other parties. This distinction between political parties and pressure groups is reflected in the fact that (in a political system with few parties) only parties are represented in parliament and, as a consequence, they also take the lead in the political campaign for seats in the legislature. Pressure groups exert political influence more secretly, in the 'underground'. In return for the support they give to political parties in many and multifarious ways, they may negotiate for electoral promises and also reserve their right to help in the selection of candidates. As a consequence, pressure groups are represented in parliament as well – though indirectly.

Since participation in the government as a rule involves a greater share in power, political parties fight for this goal. In a parliamentary democracy, the majority that enables a government to be formed is composed of party factions. Pressure groups also try to participate in governmental power. But they are interested less in a permanent and more in latent participation, because this latter gives them the chance for short-term and effective intervention whenever their special interests are at stake in some way or other. This indirect participation of pressure groups in government apparently depends on their distance from the governing and opposition parties. In some instances, the greater or smaller distance is obvious, and in the case of a change of government, there is then a shift in the influence of pressure groups. Some pressure groups, however, attach importance to neutrality in party politics and, in this way, attempt, without regard to the parties in power, to ensure that they always have access to the government if required.

The greater share in power involved by participation in government has its origin in the fact that legislative initiatives in most cases emanate from government, that government enacts administrative regulations and that with the bureaucracy it has the very instrument of power to rule at its disposal. The bureaucracy, however, develops a certain life of its own, and it has become practice to assume that the bureaucracy pursues its own interests such as to increase its influence, prestige and income. In this approach, it is, of course, not considered that parties and pressure groups act upon the bureaucracy; their influence is reflected in patronage used in bestowing public offices. Therefore, the bureaucracy's bearing upon political decision-making does not always reflect the self-interest of the public administration. Impulses, may as well emanate from the interests of parties or pressure groups.[2] We should not forget either that there still are public officials who are doing their job without regard to party or pressure-group influence or to the administration's interest (and thus work towards rationality in administration and in politics).

Finally, the influence of articulate public opinion (that is, of the press, the radio and the television and also of science as well) on political decision-making has to be taken into account. Notwithstanding the many connections with parties and pressure groups, there also exists party and pressure-group independence.

RELATIONSHIPS AMONG MEMBERS OF THE POLITICAL ELITE

Parties and pressure groups act through their leading bodies. They are the proper actors and can be considered as the political elite, together with members of the top-level bureaucracy and persons in leading positions in the mass media. Now, the relations among the (partial) elites of these organizations are multifarious. The political elite is by no means homogeneous, in so far as the partial elites represent the different and at times even opposed objectives of their respective organizations. The activity of party elites aims at direct participation in government; pressure-group leaders attempt to exert indirect influence on the government through a variety of channels. High officials and prominent persons from the press, the radio and the television (and also from science) partly act on behalf of political parties and pressure groups, but partly pursue their own interests. On the other hand, both party and pressure-group elites must devote attention to those whom they represent and whose support they want to secure – that is, potential voters and sympathizers. The degree of dependence of the 'few at the top' on the 'many at the base', and the chances of climbing from the bottom to the top as well as the eventuality of a reverse movement from top to bottom has to be, so to speak, optimal in order to ensure the efficient operation of representative democracy. Furthermore, there are interrelationships among parties, pressure groups and the bureaucracy and also among voters/sympathizers and the public opinion. These interrelationships are shown schematically in figure 7.1.

Now, the definition of the objectives of organizations is not identical to that of the motivations that determine the behaviour of the political elite. This party leads us to the question: what is a politician? There is an abundance of answers to this question, well-meaning, ironical and malicious ones, and in most cases examples exist to illustrate these answers. In what follows, I will proceed on the assumption that the prime concern of a member of the political elite is to remain there. Furthermore, I assume that these actors (as well as the other politicians who are not yet or no longer members of the

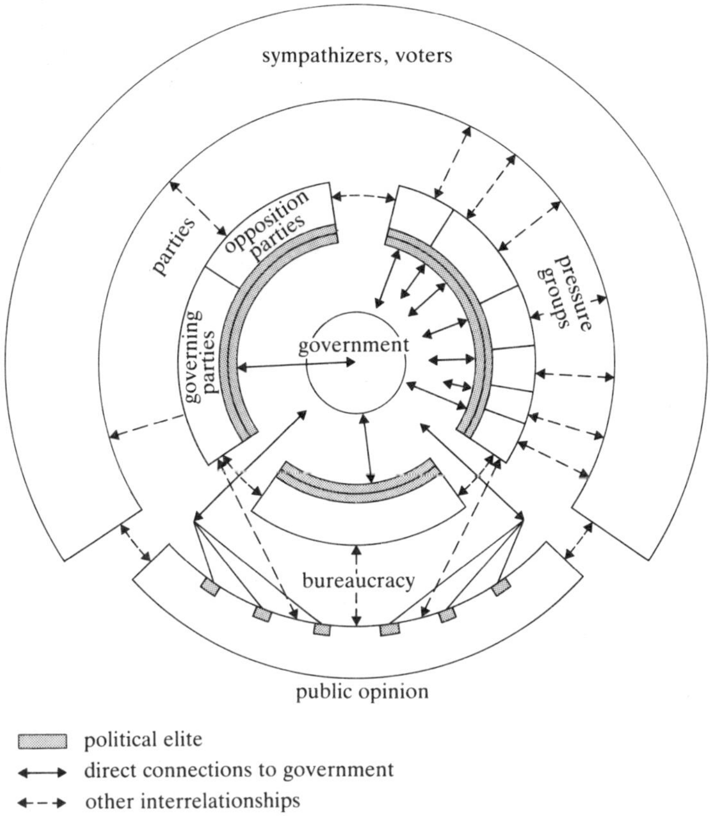

Figure 7.1 Interrelationships among political parties, pressure groups, the bureaucracy, voters/sympathizers and public opinion.

elite) are in their behaviour determined by the two following diametrically opposed motivations: power-orientation and value-orientation.[3]

The power-oriented politician is interested solely in possessing and exercising power, he wants power for power's sake and for him, therefore, everything else is of a merely instrumental nature. The value-oriented politician is characterized by the fact that he wants to preserve certain values or bring them into play. He seeks power only for this purpose, for him power is only an instrument.[4]

ATTITUDE OF THE POLITICAL ACTORS

What are the conclusions to be drawn in regard to the development of public spending over the last thirty or forty years from the above described interrelationships of political forces (that is, for a period during which the history of public finances was determined neither by war nor by big crises)? After having outlined briefly the public's ambivalent attitude to public economic activity, we are now concerned with identifying the attitude of political actors in respect of public economic activity with due regard to their value- or power-orientation and their membership of elites.

Let us first consider the party elites who, as explained, seek participation in government. Political actors who orientate their behaviour by power will, strictly speaking, care little about the problem of more or less public economic activity (to put it technically, about the rate of expansion of public spending). When in doubt, they will join the side promising the greater share in power (or the smaller loss of power). They must be aware, however, of the image attached to the parties for which they stand, the image which embraces the attitude towards public economic activity. In the case of parties, this attitude is determined by value-oriented politicians. In more concrete terms, when the public or private supply of a good is controversial, a political party has to decide whether it advocates public provision or market supply. An important point is that the political position in this respect (as in others) must not be defined in absolute terms, but in relation to other parties. As a matter of fact, political parties altogether undergo changing 'tendencies': at times there are shifts to the 'right', at others to the 'left'.

The elites of pressure groups have to defend the special interests of their respective organizations. Power-oriented actors, without any doubt, will keep this in mind – notably in regard to the position of the respective pressure group towards public economic activity. The value-oriented members of pressure-group elites may be expected, in regard to their opinion on public economic activity, to conform to the special interests of the group for which they are acting so far as these special interests are concerned, there are considerable divergencies between pressure groups. As the special interests determine also the attitude of the pressure groups with regard to the size of public economic activity, it is not surprising that in this respect there are also distinct differences.

Members of the political elite who work in the public administration or in the public media can also perform their function either in a value-oriented or in a power-oriented manner. Inasmuch as they are sympathizers of parties or pressure groups or even act on behalf of these, the above description of party or pressure-group elites will hold. The remaining part of those political actors, provided they are predominantly value-oriented, may be assumed to have differing views on the size of public economic activity. This also applies to members of the elite in the bureaucracy. Their mode of behaviour, if labelled as directed towards 'budget maximization', is described in too biased a way, and hence imperfectly, as set out above. This might hold true, perhaps, for those in the bureaucratic elite who are to be considered as power-oriented, for growing budgets can be career-promoting and the control of public money implies influence and prestige. Prominent representatives of the public media who are acting in a power-oriented way will focus their attention on the development of expenditure only when this problem is a burning issue, and will then take the position which they believe to be the most expedient for their purposes. As these persons are operating outside government and public administration, they may well be expected to be critical about public economic activity, with the purpose of improving their image and influence.

TREND OF PUBLIC ECONOMIC ACTIVITY IN THE FRG

The interrelationships of political forces as described above also illustrate the many-sided separation of powers which characterizes a modern-type representative democracy. Where such a balance of power exists, it is no surprise that in such countries the line of politics is usually determined by course corrections and not by sharp turns. Thus the spectrum of political changes is observed to have been rather narrow for quite a long time. The same is true for the size of public economic activity[5] – as demonstrated by the ratios of the public economy: the expenditure ratio (public expenditures as against GNP) and the tax ratio (tax yields as against GNP). The development in the Federal Republic of Germany shows that in the years 1951–70 the expenditure ratio ranged from only 28.2 per cent to 30.5 per cent. The variations of the tax ratio were equally moderate; over the same period, the tax ratio did not fall below 22.8 per cent and did not exceed 24.8 per cent.

As from the early 1970s, however, things have changed considerably. On the one hand, the expenditure ratio rose from 30 per cent in 1971 to more than 35 per cent in 1981; the years 1982 and 1983 showed a decrease which probably has continued in 1984, when the ratio may drop to 33½ per cent. On the other hand, the tax ratio fluctuated in the years between 1971 and 1984 within about the same range as in the period from 1951 to 1970, namely between 23 per cent and 25 per cent. Since 1974, the borrowing ratio (net public borrowing as against GNP) is substantially higher than in the years between 1951 and 1970; it has, however, been declining since 1981.

What are the reasons for the considerable expansion of public economic activity during the 1970s and for its partial curtailment since 1982, which has come about without essential changes in the many-sided separation of powers as illustrated above? In my view, both developments are mainly the result of the above-mentioned changes in the line of thought. In the Federal Republic of Germany, the changed attitude in favour of an expansion of public economic activity was more or less apparent already in the mid-1960s. It became manifest in 1959 with the change of government, which provided the political basis for an expansion of public economic activity. The general mood in the country pointed towards more public spending. Value-oriented politicians who supported an increase took the lead; likewise, power-oriented politicians bet on that horse. The spectrum of political parties and in its wake the entire political landscape shifted in this direction. All projects that required economic activity had greater chances of success than before. At the outset, financing caused little concern, but later on difficulties arose. At first, higher tax yields resulting from business upswing and inflation filled the public purse, then, except in the years 1976 and 1977, increased public borrowing took this place.

Also, the reversal became obvious earlier than was politically apparent. The late 1970s were characterized by disillusionment in respect of additional public services provided by the government, perhaps as a result of passive consumption, but more probably because of some obvious undesirable developments. In the first place, disillusionment was caused by growing public sensitivity with regard to the costs of (increased) public economic activity. Direct taxes, particularly the wage tax, rose permanently, and with increased social insurance contributions the burden of taxes and levies rose altogether; the spectacular increase of the public debt gave rise to doubts in monetary stability and even engendered enxiety for the economic future. This shift in the general mood strengthened the position of value-oriented politicians, who supported a curtailment of public expenditure. Power-oriented politicians followed the signs of the time and even expansionists among value-oriented politicians, considering the tax resistance and the strongly rising interest burden on public budgets, could not admit that sooner or later the consolidation of the public budget would become inevitable, if the government's scope of action were to be recovered.[6] The reversal in respect of public economic activity had been introduced by the previous federal government. The new government made the curtailment of the expenditure ratio one of the most important items on its agenda and pursued the course of consolidation rigorously, despite recession.

In my view, the reversal towards less public economic activity is easier to explain than the change of opinion in favour of greater government involvement after many years of an almost unchanged size of public economic activity. Diverging ideas with respect to public economic activity have, over the years, by reason of their contrary course, offset each other and, given a balance of powers, have, as a consequence, prevented greater changes in the expenditure ratio. How does one explain, then, that at a given time ideas which advocate increasing public economic activity get the upper hand and begin to exert political influence? Hirschman (1982) claims to have discovered that societies tend to alternate between 'private interest' and 'public action', and that this shift of opinion can be explained by altered preferences as a result of disappointments in the fields of private consumption and of commitment to public matters. Here, the cyclical aspect appears somewhat exaggerated, as does the dialectic pattern in Lorenz von Stein's formation of eras.[7] It rather looks as if times with an almost stable expenditure ratio are followed by times of more distinct fluctuations in the expenditure ratio. The reasons for such a shift of ideas, which moves the development 'up' (or 'down') and which hence leads away from an existing 'equilibrium' (which possibly is lasting for some time), remain difficult to determine. They may be spontaneous or suggestive, empirical or speculative. The increasing (or declining) demand for publicly provided services as well as the propensity for regulation (or deregulation) and many other factors may come into play here. Presumably, the shift of ideas that gives rise to changes in the size of public economic activity is produced by a particular constellation of circumstances, by a historical coincidence, so to speak. This would also explain the difficulty in forecasting the transition from a period where the size of public economic activity remains almost stable to a period with more distinct fluctuations.

RELATIONSHIP BETWEEN PUBLIC ECONOMIC ACTIVITY AND EXPENDITURE RATIO

Let us consider more closely the case of a shift of ideas which implies an expansion of public economic activity and which is followed by a reversal, entailing a decline of public activity. Can we, at the end of such a swing, reckon with the situation that had prevailed before being restored? To put it differently, may the increase and decrease of the expenditure ratio be expected to have the same size? As far as I can see, this is fairly unlikely; the expenditure ratio will decline for its major part, but will not be reduced to its former level.

There are several reasons for this: the most important is that people get used to additional provided public services; as a consequence a retrenchment of these services is unpopular, and politicians who plead for retrenchment are running certain risks.[8] People get particularly accustomed to those services which have served as an argument for an expansion of the public activity. In the Federal Republic of Germany, this applies in particular to the fields of social services and education. The curtailment of expenditure in these fields is awkward, in particular for politicians who have not only provided the beneficiaries with the material advantage, but who also, by means of suitable rationalization, have removed people's scruples about taking advantage of these additional public services. Certainly, politicians who have done so by mere value-orientation will oppose such retrenchments; power-oriented politicians presumably will beat a partial retreat, the scale more or less depending on the degree of consideration they have to show to their clientele.

People also get used to regulations which may have been introduced for quite respectable reasons in times of increasing public activity. However, the costs ensuing from these regulations are often very high and when government is obliged to make budgetary cuts, these measures turn out to be irreversible. The regulations concerning the construction and equipment of kindergartens, schools, gymnasiums, public baths and homes for the aged may be quoted as examples. These regulations originate for the most part from the ambition and perfectionism of associated ministries. Moreover, there is the competition and urge for a positive image of politicians who either work at the community level or who are seeking there the support of voters and sympathizers. They are using their influence to have the aforementioned facilities with the most up-to-date equipment installed in as many towns as possible.

Increasing public economic activity that is financed largely by borrowing creates constriants which, after a reversal, prevent the expenditure ratio from declining to its former level, or at least render such decline very difficult. In the Federal Republic, the share of interest payments in public expenditure clearly reflects to what extent the scope of spending has been curtailed by deficit policy. Had the ratio of the interest burden been maintained at the level of 1973, the federal government, the *Länder* and local governments would have had 30 billion DM available for tax reductions or other expenditures in 1983. Interest liabilities are for the most part a permanent burden, and hence the politicians' scope for spending and action will remain confined. This is all the more true, the closer the expenditure ratio is cut down to its original level. Less drastic cuts, then, would leave more scope – 1 percentage point of the expenditure ratio at present represents almost 6 billion DM. Surely in these circumstances, the value-oriented politicians, supported by the expansionists, will use their influence to prevent the expenditure ratio from being cut down as far as its former level.

As expenditure has to be financed, an expenditure ratio that after an expansion is not reduced to its former level, calls for higher revenue. It is fairly unlikely that public revenue can be raised substantially, although a moderate increase appears feasible, for example, by raising the tax ratio by half a percentage point and by increasing the borrowing ratio eventually slightly more. These slight alterations will meet with little resistance on the part of the people, because they are unimportant as against the former 'equilibrium'; eventually, people even will not become aware of them at all. Politicians who plead for cutting the rate of public economic activity back to its former level will presumably receive little attention, once the major portion of consolidation is achieved. Moreover, they risk being accused of petty-mindedness by opponents.

All in all, there are clearly more arguments in favour of, than against, reducing the expenditure ratio to a level slightly superior to that before the phase of expansion. If such expenditure moves arise repeatedly, they are likely to result in the expenditure ratio being slightly raised each time, that is that it increases 'sedimentarily', so to speak. The substantial expansion of the expenditure ratio which has come about in the described way will, in order to be brought under control, perhaps require a once-and-for-all 'downward displacement' (Peacock and Wiseman, 1967).

CONCLUDING REMARKS

There remain some qualifications to be made. First, I would like to emphasize that people's rejection or approval of parties and pressure groups is not determined by tax or expenditure policy measures alone, and that, in consequence, both parties and pressure groups also develop activities in other political fields in order to gain popular support. This is very obvious in times of war or of a large (economic) crisis, but it is also true for 'normal' times. Nevertheless, much evidence points to the fact that people's response to almost no other government activity is as strong as in the case of tax and expenditure policy, however vague or even erronious people's ideas of the effects may be. In fact, measures of public finance strike them more directly than any other government measures; and, above all, people are permanently affected by them. The eagerness of parties and pressure groups in matters of public finance clearly indicates people's sensitivity in this respect. Moreover, the thesis of the political rank of public finance applied always at the 'margin', that is, whenever it all depends on public finance – either because too little happens in other political fields, or because what is going on there is offsetting itself. In such a situation, what really matters, except when other reasons account for firm political fronts (for example, when committed voters constitute the majority), is what happens to those people who react to tax and expenditure policies.

Next, attention should be given to the fact that apart from measures of public finance there also exist regulations; from this it follows that the scale of public economic activity is not reflected in the budget alone and that measures of direct control should be considered as well. For our purpose, it is of relevance that there are certain possibilities of substitution between such regulations and measures of public finance. Consequently, the result of our study could be affected if regulations and the size of the budget take a contrary course. As far as I can see, this does not apply to the Federal Republic of Germany, despite some operations of substitution in the social security system. A contrary course is also very unlikely if changes in the scope of public economic activity are in essence determined by lines of thought.

I would also like to remind readers that I have left the social insurance expenditures out of this account. If we take this expenditure and social insurance contributions into account, we will find that both this comprehensive expenditure ratio and the ratio of taxes and levies started growing in the 1960s. Since 1982, this expenditure ratio is also declining, whereas the ratio of taxes and levies has remained almost unchanged. This development is presumably due to the fact that here, in reality and in the opinion of the insured, the equivalence of services and costs is greater than that of public services and taxes. Increasing costs and services in the social security system will therefore meet with less resistance than in the field of public expenditure and taxes. It is therefore not surprising that in the consolidated budget of the social insurances and of the federal government, the *Länder* and the local governments the development of these latter three budgets is sometimes overshadowed by the development of the social insurance budget.

Finally, it should be noted that for purposes of simplification I have abstained from extending my study to the constellation in a federatively organized state. In this event, as in the case of the Federal Republic of Germany, the above-described horizontal separation of powers becomes effective on various levels and another dimension is added – the vertical one.

NOTES

1 In this contribution, I am resuming, and in some respects modifying, thoughts which I have developed on earlier occasions (c.f. Schmidt, 1965; 1966; 1967; 1975).

2 The behaviour of such group representatives placed in the public administration may also be affected by whether it is predominantly a 'beneficent patronage' for deserving older-group functionaries or an 'influence-exerting patronage' with the help of career-conscious young-group functionaries.

3 Caution is recommended in respect of the term 'value-orientation'; despite its positive semantic value, it is used here, for want of a more suitable expression, as if it were value-neutral, that is, politicians whose actions are power-oriented are not classified as 'worse'. Thus, we must abstract from possible sympathies with a policy 'based on principles'. In practical terms (that is, with respect to political action), such sympathy can hardly be substantiated; in fact, the opposite is more likely, for in the case of politicians who are primarily interested in power, prediction is easier – and hence also control – than in the case of those who pursue noble (or ridiculous) objectives and want to attain them at all costs.

4 Power- and value-orientation can be conceived as being 'extremes', but at the same time as elements explaining the behaviour of politicians (and political bodies); the *Idealtypen* consequently do not stand for contradictory contrasts. It will suffice for this essay to think of politicians whose behaviour is primarily value-, or power-oriented.

5 c.f. Kurt Schmidt (1966). This does not mean that the structure of public expenditure also remains essentially unchanged. In the quoted article, I have tried to show that group-oriented (pressure-group-related and party-related) expenditure would rise at the expense of group-indifferent (general and social-related) expenditure. For a sectoral study, see Karl-Heinrich Hansmeyer (1963). In recent issues of *Public Choice*, this development would have to be subsumed under 'rent-seeking'.

6 The size of the loss of government's scope of action in the Federal Republic over the past ten years is illustrated by the increase of interest payments as against the growth of public spending. c.f. *Sachverständigenrat zur Begutachtung der gesamtwirtschaftlichen Entwicklung, Jahresgutachten 1983/84, par. 381.*

7 Lorenz von Stein developed this theory in several publications during the second half of the nineteenth century.

8 This also applies to a good deal of passive consumption; for people will be more aware of a retrenchment of public services than of their supply, which they have learnt to take for granted.

REFERENCES

Hansmeyer, K. H. (1963), *Finanzielle Staatshilfen für die Landwirtschaft*, Tübingen:

Hirschman, A. (1982), *Shifting Involvements: Private Interest and Public Action*, Oxford:

Peacock, A. T. and Wiseman, J. (1967), *The Growth of Public Expenditure in the United Kingdom, 1980–1955*, rev. edn. London: George Allen and Unwin.

Schmidt, K. (1965), 'Zu einigen Theorien über die relative Ausdehnung der öffentlichen Ausgaben', *Finanzarchiv*, vol. 24.

Schmidt, K. (1966), 'Entwicklungstendenzen der öffentlichen Ausgaben im demokratischen Gruppenstaat', *Finanzarchiv*, vol. 25.

Schmidt, K. (1967), 'Zur ordnungspolitischen Problematik wachsender Staatsausgaben', *Schriften des Vereins für Sozialpolitik*, vol. 47.

Schmidt, K. (1975), 'Zur politischen Reaktion auf Nachfragewogen in der Staatswirtschaft', *Finanzarchiv*, vol. 33, Published also in English: 'On political reactions to demand waves in the public cconomy', *German Economic Review*, vol. 15.

8

Control of Public-Spending Growth and Majority Rule

Francesco Forte

PUBLIC EXPENDITURE AND THE UNANIMITY RULE

According to the well-known proposition of Buchanan and Tullock (1962), the adoption of voting rules deviating from unanimity is one of the main structural causes of anomalous expansion of public expenditure and, by inference, of deficits (but this is a less clear point). This is so because the (representatives of the) majority groups may cover the costs of collective goods that provide a benefit to them by exploiting minorities through differential burdens of taxes or debts raised to finance these expenditures. A Pareto-inefficient expansion of public outlays is thus generated and maintained, because although marginal costs for the collectivity exceed its marginal revenue, costs for the majority at the margin are less than its benefits. There is no equality at the margin of these costs and revenues for the majority, because it has to undergo considerable 'transactional', that is, bargaining costs, to reach internal consensus. From the Buchanan–Tullock theorem, it follows that not only an excess of supply of public goods in the narrow sense, but also an excess of supply of (social) transfers may result. In the light of the 'Pareto optimal redistribution' theory, one may argue that although under the unanimity rule redistribution will be possible only in so far as it corresponds to the preferences of everybody (whether egoistically or altruistically motivated), under the majority rule an 'irrational redistribution' may emerge because the majority may offload part (or the whole) of its costs on minorities, the outcome being a 'cheap altruism'. Assuming less restrictive postulates on optimal redistribution, and taking some utilitarian 'rational' rule such as that of Harsanyi (which could be accepted by most contractarians as an 'economic' rule), one may still argue that majority systems of voting favour oversupply of transfer outlays because the costs of redistribution need not be paid by those who obtain long-term (probabilistic) benefits, in proportion to them. In other words, under majority rule there may be an oversupply of redistributive transfers in comparison with the exact preferences of the individual members of the majority. Perverse redistribution through transfers favouring the rich or the average-income citizens at the expense of the less affluent may also emerge, as a result of the 'exploitation' of minorities by the majority. Thus there might also be an oversupply of social transfers (perhaps in the form of 'tax expenditures') also from the point of view of theories favouring an intense redistribution, such as the Rawlsian difference principle. This may be particularly true where, as in most industrialized countries, the 'have-nots' are a minority and may hardly be able to become significant members of the political majorities.

It follows from the above that the adoption of unanimity rules in the purest sense minimizes public outlays and avoids 'irrational expenditure', even if, from a neo-utilitarian or from neo-Kantian–Rawlsian point of view, what can be considered a 'just result' does not always materialize. Unanimity is also likely to bring about a smaller public deficit and, consequently, less inflation.

However, as control of economic fluctuations, timely fiscal and monetary policy measures are sometimes required, the unanimity rule may aggravate economic instability. It may also be damaging in other circumstances, for example, ensuring supply of defence and public order where timely decision-making may be essential. Buchanan and Tullock recognize that even the unanimity rule may be highly Pareto inefficient, given the costs of not reaching a decision. Government implies power and power is inconsistent with unanimity.

QUALIFIED AND SIMPLE MAJORITY RULE

However, Buchanan and Tullock reconcile these two conflicting propositions – that under majority rule there may be a tendency towards 'excessive' public expenditure and deficits, and that the unanimity rule may be dangerously inefficient – by arguing, using a diagram (figure 8.1), that a qualified majority emerges as the optimal (or 'second-best'?) solution.

The extent of exploitation of minorities causing excess of public spending is represented by the curve of the social cost of a collective decision, which declines as the rules for consensus are made more severe, that is, the percentage of votes required to approve a decision increases over the number of potential voters. Thus a qualified majority is always 'less expensive' for the public budget and for individuals who dislike risks of mutual exploitation rather than a simple majority rule.

The cost of bargaining to reach consensus, on the other hand, is represented as an increasing value curve: it increases as the percentage of required majority increases. This is so because the greater the need by any would-be majority of acquiring votes, as a proportion of the supply of votes, the higher appears to be the bargaining power of each voter and the smaller the risk that other

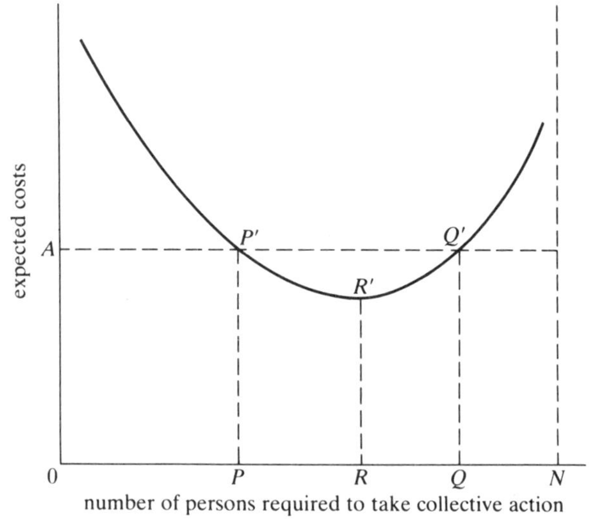

Figure 8.1 Cost comparison of simple and qualified majority rule.

would-be majorities might collect competing votes to such an extent that they achieve consensus on their platform.

From the shape of these two curves, it follows that an equilibrium point may be found where the addition of the values of the decreasing exploitation-cost curve and of the increasing bargaining-cost curve gives a minimum.

It is not clear to my mind why this minimal value should necessarily be in a zone where qualified majority rules are in force. Even assuming that the exploitation-cost curve is continuously increasing, one might be faced by U-shaped bargaining-cost curves, which, after an initial period, during which they are increasing because of instability of decisions due to instability of relative majorities, they might sharply decline, although they would rise again with qualified majorities, because of the cost of not deciding. The minimal values of the addition of the two curves would then be found in a zone between simple absolute majority and high relative majorities, that is, minority decisions.

This, however, belongs to the realm of what might be. What matters for the argument of the present chapter is a *stronger* result. It seems to me that what is untenable is the (crucial) assumption that qualified majorities are 'less expensive' than simple majorities, and the related shape of the exploitation curve (represented as a 'decreasing cost' curve). Why should this curve be continuously increasing?

The evidence of parliamentary activities demonstrates that governments, in order to stay in power, are obliged to increase public expenditure and deficits (since it is increasingly difficult to find taxes agreed by the majority) in order to accommodate the requests of the marginal supporters. Before elections, public expenditure shows a tendency to increase and deficits soar because of the efforts by the rulers to seduce marginal voters.

Since this takes place under rules which are officially described as a 'simple majority', where, by definition, marginal support is less necessary than under a qualified majority, why should one argue that a restraint to public expenditure and to deficits should take place, if a qualified majority was officially required?

It is true that those who add to the majority do not expect to be exploited by it, but it is also true that they also expect to be able to participate in the exploitation by the majority of the minority. They also expect to get benefits from public outlay (and other public policies) at the expense of other people and to obtain exemption from general taxes. The tendency towards an 'excess' of public expenditure and towards public deficits will thus be reinforced by the increase of the proportion of votes required for the approval of parliamentary decisions.

DIRECT AND REPRESENTATIVE DEMOCRACY

There is another oversimplification in the Buchanan–Tullock theorem: the transposition of the criteria of optimality for consensus rules from direct to representative democracy. To be precise, Buchanan and Tullock actually point out that, for the containment of public expenditure to the 'benchmark level' (and the same may be said for the containment of deficit), what matters is not only the rule of choosing applied in parliament, but also the degree of representativeness of its members, since it cannot be taken for granted that they pursue the interests of their electorate. From this it follows that there is no guarantee that even a unanimity rule applied in parliament avoids any possible exploitation of minorities, since it may well be that no one in parliament pursues the true interests of some (unfortunate) minorities. On the other hand, if unanimity or large majority rules are applied in parliament, consensus will replace competition and coalitions of politicians will easily be formed. Through them, maximization of narrow parliamentary interests will prevail over the collective interests of voters. This also may be a cause of increased expenditure and deficit, because every pressure group represented in parliament will be accommodated at the 'unsound public finance' banquet. No competition among political parties will develop. Thus what may be apposite for direct democracy may be wrong for representative democracy. Here one has to consider that the larger is the majority rule applied, the smaller is the room for confrontation and for the application of the law of selection.

COMPETITION AND COALITION

If one assumes that there are genuine collective goods, interesting a majority of citizens, among them such immaterial goods as monetary stability, availability of investment money for growth, independence from a large foreign debt, a tolerable burden of public debt interest, one must argue that competition in supplying public goods among the political class will be more likely to provide these goods than a system in which coalitions predominate. Coalitions prevent competition in much the same way as monopolies, and so violate the conditions which ensure, as with ordinary commodites such as bread and meat, that supply conforms to voters' demands.

Thus, for collective goods of 'general interest' what matters is whether there is enough stimulus in the political market to supply them through innovations. And since the higher the degree of competitiveness, the more likely are these innovations, it follows that the smaller the majority required to rule, the greater will be the pressure for 'sound finance'.

There is a further point to be made in this respect. Interests of the executive power are normally different from those of the majority supporting it, because it is the government that is specially charged with the responsibility for such objectives as monetary stability, economic growth, balance of payments equilibrium, availability of credit for the market economy, employment and the like. The majority thus may be viewed as consisting of a group of 'rulers' (that is, the members of the government), judged chiefly on the basis of the performance in achieving these general (and to an extent conflicting) objectives, and members of parliament who carry sectoral interests, in addition to general ones, and press government to take care of them. The broader the majority required to support the government, the more its programme will be 'qualified' by sectoral interests and the less will be the room left for the pursuance of broad general interest. Governments constrained by the daily need of assembling a large majority are pushed against their will to inflate public expenditures, to distort taxes, to increase deficits beyond their plans, in order to stay in power.

Thus, one may say that a qualified majority as applied to parliaments implies both a strong limit to the selection process relating to the ruling class and to efficient behaviour of rulers in terms of their own programme.

Under simple majority rule (that is, a system where the majority consists of actual vote counts, net of abstentions), governments have a minimum of parliamentary democratic constraint in pursuit of their policies, and thus can more easily be judged according to their real aims and capabilities. Rulers who voluntarily disregard 'sound finance' will then be sharply exposed to the competition of those who, sponsoring sound budgets, can reach a broader consensus.

HYPOTHETICAL CASE OF TWO POLITICAL ENTERPRISES

In figure 8.2, D_s is the demand curve for political enterprises (that is, the maximum potential exploitation curve) (Buchanan's external costs' curve), and it decreases as the percentage of parliamentary votes required to exert power increases. D_s, however, does not tend to zero for a hypothetical 100 per cent voting requirement, since the political enterprise (that is, the representatives) can always exploit the represented citizens. On the right side, we have C_I, the average cost curve of political enterprise I, which is the more efficient curve. On the left side, we have C_{II}, the cost curve of political enterprise II, which is less efficient than enterprise I.

Both enterprises are coalitions of political forces and become more and more heterogeneous the larger their size, measured as a percentage of parliamentary votes. Their cost thus initially decreases, because of the fixed-cost component (organizational expenses for elections, news coverage, minimum party machine costs, etc.), and then it increases (costs incurred bribing pressure groups and other political forces, which increase, as a function of parliamentary votes, because of their increasing heterogeneity to the core of the political enterprise and of their increasing 'scarcity' as the voting requirement increases). C_{II} has the same characteristics as C_I, but it is higher.

Under a simple majority, political enterprise I is able to run the public economy (that is, obtains political power) with an average exploitation cost *AP* (that is, a social cost of the exploitation) corresponding to the 'exclusion price', which is equal to the average cost *BP* of political enterprise II for the same majority.

Managers of enterprise I get an aggregate rent of *PTCV*, and the total 'production cost' of enterprise I is $TT'A'A$. Increasing the voting requirement to 60 per cent, the average cost for enterprise II increases to $B'P'$, and enterprise I will impose on the citizens an average exploitation social cost $A'P'$ and a total social cost of $P'A'0V'$, with an average rent for the managers of enterprise I of $P'T'$ and an aggregate rent of $P'T'VV'$.

Assuming a 65–70 per cent majority requirement, enterprise II is excluded from the 'political market' because its average costs exceed the demand price. Thus enterprise I is able to exploit entirely its demand curve. With a 70 per cent majority, it imposes on the citizens an average social exploitation cost of $A''S''$ and a total social exploitation cost of $S''A''0V''$. With a majority greater than 70 per cent, average costs exceed the demand price for enterprise I too. Therefore a coalition of enterprises I and II is needed to avoid anarchy. Assuming a majority of 80 per cent, we may have three possible situations:

1. politicians supporting enterprises I and II agree to exercise political power monopolistically (that is, to run the public economy);
2. the country is reduced to chaotic political conditions;
3. the voting is modified, assuming that to have the 80 per cent majority

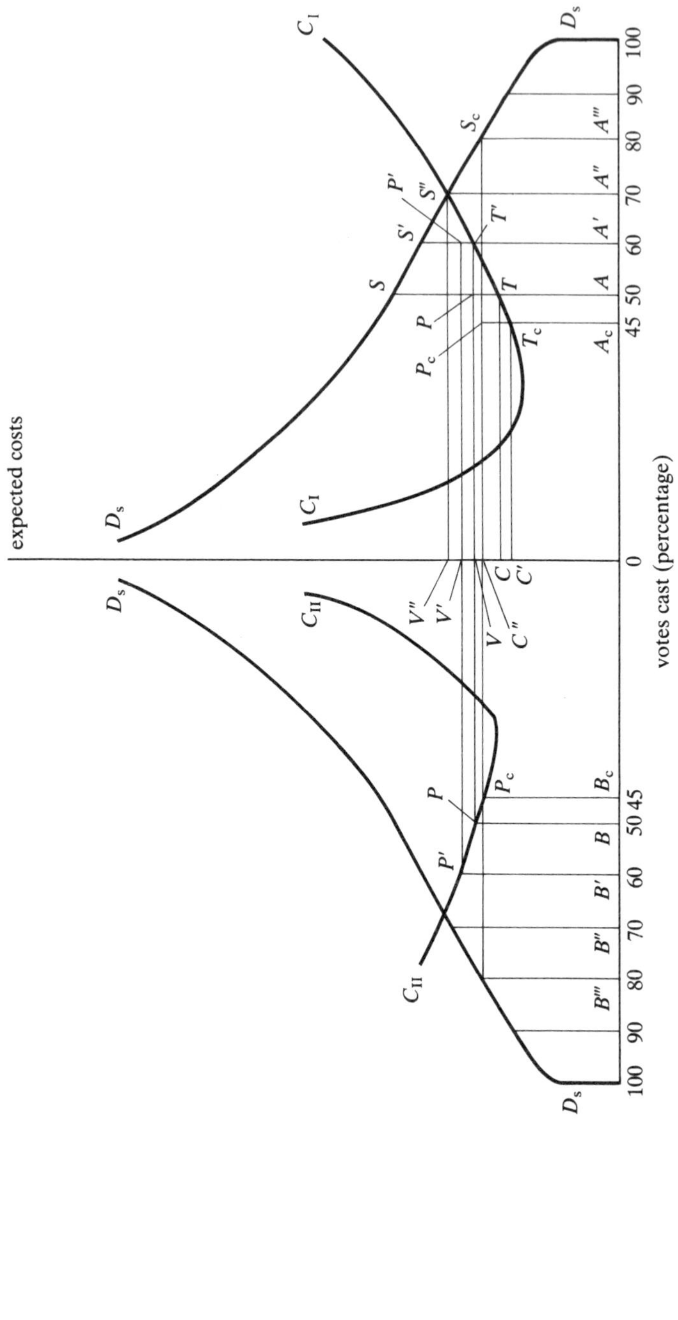

Figure 8.2 Costs of exploitation: the case of two political enterprises.

each political enterprise puts together 45 per cent of the votes (5 per cent being a strategic reserve).

Enterprise I will have an average exploitation cost A_cP_c and enterprise II a cost B_cP_c; the revenue of the coalition will be $A'''S_c \simeq B'''S_c$, assuming equal sharing among the two enterprises. Enterprise II covers its costs, and enterprise I has a rent of $T_cP_cC''C'$.

It should be emphasized that figure 8.2 deals with the Buchanan–Tullock external costs (or social costs) of exploitation, to which one must add the transaction costs borne by the community because of the delays and the irrationality of the bargain process needed to reach agreement.

THE QUALIFIED MAJORITY SYSTEM

It is my contention that the observed fact that democracy so often leads to inflated budgets, even when 'conservative' governments are in power (and some times more so under these governments), does not depend on the existence of the simple majority rule, but on the several (often concealed) hindrances to the true application of the rule; in fact these hindrances actually lead to a *de facto* qualified majority system.

Since US Primaries relate to a platform of consensus different from that existing in the country, they act as a qualified majority rule in the sense that some votes must be *overweighted* to be *added* to the others, as if the consensus of the groups to which they belong was needed. Likewise, the cumbersome procedures to get control of the party, which condition political life in so many European countries, produce a similar result. Direct election of the president of the government may reduce the amount of conditioning, thus reducing the need for adding different majorities.

A bicameral system – as Buchanan and Tullock have demonstrated – also may be viewed as a qualified majority procedure. Another way to deviate from sharp majoritarian rules is the uni-nominal system of elections to parliament. Since it is normal in each constituency that the composition of the electorate – by income classes, sectors of economic activity, religious beliefs, ethnic composition, etc. – differs, a political party must have a heterogeneous political platform adapted to the most diverse interests, if it is to hold on to the constituency. Some otherwise irrelevant minorities may thus become decisive.

A similar result is produced by the preferential-vote mechanism through which, in each party list, those who get a larger number of personal votes win. Sectoral interests have a very important role in preferential votes, both directly through the vote system itself and indirectly through financing political campaigns to capture public opinion. Interests of pressure groups who provide these votes, whether indirectly or directly, need not be included in the platform of the political parties concerned. They come in through bargaining at the personal level with candidates of the different lists. Actually this type of political bargain may be the way for a pressure group, which, as such, belongs to a minority, to infiltrate the majority.

The checks and balances that have been introduced in the parliamentary system to protect the citizens from abuses of the executive power imply a deviation from a sharp simple majority rule. More consensus is required than otherwise.

Secret ballots also increase the required majority, because it becomes uncertain how many members of the official majority support each decision proposed by the government. Those who vote against it cannot be excluded from the benefits of being members of the majority, since they remain unknown. As the existence of free-riders makes it more difficult to cover the costs of collective goods yielding benefits exceeding expenditure, then some goods will be undersupplied. Thus under secret ballots there will be an undersupply of choices of interest to the majority, while additional interests will be taken care of, adding further claims on the budget.

To my mind, it is clear why most of the reviewed rules receive staunch support in our (democratic) political system. It is so, chiefly, because they reduce the scope and sharpness of competition and of the law of selection in political markets and institutions. Members of the political class, and particularly bureaucratic parties, do not like selection and competition, and much prefer coalitions and agreement. Inflation, however, is the likely result of artificial agreement among different 'parties', in situations where it is extremely difficult to find a general consensus to diminish or abolish an existing item of expenditure whose utility has markedly declined. Additional expenses are approved which favour particular interests, with the additional costs divided among the whole electorate, but the obsolete expenditures stay where they are.

THE 'HIDDEN' QUALIFIED MAJORITY RULE

The worst case is that in which a 'hidden' qualified majority rule is in operation because some political group needed to secure a majority does not officially participate in it, and yet it is needed to facilitate efficient decision-making. (For example, they might agree to renounce filibustering, a practice all too easily accepted.) Members of the 'hidden majority' will get the benefits of every increase of public expenditure they are able to obtain, without being held responsible for its results such as inflation or high public debt, which are problems associated with the government and its official majority. Since members of the hidden majority are officially part of the opposition, they will still be free to denounce the 'unsound' financial practices of the government, when such criticisms help them to increase their popularity. The more severe the requirement of legislative provision in parliament is, in order to pursue economic policy, the more room there will be for hidden majorities.

I do not argue that clear majority rules and efficient majoritarian voting procedures suffice to hinder 'unsound finance'. In any event, they would not prevent fiscal injustice and fiscal exploitation. Public expenditure may grow improperly also under a sharp majoritarian system, both because of the Buchanan–Tullock 'external-costs' effect and because of the difference of interests among citizens and members of the ruling group and lack of information on the precise nature and effects of expenditure changes. The interests of future generations, in any case, are not represented by present voters.

The more clear-cut the majoritarian system applied in current political and economic affairs, the greater is the risk of (extreme) exploitation and of (extreme) disregard of the needs of the less favoured. Here, the constitutional contract may have to come into play, imposing rules designed to promote fiscal soundness and equity and conformity to the rule of law.

A POLITICAL AND FISCAL CONSTITUTION

In my scheme, the political and fiscal constitution would act as a set of constraints against the risks and temptations of the highly selective political process that is dominated by a clear leadership produced by an efficient simple majority system.

In this constitution one should ideally include five kinds of rules:

1. Principles designed to make it extremely difficult to practise fiscal illusion and to reduce the scope for bad practices by 'powerful government'. This must require that there be some independent body which will have to state whether and to what extent the issue of public debt and running public enterprises in deficit causes inflation, increases interest rates, creates external imbalance, crowding-out of investments, difficulties in promoting economic growth and employment.[1]
2. Principles designed to protect future generations from exploitation by the present ones: a limit should be imposed consitutionally on the issue of 'real' internal and external debt.
3. Principles designed to limit the share of tax burden in national income.
4. Principles designed to protect property rights, whether large or small (these are generally more exposed to exploitation) from retroactive or confiscatory laws, excluding, obviously, the case of property acquired through criminal activities, where the concept of crime should be carefully defined. Similar principles designed to protect entrepreneurs from personal discrimination and prohibitive legislation, for example, prevention of taxes on particular categories of individuals.
5. Principles designed to protect the living standards of the poor and to provide, wherever possible, vocational training and job opportunities for the less favoured, protecting, as much as possible, their freedom of choice.

Some of these principles are actually included–even if vaguely–in many present-day consitutions. Several are commonly accepted.

The intention of the Buchanan–Tullock rule of qualified majority, it seems to me, would be better preserved (with a net gain in the area of fairness), if it were replaced by a two-part system where, at the first stage (the operational one), a sharp majoritarian system is applied and, at the second stage (the constitutional one), constraints are set to strategic action and to the collectively 'irrational' (in some neo-utilitarian or neo-Kantian sense) maximizing behaviour of the majority.

How much public spending would thereby be reduced is a matter for speculation. Clearly, under the system here suggested, public debt would be constrained. And since exploitation of particular individuals or groups through taxation would be prevented, one should expect that the tendency to promote 'irrational' public expenditure (that is, expenditure whose costs exceed the benefits) will be reduced without damage to equity. What chances such suggestions have of being approved is a question that has to do with the conditions governing the ways in which constitutional changes reach the statute book.[2]

NOTES

1 For these principles and those under (4), see my forthcoming paper.
2 On this point, see chapter 2 above.

REFERENCES

Buchanan, J. M. and Tullock, G. (1962), *The Calculus of Consent: Logical Foundations of Constitutional Democracy*. Ann Arbor, Mich: University of Michegan Press.

Forte, F. (forthcoming), 'Monetary and Fiscal constitution, a contractarian approach' (in Italian).

9

Macro-economic Controls of Spending as a Device for Improving Efficiency in Government

Alan Peacock

INTRODUCTION

The dilemma facing Western-type societies in regard to the future of public spending has been vividly demonstrated, even given one's own reservations about its assumptions, in the propositions derived from Baumol's model of unbalanced growth (for an exposition and critique of this model with reference to public expenditure, see Peacock (1983b)). Assuming no growth in productivity in the public sector, but positive exponential growth in the private sector, and equalization of wage rates in the public and private sectors, the average tax burden (as measured by the ratio of total taxes to GDP) would grow through time, even if the proportion of publicly produced goods and services to all goods and services produced were to remain constant. Put in another way, even if the demand for publicly produced goods and services had a 'communal' elasticity of unity, the taxpayers as a whole would face a fall in the proportion of disposable real income to their gross income. A corollary of this proposition is that the continuous transfer through time of resources to the public sector will automatically reduce the overall rate of economic growth.

Even if there are doubts and reservations about the unbalanced growth thesis, it presents the kind of scenario which dominates public discussion of control and appraisal of government expenditure. It immediately gives rise to the fascinating question as to whether some equilibrium growth in public spending will be achieved as taxpayers, after a lag, react to growing tax burdens. Other chapters in this book consider the question whether market economics which are transformed into mixed economies can generate some 'built-in' mechanisms that will exorcise the 'Buchanan-Tullock bogey' of a public sector that takes the whole economy over (see Buchanan and Tullock, 1977). All of us must surely share some scepticism of public-choice theorists, myself included, of the strength of the 'built-in' forces tending to stop public-expenditure growth. Taxpayers are beset by the 'isolation paradox', for while they may generally be in favour of lower tax burdens, they have no incentive as individuals to forgo the benefits of public services which they currently enjoy. As the public sector grows, the employment opportunities of a growing proportion of the working population depend on the production of non-market goods. There is a presumption (though the evidence does not entirely support it) that public employees will favour growing public spending, and may be able to offset growing burdens as taxpayers by greater ease of access to non-pecuniary benefits than taxpayers employed in the private sector. Members of Cabinets seek to resolve their differences by a kind of perverse application of Paretian welfare principles. Some ministerial departments may be made better off by a rise in their budget in real terms, but none must be made worse off, if agreement is to be reached, resulting in upward pressure on real public spending. Whereas all agree on the remedies – closer control on overall public spending and greater efficiency in the public sector – no group involved in the bargaining process which determines the growth of public spending has a pronounced incentive to apply these remedies.

This scenario might lead one to the pessimistic conclusion that the institution of any form of control of public spending is a forlorn hope, other than as the consequence of a disastrous crisis which might destroy democratic government. However, there is a presumption that some *general* rule designed to control *overall* public spending is much more likely to command agreement than methods of control that presuppose a clear identification of gainers and losers, *before* the political process begins to make public-spending decisions. This presumption justifies much closer consideration of the content of such general rules, even if it does nothing to establish their feasibility.

In this chapter I shall make two assumptions:

1. macro-economic controls are those controls that work through movements in budget aggregates;
2. efficiency is used in the conventional economic sense with a distinction being made between allocative and technical 'x'-efficiency.

These assumptions call for a few comments. So far as the first is concerned, one might have taken a broader view in order to consider non-fiscal controls such as incomes policies, which cover both the private and public sector, and also constitutional reforms affecting the decision rules which apply both in the election of legislatures and governments and in the passing of legislation relating to government expenditure. My reason for not including such matters in this contribution is simply to reduce the subject to manageable proportions.

So far as the second assumption is concerned, it is common to associate macro-economic controls and the associated budgetary rules with a much wider range of objectives. We have to face up to the problem that the use of macro-economic controls for purposes of achieving efficiency in the economist's sense may place constraints on their use for other objectives, such as preserving economic stability and altering the distribution of income. An associated problem arises from the fact that economists disagree fundamentally over the extent to which these constraints are important. It is quite possible for a 'supply-side' economist to hold that commonly discussed methods for restraining government spending and balancing the budget are not only fully in accord with macro-economic policy in the more conventional sense, but are a pre-condition for the pursuit of that policy. On the other hand, some latter-day Keynesians will argue that the price one has to pay for promoting economic stability and equity objectives may be a large and growing public sector and fiscasl targets involving unbalancing of budgets. No attempt is made in this chapter to resolve this issue. Broadly speaking, the author takes an intermediate stance in the technical debate. He accepts that strictly balanced budgets make policies designed to promote economic stability more difficult to carry out than otherwise. At the same time, he recognizes that unbalanced budgets may cause changes in money supply and interest rates whose effect on output prices and employment, brought about by changes they induce in money GDP, cannot be ignored.

A prior question to this analysis is why macro-economic controls for efficiency purposes are necessary, and this question is considered in the next section. Some of the control measures which have been or might be instituted for efficiency purposes are then discussed, before considering the problem of how effective any macro-economic solution is likely to be within the context of Western industrial countries.

WHY HAVE MACRO-ECONOMIC CONTROLS?

There is still an influential body of opinion among economists who would argue that macro-economic instruments are unnecessary, at least for controlling economic aggregates as distinct from their constituent parts. Thus it is claimed that if government action is confined to ensuring that property rights do not confer monopoly privileges on any sector of the economy and free international trade is allowed, the economy will generate allocative efficiency and technical efficiency (through the 'threat' of freedom of entry) largely of its own accord. Moreover, it will also generate the best achievable 'natural' rate of unemployment, and the growth rate most consistent with optimal allocation of resources through time.

What happens to this argument when we introduce a public sector? The proponents of the argument might first of all make the point that several important forms of public production need not be carried out by the public sector at all, although they might concede that such activities might be financed by the public sector, directly or indirectly. Be that as it may, in the case of goods containing a major element of 'publicness', the major problem encountered in obtaining the optimal amount of these goods is how to invent an acceptable and efficient system of preference revelation. (For a useful summary of the problems and issues see, for example, Mueller (1979).) I believe that I am safe in assuming that the experts in this area, whether arguing for some kind of insurance scheme to protect individuals from 'adverse' collective decisions, or some demand-revealing process, or some kind of right of veto by individual voters, would agree that the present state of knowledge is summed up in the cryptic statement: 'We're still working on it.' This is not to imply that some form of macro-economic control will perform any better in achieving something like a Lindahl-type solution which would denote allocative efficiency.

In any case, the preference revelation approach normally takes the cost of producing various government outputs as given, therefore avoiding the problem of discussing whether public goods will be forthcoming at the amounts required and at minimum cost. The economic analysis of the presence of both allocative inefficiency and 'x'-inefficiency in government bureaux is a growth industry which need not be examined here, except to say that considerable ingenuity has been exercised in trying to devise schemes which would simulate competitive conditions in the provision of public services. As I have argued elsewhere (Peacock, 1983a), the moot point is how to make bureaux conform to 'rules' designed to implement these schemes. The very basis of the economic analysis of bureaucracy seems to deny the possibility that effective rules will be generated 'from within', at least if the scope of public-sector activities remains more or less as it is. According to that analysis, the maximizing bureaucrat is not characterized by the 'self-discipline' that would have to act as a substitute for the discipline of the market. Perhaps macro-economic controls might generate these 'from outside'.

There is a neglected feature of the analysis of public-sector inefficiency which calls for special comment. This is the influence that a growing, centralized public sector exercises on the behaviour of firms and households in the private sector placed in a bargaining position with the various departments and layers of government. Thus the dominance of the government as a purchaser in a particular market for goods or for labour inputs may promote the growth of countervailing power through merger of suppliers or through extension of unionization to professional employees. Indeed, it may be in the interests of bureaucrats to encourage this growth in market imperfection, for it is simpler and more convenient to negotiate with a few suppliers. In short, the growth of the public sector produces distortions in the allocation of goods and factors which proliferate *outside* itself, that is, in the private sector. In addition, as private enterprises become dependent on government, both as a customer and as a source of grants and tax concessions, it may pay them to invest in activities which improve their bargaining skills with government at the cost of produce and process innovations, which would improve their technical efficiency. (For further analysis of 'collective failure' in this form, see Peacock (1980).)

METHODS OF MACRO-ECONOMIC CONTROL

Aggregate revenue limitations

Considerable attention has been paid to the spate of tax limitation proposals for a number of US states, following the famous Proposition 13 supported by the Californian voters in 1978. There is no doubt that in the various states in which amendments of this kind were proposed, voters did have in mind associated spending limitations which would reduce the size of bureaucracy, although empirical evidence reveals a striking lack of clarity about the details of the cause-effect relationship. It must also be remembered that such proposals referred to state governments and therefore related to a limited range of state taxes and to state expenditures, which were also financed by federal grants. The question is how relevant such limitation agreements might be in a national context.

The first point to note about the transference of a scheme for state governments to a national government concerns the attainment of an overall tax limitation which operates as an effective check on aggregate spending. This presumably requires that *overall* revenue yields are specified, probably by reference to a yield which is expressed as a proportion of some such magnitude as GDP at market prices. It follows that this object could not be attained unless there were comprehensive coverage in the control of tax rates of a kind which would result in control over overall tax yield. There are two major problems encountered in fulfilling this condition.

First, the concept of taxes as a proportion of GDP is not one which has much significance to individual taxpayers (cf. Brennan and Buchanan, 1980). If taxpayer support for tax limitation is to be engendered, it is much more likely to succeed if limitations are placed on rate schedules and on the size of tax base of taxes which are visible to taxpayers. Such are incomes, wealth and property taxes. On the other hand, if tax-limitation measures are confined to rates and tax bases covering only a limited range of taxes, it is open to governments to defeat the general purpose of tax limitation by upward adjustments in the rates of other taxes. They may be able to rely on an element of 'fiscal illusion' in order to reduce the 'visibility' of taxes and to maintain the growth in tax-financed spending.

Second, even if it were possible to produce a tax regime that reflected a high degree of tax consciousness among voters, it must be remembered that governments do not have direct control over tax yields, but only over rates and tax bases. Fiscal 'marksmanship' of a high order is necessary to hit the tax/GDP target, particularly because the yields of different taxes are interdependent. Thus if taxpayers concentrate on obtaining limitation requirements on income taxes which result in a lowering of rates, the 'first-round' reduction in the income-tax yield will be partly compensated for by the effect of the rise in disposable incomes on the yields of taxes on expenditure as a result of multiplier effects which may themselves alter the income-tax base and result in 'second-round' effects on income-tax yields. No doubt sophisticated macro-economic policy models can lay bare these interdependencies and help in the forecasting of tax changes, but as tax-rate changes may affect both the numerator and denominator in the tax/GDP ratio, quite apart from random changes in aggregate incomes and expenditure from sources other than government which influence tax yields, fiscal planners may have to contemplate large margins of error in the planned aggregate tax yield. The requirement of a close correspondence between tax yields and expenditure is not likely to help expenditure planning and control, if there are liable to be big forecasting errors in global revenue.

This latter problem is closely connected with the second point at issue concerning tax limitation. Clearly, the growth in government expenditure need not be wholly dependent on the total tax yields and fluctuations in that total, for governments can borrow and lend. However, once it is accepted that the nexus can be severed between tax yields and government expenditure, it is all too easy for governments seeking to balance their popularity with those who benefit from tax cuts against their unpopularity with those who benefit from expenditure programmes to try to satisfy both by incurring deficits. This follows from the obvious proposition that whatever the long-term disadvantages of debt issue, the short-term popularity gains from selling debt to willing bondholders are to be preferred to the odium incurred from compulsory levies on unwilling taxpayers. Clearly, then, if the tax-limitation system is to achieve its objective, it must be buttressed by a 'balanced-budget' rule of some kind, if the object of tax limitation is not to be defeated.

The third issue arises directly out of the second. Whether or not one accepts a strictly Keynesian view or a monetarist view of macro-economic policy, the combination of a rigid tax/GDP ratio and a balanced-budget condition (with capital expenditure of government financed out of taxation) must place very firm constraints on the use of fiscal measures in order to stabilize the economy. In Keynesian terms, stabilization of the economy using fiscal policy constrained by a balanced-budget condition will be impossible, unless the tax/GDP ratio can be altered frequently and significantly. In monetarist terms, control over money supply and interest rates will have to be exercised through alterations in the composition of the annual public-sector borrowing requirement (which could be positive or negative).

The main problem, therefore, with tax limitations is to establish the link between taxes and expenditure in an effective way and without placing constraints on the use of budgetary policy for the pursuit of other policy objectives. There is no obvious way in which tax limitations would offer a *unique* solution to the problem of implementing efficiency criteria, unless it be in making voters more closely aware of the budgetary process and more willing to monitor the actions of government. However, this must entail that tax limitations are expressed not only in terms of some overall tax/GDP ratio, but also in terms of the rate schedules of particular taxes which are clearly visible to the taxpayer.

I have raised enough problems about tax limitation being used on its own as a control device for government expenditure without considering some practical problems concerning the choice of tax/GDP ratio, the definition of taxes, etc. One particular problem raised by a general control device of this kind concerns its range of operation, and particularly whether it is to be applied to all layers of government, how this is to be done and what its efficiency implications will be. This is a problem common to both tax and expenditure limitations and is further considered below.

Limiting the growth in public spending

At first sight, an expenditure rule which requires that government spending in aggregate should not rise above some given ratio of expenditure/GDP (or should only fluctuate within some narrow band) seems to have distinct advantages over tax limitation and balanced-budget rules. A balanced-budget provision does not by itself promote control over government expenditure growth, for the budget can be balanced at different levels of expenditure and taxation. A tax-limitation proposal unaccompanied by a balanced-budget rule still leaves open the possibility that government expenditure can be financed by borrowing. Furthermore, an expenditure rule, while restricting the use of government expenditure as a stabilizer of income, employment and prices, still leaves open the possibility of altering the tax/borrowing 'mix' for stabilization purposes.

A preliminary observation must be made about the nature of the ratio. In the 1960s and early 1970s, the overall level of public spending and efficiency in public spending were supposed to be controlled by a dual system. Techniques such as cost-benefit analysis and programme budgeting were to be employed at the micro-level, and overall spending was based on a comparison between the real growth in public spending and in real national expenditure. The system broke down when it became clear in the 1970s that claims by government departments for funding based in real terms turned out to be a method by which the public sector, in current-price terms, grew at the expense of the private sector. Governments had to learn the bitter lesson that account has to be taken of changes in the 'the terms of trade' between public and private spending. The changes in the terms of trade have fluctuated considerably and strikingly in recent years, when inflation has affected the private and public sector differentially.

The dilemma presented for expenditure control may be illustrated by looking more closely at this problem of the change in the terms of trade, which has been extensively discussed in recent literature (see Beck, 1981; Heller, 1981; Todd, 1983). Our tables are based on Todd's data.

In table 9.1, a comparison is made between the unweighted government expenditure on final consumption (GC) as a proportion of GDP and a weighted proportion. The unweighted proportion is simply the expression of the numerator and the denominator in current-price terms. In the weighted comparison, the GDP is deflated by the usual type of GDP deflator and government expenditure on final consumption by a price index of government inputs. In all three examples, the weighted series of GC/GDP actually falls over the period, whereas the unweighted series rises. (Of course, such a comparison has to accept the usual convention that changes in productivity in the public sector are assumed to be zero.) In table 9.2, the weighted series is obtained by the deflation of current transfers by the consumer price index (CPI), and the relative closeness in both the absolute size and movements through time in the ratios indicates that the CPI and GDP deflators in all three countries moved together. Consequently in table 9.3, the weighted series of total government current expenditure (G) is closer to the unweighted series in all three cases, although it rises at a much slower rate. The obverse to these ratio changes is to be found in the growth rates in privately financed consumption (that is, ignoring transfers as part of personal incomes). In Italy, privately financed consumption grew at an annual average rate of 5 per cent between 1960 and 1973, but fell to 1.5 per cent between 1973 and 1981. The corresponding figures for the UK were 2.5 per cent and 0.1 per cent, respectively.

Whatever its virtues may be as a way of setting out the resource implications of public-sector policies (that is, as some sort of planning framework), budgeting based on movements in the real growth of government expenditure compared with GDP is not going to operate as a system of control over the efficient use of resources. If government expenditure control is based on G/GDP in real terms, this is tantamount to accepting that productivity gains in the public sector are neither possible nor desirable. In what follows, therefore, we assume that any expenditure limitation 'rule' is based on current-price movements in government expenditure and GDP.

We can illustrate the characteristics and problems of operating some such rule by reference to the 'cash planning and control' system developed by the Conservative government in the UK in the early 1980s. Though originally and primarily justified on the grounds of its contribution to economic stability, it has been claimed that the system will contribute towards greater efficiency in public spending through greater financial discipline.

The system is a 'control system', in the sense that for the fiscal year ahead cash limits are placed on spending by each central government department, practically without exception, and on the grants paid to local governments. If for policy reasons this limit is exceeded, provision may be made for extra cash from a contingency reserve, but the reserve itself is a control figure for that year. The system is also a 'planning system', in the sense that

Table 9.1 *Government expenditure on final consumption as a ratio of GDP*

	1960		*1973*		*1981*	
Country	*UWS*	*WS*	*UWS*	*WS*	*UWS*	*WS*
Italy	12.75	16.71	15.50	14.58	18.00	14.17
UK	16.52	21.96	18.39	20.20	22.21	21.92
USA	17.36	21.00	17.68	17.66	20.32	17.80

UWS unweighted series.
WS weighted series.
Weighted series based on OECD consumer price index (CPI) and public-consumption price-index data for relevant countries.
Source: Compiled from Todd, 1983, tables 4 and 5.

Table 9.2 *Current transfers by government as a ratio of GDP*

	1960		*1973*		*1981*	
Country	*UWS*	*WS*	*UWS*	*WS*	*UWS*	*WS*
Italy	11.91	11.29	16.37	16.75	20.59	20.77
UK	9.18	8.88	12.13	12.01	15.74	16.64
USA	6.26	5.98	9.80	9.80	11.08	11.02

Source: As table 9.1.

Table 9.3 *Total government current expenditure as a ratio of GDP*

	1960		*1973*		*1981*	
Country	*UWS*	*WS*	*UWS*	*WS*	*UWS*	*WS*
Italy	24.66	28.00	31.87	31.33	38.67	35.54
UK	25.70	30.84	30.52	32.21	37.95	38.56
USA	23.62	26.98	27.48	27.46	31.40	28.82

Source: As table 9.1.

public-expenditure plans for three years ahead are to be expressed in cash and no longer in volume terms, and these plans will be related to movements in GDP at current prices. This is a major departure in British planning procedures (see Likierman, 1981 and 1983).

The difficulties associated with cash planning and control are obvious and are well illustrated by UK experience. First, strict cash limits cannot be applied in a truly comprehensive manner for two main reasons. The first reason is that the central government is not the sole spending authority. Alongside it there is a motley of local authorities, including locally elected councils, police authorities, passenger transport executives, etc., as well as public corporations with a substantial degree of financial independence. Their operations can only be directly controlled through budget procedures by 'cash-limiting' grants or subsidies received from central government. The second reason is that important segments of public expenditure are demand-determined, at least in the short run. For example, the government can only control the scope and the rates of payments to social security beneficiaries, but the volume of payments will depend on the number of qualified applicants. In fact, in the fiscal year 1982/3 only 40 per cent of total government expenditure was cash-limited in the strict sense.

The second difficulty is that the current expenditure estimates adjust the volume estimates of expenditure by expected changes in prices. No government will willingly reveal price assumptions in case these will affect the price expectations of the private sector and, through private-sector reactions, alter the assumptions on which the expenditure estimates have to be based. So far as cash-limited expenditure is concerned, price estimates may be disguised, at least in presenting data, but in the case of demand-determined expenditure it may not be too difficult for the outside investigator to work out the implicit movements in the price index. The UK Treasury has been able to get round this difficulty by revealing that projections of social security transfers are based on a positive, but *declining* rate of inflation! Presumably no government using cash limits as a means of controlling the public-sector borrowing requirement in the name of anti-inflationary policy could ever admit to assuming otherwise!

Thirdly, with a considerable proportion of current expenditure goods and services incurred by local governments, the cash-limit system has to extend its grip very firmly on other spending authorities. In the short run, it has been possible for local governments to erode the policy by offsetting the fall in the growth in grants from the central government by substantial increases in revenue from the local property tax, the local rate. In fiscal year 1981/2, for example, the cash expenditure target was exceeded by £1½ billion which, although only a little over 1 per cent of total expenditure, was almost entirely the result of local government overspending. However, attempts to control local authorities' spending directly by penalizing those who overspend – for example, by reducing central government grants or by seeking to limit their tax increases – is regarded as an unwarranted interference with local democracy.

MACRO-ECONOMIC CONTROLS AND EFFICIENCY

The mechanics of expenditure and tax-limitation controls, as observed, are complicated but, assuming that some method of expenditure limitation is embodied in a constitutional code, how sure can one be that it will promote efficiency?

A rigid test to apply is to examine how far such a limitation would constrain a government unsympathetic to the object in view, perhaps because it relied on voting support from median voters who wished to maximize distributional gains from public spending. (For models of government expenditure growth which are based on this scenario, see Peltzman (1980) and Meltzer and Richard (1981).) Even if it is assumed that such a government could not carry through a constitutional amendment that altered or destroyed the expenditure limitation, there are various strategies it could adopt to erode its influence.

1. Juggle with the definitions of government expenditure and GDP. One can hardly imagine that such definitions could be incorporated in constitutional provisions. As Senator Muskie put it: 'Our Constitution does only two things. It blueprints the structures by which we govern ourselves, and it defines the human rights we respect. Do we really want to devalue the currency with algebra and bar graphs?' (Quoted in MacLaury, 1979.) On the other hand, the very imprecision of constitutional provisions plays into the hands of the jugglers.
2. Substitute tax-relief policies for transfers, so reducing the claims on government spending. To prevent this strategy from being successful, the expenditure limitation would then have to be backed up by a further constitutional provision requiring annually balanced budgets.
3. Exploit non-budgetary means as a substitute for government expenditure in order to further distributional aims. These might include incomes policies which concentrated on a statutory limitation on profits, coupled with controls over the export of capital.
4. Even if all such loopholes were closed, a government which gave overriding priority to equity considerations could promote its aims by alterations in both the composition of taxes and expenditure within the limitation provisions. It could also derive support from the economic argument that a definition of allocative efficiency which includes efficiency in the allocation of public goods must embrace income redistribution itself as a public good!

On the other hand, it could reasonably be argued that there is no point in applying any test which does not assume that there is voter support for the policy of improving efficiency in government as well as the reduction of average tax burdens, and that the question at issue is simply that of finding out whether, given the will to achieve efficiency, a macro-economic rule will work. Given such circumstances, I will make the following observations.

First, so far as allocative efficiency is concerned, there is little doubt that if government departments know that they are competing with one another for resources fixed in money terms, they have to go through much more stringent processes of scrutiny of their costs and produce arguments for their ministerial heads which take much more account of economic logic. Likewise, pressure groups seeking to influence ministers either by direct appeal to them or through their sponsors in the legislature know that they will encounter strong resistance to special pleading. A useful, though not particularly important example, as measured by the government expenditure involved, is provided by public support for the arts. The Arts Council of Great Britain, which administers a major part of such support, only began to offer cogent arguments in favour of expansion of its budget in its 1980/1 Annual Report in which one can recognize standard 'externality' arguments. Similarly, their beneficiaries, such as the major national theatre and opera companies, having found themselves no longer in a position where they could assume annual increases in real terms, have offered evidence to the Parliamentary Committee on Education and Science that emphasizes the uncovenanted benefits emanating from their activities in the form of 'national prestige' and 'conservation of cultural resources' as well as rather dubious economic benefits such as their contribution to the balance of payments and to employment. One cannot conclude from this and other examples that I might give (for example, from the large education sector) that the resultant pattern of government expenditure more closely reflects voter preferences, but what it does do is to reduce the costs voters/taxpayers of obtaining information about the activities of interest groups in receipt of government funding. This at least offers the voters/taxpayers a better basis for judging whether such activities deserve their present level of support.

Second, it is over-optimistic to expect that 'x'-efficiency gains will be the inevitable outcome of stricter budget constraints on government services, unless, simultaneously, there are major changes made in their organization. If their outputs are difficult, if not impossible, to measure and their output is not or simply cannot be marketed, then the very nature of the *potential* gains is difficult to determine. Consequently it comes as no surprise to find that those in charge of government services will generally deny that cross-inefficiency exists at all, and will claim that the only action they can take is to reduce the quality and/or quantity of the services on offer.

Thirdly, a major dilemma arises if the aggregate spending rules extend to 'lower-level' decision-makers, such as state and local governments, in receipt of funds from central government. On the one hand, given that grants to such bodies form a major part of central government expenditure, a comprehensive rule loses credibility if it is not backed up by equally strict controls on the overall spending of lower layers of government. On the other hand, the kernel of the economic argument for a decentralized system of government, albeit one which includes an inter-governmental system of grants, is that lower-level spending authorities may be more sensitive to voter/taxpayer needs. 'X'-efficiency may be promoted at the cost of allocative efficiency.

CONCLUDING REMARKS

It is easy to agree with Wildavsky (1983) that 'To the extent governments are serious about limiting spending . . . they will be concerned about overall spending limits', and that 'whereas old-line reforms sought to directly impose detailed methods for improving decisions, the new, stream-lined models will work indirectly to increase incentives to value programs according to their best alternative use'. Although Wildavsky is careful to qualify his position and would presumably not claim to be making a political prediction, there is an underlying tone of optimism in his position about the feasibility of introducing spending limits. This optimism is based on the changing attitude of *governments*, but presupposes that the 'rational expectations' of bureaucrats are conditioned by the belief that successive governments are going to be committed to macro-economic controls of a sufficiently stringent character to make it incumbent on them to carry out the necessary organizational reforms which complement such controls.

Even if it can be presupposed that governments are resolute in their desire to limit spending increases, whether or not this means that they feel compelled to introduce some constitutional rule to buttress their position, qualitative as well as quantitative control will be necessary if control is designed to improve efficiency in the production of publicly provided goods and services. It is no doubt for this reason that governments, if disillusioned about the possibility of deploying 'in-house' methods for improving efficiency, are increasingly interested in exploring the feasibility of 'privatization' of services. But let harmony prevail between the political scientist and the economist to the extent of agreeing with Wildavsky that 'limits on total spending do not guarantee control, but without limits on total spending there can be no control'.

REFERENCES

Beck, M. (1981), *Government Spending: Trends and Issues*, New York: Praeger.

Brennan, G. and Buchanan, J. M. (1980), *The Power to Tax: Analytical Foundations of a Fiscal Constitution*, Cambridge: Cambridge University Press.

Buchanan, J. M. and Tullock, G. (1977), 'The expanding public sector', *Public Choice*, vol. 15, Fall.

Heller, P. (1981), 'Diverging trends in the shares of nominal and real government expenditure in GDP: implications for policy', *National Tax Journal*, vol. 34, no. 1, pp. 61–74.

Likierman, A. (1981), *Cash Limits and External Financing Limits*, Civil Service College Handbook, no. 22, London: HMSO.

Likierman, A. (1983), 'Maintaining the credibility of cash limits', *Fiscal Studies*, March. pp. 29–43.

MacLaury, K. (1979), 'Proposals to limit federal spending and balance the budget', in J. Pechman (ed.), *Setting National Priorities: The 1980 Budget*, Washington, DC: Brookings Institution.

Meltzer, A. H. and Richard, S. F. (1981), 'A rational theory of the size of government', *Journal of Political Economy*, vol. 89, no. 5, pp. 914–27.

Mueller, D. C. (1979), *Public Choice*, Cambridge: Cambridge University Press.

Peacock, A. (1980), 'The anatomy of collective failure', *Festschrift für Paul Senf*, *Public Finance*, no. 1, pp. 33–43.

Peacock, A. (1983a), 'Public X-inefficiency: informational and institutional constraints', in H. Hanusch (ed.), *Anatomy of Government Deficiencies*, Berlin: Springer-Verlag.

Peacock, A. (1983b), 'Reducing government expenditure: a British view', in H. Giersch (ed.), *Reassessing the Role of Government in the Mixed Economy*. Tübingen: JCB Mohr (Paul Siebeck).

Peltzman, S. (1980), 'The growth of government', *Journal of Law and Economics*, vol. 23, no. 2, pp. 209–87.

Todd, D. (1983), 'The growth of public expenditure in the EEC countries 1960–81: some reflections', mimeo., Directorate-General for Economic and Financial Affairs, EEC.

Wildavsky, A. (1983), 'From chaos to opportunity: the movement towards spending limits in American and Canadian budgeting', *Canadian Public Administration*, no. 2 (summer).

10

Monetary Policy and Control of Public Expenditure

Vito Tanzi

By monetary policy, I mean a policy directed at the control of the supply of nominal money to achieve whatever objective the monetary authorities wish to achieve. I shall assume that the monetary authorities can control the money supply. This assumption is necessary because countries with very open economies or with the possibility of currency substitution may not be able to control the money supply. One of the basic conclusions of monetary theory is that the monetary authorities may be able to control the supply of *nominal* money in circulation, but not the amount of *real* money. Real money is determined by the demand for money, which in turn depends on the rate of inflation, the rate of interest, and some other variables such as wealth.

The chapter is structured in the following way. First, I discuss briefly the effects of monetary policy on the economy. Once these effects have been explained, I discuss their impact on public expenditure. Finally, I discuss the process of controlling expenditure in an inflationary period.

EFFECT OF MONETARY POLICY ON THE ECONOMY

One could consider two situations. First, that the government controls directly monetary policy. In other words, the central bank is not independent, but is under the direct control of the Treasury or some other ministry. Alternatively, one can assume that the government does not have a direct control over monetary policy. This, for example, is the situation characteristic of the United States, where the central bank is legally independent. Although this distinction is important in the short run and in theory, in reality, and especially over the longer run, it may become rather vague, as inevitably the central bank will be influenced by the political process. It will be subjected to governmental pressures and it is unlikely that those pressures can be ignored, even though they may be resisted for some period. To simplify the discussion, or in fact to make the discussion possible, I shall, none the less, assume that, in the short run, monetary policy is exogenous to the budgetary process. In other words, the budgetary authorities that what is happening in the monetary field as given and cannot influence it.

Monetary policy can influence the economy through its effect on (1) the inflation rate; (2) the interest rate; (3) the unemployment rate; and (4) the rate of real economic growth. Each of these can have an impact on public expenditure and, of course, on revenue. The effect on revenue will be largely ignored here, as the emphasis is on expenditure.[1] There is a close link between the inflation rate and the interest rate (the Fisher effect). Therefore, these two aspects will be discussed jointly. There is a close link between the unemployment rate and the rate of real economic growth (Okun's law). Therefore these two aspects will also be discussed jointly. As stated earlier, the monetary authorities can control the growth of nominal money (especially over longer periods), even though they may not be able to do so for short periods. I shall assume that the only influence of monetary policy comes through that control. Administrative policies such as those that regulate banks, interest rates, etc. are ignored in this discussion.

There are three basic issues in monetary theory that are central to our discussion. The first is the effect of a change in money supply on the price level. Given lags that can be quite long, and possible changes in the demand for money due to institutional factors or to changes in the rate of interest or the rate of inflation itself, the relationship between changes in nominal money (ΔM) and changes in the price level (ΔP) is well established. It is generally agreed by monetary theorists that when the change in the money supply is anticipated, the price level is affected more quickly and systematically. In this relationship, *systematic* changes in velocity need to be accounted for. In the United States, for example, until the early 1980s velocity had grown at 3 per cent per year over many years.[2] As pointed out by Friedman and others, if the real side of the economy is growing at a fast pace, or if the rate of interest is falling, some increase in the money supply may be sidetracked to accommodate the larger demand, so that the effect on prices may be less than anticipated. But all of these factors may be accounted for as long as the change in the supply of money is anticipated. If the change in the supply of money is not anticipated, the relationship between money and prices becomes more complex.

The second basic issue is the effect of a change in nominal money on the nominal rate of interest. Here the channels are two: first, the change in the money supply will affect the rate of interest through its effect on inflationary expectations. To the extent that the change in money supply is anticipated, it will more rapidly influence the rate of inflationary expectation. This latter will be incorporated in the rate of interest that people expect to receive or pay. This is the well-known Fisher effect, and there is a voluminous literature that supports it. There is little disagreement about its existence and the only question still under discussion is whether the theory suggested by Fisher is fully or only partly supported by reality.[3] There are many reasons why the one-to-one relationship between inflationary expectation and interest rate hypothesized by Fisher might not fully hold. The other channel through which changes in nominal money may affect the nominal rate of interest is the liquidity effect. This is the effect emphasized by Keynes and his followers. Contrary to the Fisher effect, the liquidity effect exists largely when the growth in money is not fully anticipated. When inflation is an ongoing phenomenon, and individuals come to realize that there is a connection between changes in money and changes in prices, the liquidity effect largely vanishes, whereas the Fisher effect becomes dominant.[4]

The third issue in monetary theory is the effect of changes in the money supply on output and employment. This effect again depends largely, though not entirely, on whether the change in the supply of money is anticipated or not. If it is unanticipated, it will almost certainly have real effects on the economy. For example, the liquidity effect that would accompany an acceleration of money growth would reduce the real rate of interest, thus stimulating some interest-sensitive spending. It may also have real balance effects, as the additional liquidity that some individuals experience, in the face of yet unchanged inflationary expectations, may induce higher spending. The fall in the rate of interest will be associated with a rise in the value of existing debt, thus inducing higher spending.[5]

These factors may stimulate aggregate demand and lead to (a) balance of payment problems, as the monetary approach to the balance of payment argues; (b) changes in output, if there are usable unemployed resources; (c) price changes, if the resources are already relatively fully employed, or, if unemployed, have been made obsolete by changes in relative prices or in the composition of demand, or if there are structural factors that limit their mobility; or (d) any combination of these.

As time passes and monetary expansion continues, whereas its effect on prices becomes more important as the experiences of many countries throughout the 1970s show. The liquidity effect tends to vanish; the Fisher effect becomes better established; and distortions caused by the interrelationship of the rate of inflation with the tax system begin to have negative effects on the real rate of growth.[6] To a large extent, the issue of the impact of monetary policy on the economy comes down to one of distinguishing equilibrium from disequilibrium or expected from unexpected changes.

In theory, one can distinguish four cases. First, money supply grows at a relatively steady and sustained pace, and its change comes to be expected. Second, the growth of money supply accelerates over its trend and the acceleration at least for a while is not anticipated. Third, money is growing at a steady pace, but one consistent with a low or zero rate of inflation. Fourth, the growth of money decelerates brusquely and the deceleration, at least for a while, clashes against ingrained inflationary expectations, as it was not anticipated. Because of space limitation, and because they are the most interesting in relation to recent experiences, in the discussion that follows I shall only deal with the first and fourth of these cases.

EFFECTS OF MONETARY POLICY ON PUBLIC EXPENDITURE

There is not much literature that discusses the impact of inflation on public expenditure, although there have been many articles that have discussed the impact of inflation on revenue, (see Tanzi, 1977 and 1980). There are several reasons why public expenditure is likely to grow, as a share of gross national product (GNP), whenever a country undergoes a period of steady monetary expansion with inflation. In this section, I shall discuss the effect of a steady monetary expansion on public expenditure and, briefly, the implications of a policy of monetary restraint. As different parts of the budget respond differently to inflationary pressures, and space limitations prevent a detailed item-by-item discussion, it is necessary to introduce some broad distinctions. The first type to be considered are exhaustive expenditures, namely, those that directly use goods and services. Next, transfer payments are discussed. These provide incomes to individuals without demanding (at the time they are received) anything in exchange from them. Exhaustive expenditures are divided into capital and current. Transfer payments are divided into pensions, subsidies and interest payments.

Exhaustive expenditures

Capital expenditure

The deflator for governmental captial expenditure can be expected to increase faster than the deflator for the rest of the economy, or even faster than the deflator for investment in the private sector. As a consequence, and provided that the volume remains constant, capital expenditure is likely to rise as a share of GNP. The main reason for this is that government capital expenditure is heavily biased toward dwellings and structures, whereas the private sector's capital expenditure has a higher component of machinery, vehicles, etc. Since, during inflation, the prices of dwellings and structures increase faster than the prices of machinery and vehicles, as long as the volume remains unchanged government capital expenditure will grow as a proportion of GNP.[7]

Current expenditure for goods and services

Current expenditure for goods and services is labour-intensive and benefits little from productivity growth (Baumol, 1967). This is especially true for educational services, health services, police, the administration of justice, etc.[8] Thus, what happens to wages in the economy in general, and in the public sector, in particular, is all important. Wages may be indexed or non-indexed. Their degree of indexation may be high or low. In some countries it is 100 per cent of the price increase; in others the proportion may be lower or higher.[9] The indexation mechanism may be associated with frequent or infrequent adjustments for price changes.[10] The index used may or may not reflect realistically inflationary pressures. Apart from the indexation mechanism itself, which would determine the *automatic* increase in wages, real wages may grow because of pressures by unions or because of tax-push effects. Tax push can be particularly significant when marginal tax rates on wage increases are progressive and high. (See Tanzi, 1980, ch. 12; Tanzi and Iden, 1982.)

There is evidence that the terms of trade between public and private sector tend to deteriorate over time (Baumol, 1967), thus increasing the relative prices of goods and services bought by the public sector. *Ceteris paribus,* this 'relative price effect' leads to a rise in the share of exhaustive current public expenditure in nominal GNP, even when real public expenditure has not changed. It would exist even in the absence of inflation, but it is likely to be accentuated by it. Empirical evidence from national accounts statistics supports the conclusion that the implicit deflator applied to government expenditure generally increases at a faster rate than that applied to GNP (see Beck, 1979; Heller, 1981). This difference exists even when one compares public-sector with private-sector capital spending and public-sector with private-sector current spending on goods and services.

Transfer payments

Transfer payments are associated with many programmes; only general categories are considered here.

Pensions

Like wages, pensions may be indexed or not. In most industrial countries, the demand for indexation in pensions has accompanied closely the rate of inflation. Throughout the late 1960s and 1970s, as the rate of inflation accelerated, so did the introduction of indexation schemes. Between 1970 and 1979, the number of countries that introduced indexation arrangements for government pensions rose from 18 to 33 (Holmes, 1982, p. 8).[11] These schemes were presumably introduced to insulate certain parts of the budget from the political process; but they often resulted in increased spending. In some countries, pensions are tied to the lowest wage rates. These frequently have received higher than average wage increases in general wage settlements. For example, up to 1976 the degree of indexation in federal retirement programmes in the United States exceeded the rate of inflation, so that the real income of the retired population rose with inflation.[12] Since pensions were mostly untaxed, the net-of-tax increases for pensioners substantially exceeded those for wage-earners.

The use of cost-of-living indices has implied that terms terms-of-trade effects (associated, for example, with the increase in the price of oil), interest-rate effects (associated with increases in mortgage rates), or increases in the price of existing assets, such as houses, have generated increases in pension payments, which have left those who receive them with higher real incomes than if no inflation had occurred.[13] Interest-rate effects exaggerate the actual level of inflation, as they contain an element of repayment of principal that is not thus a real-cost increase. Also retired people generally borrow little, as they do not enter into mortgage agreements associated with house buying.[14]

Lags between increases also play some role – the longer the lag, the greater the loss that the recipients experience, especially when the rate of inflation increases. It is difficult to generalize about the effects of inflation on pensions, but on balance the factual evidence available, as well as theoretical considerations, indicate that those effects have been positive, thus increasing this type of expenditure.

Subsidies

Many countries have maintained political prices for some goods and services, especially for those sold by public enterprises. As inflation accelerated, there was political reluctance to adjust those prices to maintain their real value. As a consequence, there were growing losses associated with the maintenance of these prices and these losses associated with the maintenance of these prices and these losses had to be covered by budgetary transfers. Therefore inflation brought about an expansion of this expenditure in real terms.

Interest payments

The area where the effect of inflation on expenditure is most striking is interest payments. As inflation gets established, the market or nominal rate of interest on financial assets increases. Depending on the size of the public debt, the average maturity of the debt, and the fiscal deficit of a country, the increase in interest payments associated with inflation can be high indeed. Table 10.1 shows what has been happening to this category of expenditure in industrial countries in recent years. Of course not all the increase is due to inflation, as all of these countries were running sizeable deficits and accumulating debt. The experience of Italy in this context is illuminating. There are projections that indicate that, under present policies and economic conditions, interest payments as a proportion of GNP would reach extremely high figures within a few years. Similar, though less dramatic projections have been made for some other countries (see, for the United States, Stein, 1983).

Table 10.1 tells the conventional statistical story. I should report, however, that it is becoming increasingly fashionable to argue for the government, as has been done for several years for individuals, that, when there is inflation,

Table 10.1 *Central government interest payments as a percentage of government expenditure and gross national product*

	1975	*1976*	*1977*	*1978*	*1979*	*1980*	*1981*	*1982*	*1983*
Percentage of expenditure									
Belgium	6.1	6.2	6.8	7.2	8.1	9.7	12.0	14.2	17.0
Canada	10.5	11.7	11.6	13.1	15.3	16.2	19.0	19.4	18.0
France	4.1	4.0	4.2	4.1	4.9	4.8	6.7	6.5	7.2
Germany	1.7	2.1	2.4	2.4	2.6	3.0	3.6	4.2	5.0
Ireland	9.7	11.3	12.3	12.8	13.0	14.0	14.1	16.8	18.2
Italy	6.3	8.6	12.5	13.5	14.6	14.4	15.9	16.4	16.2
Japan	3.8	5.5	6.8	7.8	8.9	10.5	12.3	14.3	16.6
United Kingdom	7.6	8.5	9.1	8.9	9.1	9.5	10.3	10.5	9.4
United States	7.6	8.6	8.5	9.4	10.5	11.3	13.2	14.6	14.8
Percentage of GNP									
Belgium	2.7	2.9	3.2	3.6	4.1	5.1	6.6	7.8	9.4
Canada	2.2	2.4	2.4	2.8	3.1	3.3	4.1	4.7	4.5
France	0.9	0.8	0.8	0.9	1.0	1.0	1.5	1.6	1.7
Germany	0.6	0.7	0.8	0.7	0.8	0.9	1.2	1.4	1.6
Ireland	4.4	5.0	5.4	6.0	6.3	8.1	9.1	11.2	12.0
Italy	1.7	2.5	4.2	5.3	5.3	5.7	6.8	8.3	8.6
Japan	0.6	0.8	1.1	1.3	1.5	1.9	2.2	2.6	2.9
United Kingdom	3.3	3.5	3.4	3.4	3.6	3.9	4.3	4.3	3.9
United States	1.7	1.9	1.8	2.0	2.2	2.6	3.1	3.5	3.7

Source: National statistics.

part of the expenditure on interest is actually a repayment of debt. It can thus be financed through borrowing. At a recent conference on this issue, several papers were presented that showed that this adjustment would considerably reduce the level of public expenditure (though not that of public-sector borrowing).[15] As real interest rates fall when inflation accelerates, and rise when inflation decelerates, this correction would reduce (adjusted) expenditure for much of the 1970s, but increase it for the late 1970s and early 1980s.

Indirect effects

The effects discussed above are direct ones, but inflation affects public expenditure also indirectly. Given the short space available to me. I can only refer to a couple of these ways.

First, given the structure of the tax system, inflation may lead to an increase or a fall in real revenue. An industrial countries, where collection lags are short and income taxes important, the effect of inflation on revenue is almost always positive. In developing countries, where collection lags are long and the use of specific taxes widespread, inflation may have a negative impact on real revenue (see Tanzi, 1977). If governments experience automatic increases in tax revenue, increases that do not require politically embarrassing tax reform, they may find the temptation to increase spending hard to resist, as public spending is generally popular. The experience of the 1970s indicates that inflation brought about an increase in the tax ratio and, probably because of this, it increased the share of public expenditure in GNP in many countries.

Second, and more importantly, inflation is likely to bring about a deterioration of the budgetary process. The officials in charge of public programmes will make budgetary requests that guarantee the continuation of at least the present real level of expenditure for the programmes under their responsibility. But assume that, although the mean expected rate of inflation over the fiscal year is, say, 10 per cent, that expectation is surrounded by uncertainty.[16] For example, inflation could be anywhere between 5 per cent and 15 per cent. Would the budgetary requests still be for a 10 per cent increase in nominal expenditure? One can be sure that the programme managers would press hard for requests that would assure the continuation of existing levels of real expenditure, should inflation actually settle at the higher end of the probability distribution.

I will now briefly discuss the situation in which a prolonged period of sustained inflation is followed by one in which monetary growth slows down rapidly. This, for example, happened in the United States in 1980–2: the rate of money growth slowed down dramatically, while the rate of inflation was still high. In such a situation, *real* interest rates rise sharply, output declines, and the rate of unemployment goes up. The fall in output, and subsequently in the rate of inflation, reduces the level of revenue, while expenditures tend to rise because of lags in indexation mechanisms (that adjust expenditures for past rates of inflation), because of higher unemployment compensation and, especially, because of higher interest costs. Table 10.1 shows an acceleration in the ratio of interest expenditure to total expenditure or GNP since 1980.

INFLATION AND BUDGETARY CONTROLS

In the earlier part of this chapter, it was argued that monetary policy that allows inflation to become established induces pressures that increase the share of public expenditure in GNP. Some of these pressures are automatic and thus largely unavoidable. This, for example, is the case related to the 'relative price effect' and to the growth in interest payments. For exhaustive expenditures, maintaining their nominal share of GNP unchanged requires a reduction in real terms. For interest payments, inflation brings about a more than proportional rise in interest rates and causes an almost unavoidable increase in the share of interest expenditure to GNP or to total government expenditure. One could of course attribute this increase to presumably faulty accounting conventions, that label all nominal interest payments as interest payments, rather than partly return of capital. But the fact remains that, from a purely budgetary point of view, these are expenditures that somehow must be financed.

Pension payments do not need to rise by more than, or even by as much as, the rate of inflation. But the beneficiaries of these payments generally constitute politically influential groups, and it is only at great political risk that governments can attempt to hold them down. Governments have often preferred to take pension payments out of the political arena by indexing them for inflationary changes. This decision, however, has not just taken this expenditure out of the political arena, but it has also shifted the burden of macro-economic adjustment to other groups, even though all groups should ideally have to share in the adjustment. Furthermore, the index used was often highly favourable to pensioners.

Theoretically, subsidies and wages of government employees are the most 'controllable'. Cuts in subsidies, however, are politically difficult and real-wage reductions are more feasible in the short run than in the long run, as low wages eventually but inevitably bring about a deterioration of the quality of the public-sector workforce.

Perhaps the most controllable expenditure is that for infrastructures and real investment in general. The benefits from these expenditures often come far in the future, so that they are heavily discounted by governments whose time horizon is often much shorter. This means that inflation may bring about a reduction in real capital expenditure and thus a deterioration of the basic infrastructures, which in turn may affect a country's future rate of growth. Recent press reports in the United States have called attention to the deteriorating state of bridges, roads, aqueducts, etc. There is statistical evidence which indicates that much of the growth of public expenditure in industrial countries in recent years has been in the form of transfer payments. This result, together with the 'relative price hypothesis', implies that real public-sector capital expenditure may actually have fallen during the past decade.

A high and varying rate of inflation upsets the traditional equilibrium that inevitably comes to exist in the budgetary process. It threatens acquired positions and promotes the creation of pressure groups that demand larger shares of the budgetary cake. These pressures are likely to result in high spending. For this reason, price stability may be associated with a slower rate of growth of public expenditure. Thus a monetary policy that promotes price stability will also promote a slower growth of public expenditure.

NOTES

1 Some expenditures, however, are closely related to revenues. This happens for interest payment, as lower revenue resulting in larger deficits raises the level of

public debt and thus future interest expenses. It also happens in the area of 'tax expenditures', if the government opts to reduce taxes on some activities rather than increase expenditures for those activities. Of course, there may be expenditures that depend totally on earmarked taxes.

2 In the early 1980s, for various institutional reasons, the growth of velocity slowed down considerably.

3 In technical parlance, the question is whether the coefficient of the variable representing inflationary expectation is or is not significantly different from one.

4 This assumes that individuals are fully and immediately informed about changes in the supply of money. This assumption is far more realistic for the United States than for Italy. In the United States, several papers have shown that the liquidity effect largely vanished in the early 1980s.

5 Households are generally net creditors *vis-à-vis* corporations and the public sector.

6 For example, the net-of-tax rate of interest may become negative, thus discouraging financial saving. These negative effects may also put pressure on the government to subsidize enterprises that are in trouble, increase unemployment benefits, or expand public expenditure in other ways.

7 If there is uncertainty about the mean rate of unexpected inflation, those who present bids for contracts for capital projects are likely to push their prices even higher than one would expect from the mean rate of inflation. This tendency will be strengthened, if these contractors expect to be paid with delays. It is difficult to reach strong conclusions on this aspect, as real expenditure on capital projects is likely to change during inflationary periods. For industrial countries, from the mid-1960s to the mid-1980s, the ratio of public investment in GNP went up in some, but fell in others without any clear trend.

8 National income accounting conventions assume no productivity improvement in the public sector. Studies for the United States have found examples of productivity growth for some government programmes (see Searle and Waite, 1980).

9 In the early 1980s, attempts have been made in various countries to reduce the degree of indexation to below 100 per cent of the increase in the legally-relevant price index.

10 In earlier years there were strong pressures on governments to shorten the lags by increasing the frequency of adjustments. More recently, governments have tried to reduce the frequency in order to contain the growth of expenditure.

11 In the United States, 'between 1966 and 1980 the number of individual programs containing indexed provisions grew from 17 to 90' (see United States, Congressional Budget Office, 1981, p. XIII). The first programme to be indexed was military retirement benefits in 1963.

12 In 1969, Congress felt the need to add a 1 per cent 'kicker' to cost-of-living adjustments in federal retirement programmes. It was removed in 1976. Between 1969 and 1976, benefits for federal retirement programmes rose by 9 per cent above the cost-of-living index.

13 In 1979 and 1980, these effects may have given pension recipients real-income increases of about 2 per cent per year in the United States.

14 Because of these factors, there has been a lot of discussion in the United States about the possibility of using alternative indices (see United States, 1981a and 1981b).

15 International Conference on Economic Policy and National Accounting in

Inflationary Conditions (Bergamo, Italy, 26–28 January 1984). See especially the papers by Taylor and Saville, and by Cukierman and Mortensen. See also the paper by Eisner and Pieper in the March 1984 issue of *American Economic Review*.

16 Observed data on inflationary expectations support this assumption.

REFERENCES

Baumol, W. (1976), 'Macroeconomics of unbalanced growth: the anatomy of urban crisis', *American Economic Review,* vol. 57,pp. 415–26.

Beck, M. (1979), 'Public sector growth: a real perspective', *Public Finance,* vol. 36,no. 3,pp.313–56.

Cukierman, A. and Mortensen, J. 'Monetary assets and inflation induced distortions of the national accounts-conceptual issues and correction of sectoral income flows in five EEC countries', *Economic Papers of the Commission of the European Communities,* no. 15.

Eisner R. and Pieper, P.J. (1984), 'A new view of the federal debt and budget deficits', *American Economic Review,* vol. 74,pp. 11–29.

Heller, P.S. (1980), 'Impact of inflation on fiscal policy in developing countries', *IMF Staff Papers,* vol. 27,no. 4,pp. 712–48.

Heller, P.S. (1981), 'Diverging trends in the shares of nominal and real government expenditure in GDP: implications for policy', *National Tax Journal,* vol. 34,no. 1,pp.61–74.

Holmes, M.R.G. (1982), 'Control of government expenditure: some institutional considerations', mimeo, IMF.

Premchand, A (1983), *Government Budgeting and Expenditure Controls, Theory and Practice,* ch. 8. Washington, DC: MF.

Searle, A.D. and Waite, C.A. (1980), 'Current efforts to measure productivity in the public sector: how adequate for the national accounts', in J.W. Kendrick and B.N. Vaccara (eds), *New Developments in Productivity Measurement and Analysis,* Chicago: NBER, Studies in Income and Wealth, no. 44.

Stein, H. (1983), 'Controlling the budget deficit: If not now, when? If not us, who?, '*The AEI Economist,* December.

Tanzi, V. (1977), 'Inflation, lags in collection, and the real value of tax revenue', *IMF Staff Papers,* vol. XXIV,no. 1,pp. 154–67.

Tanzi, V. (1978), 'Inflation, real tax revenue, and the case for inflationary finance: theory with an application to Argentina', *IMF Staff Papers,* vol. XXV,no. 3,pp. 417–51.

Tanzi, V. (1980), *Inflation and Personal Income Taxation,* Cambridge: Cambridge University Press.

Tanzi, V. and Iden, G. (1982), 'The impact of taxes on wages in the United States: an example of supply—side economics?', *Economic Notes,* vol. 11,no. 3,pp. 5–19.

Taylor, C.T. and Saville, I.D. (1984), 'Adjusting the balance of payments: general principles and four case studies'. Paper prepared for the Conference on National Accounting and Economic Policies in Inflationary Conditions, Bergamo, Italy, 26–28 January 1984.

United States, Congressional Budget Office (1981), *Indexing with the Consumer Price*

Index: Problems and Alternatives. Washington, DC: Congressional Budget Office.

United States, Congressional Budget Office (1982), *The Economic and Budget Outlook: An Update,* appendix B. Washington, DC: Congressional Budget Office.

United States, Executive Office of the President, (1981), *Report on Indexing Federal Programs.* Washington, DC:

United States, Office of Management and Budget, (1984), *Budget of the United States Government, Fiscal Year 1984,* pp. 2–19 to 2–24. Washington, DC:

11

Monetary Policy and Control of Public Expenditure with Special Reference to the Netherlands

Nout Wellink and Victor Halberstadt

INTRODUCTION

This chapter focuses on the question whether and to what extent monetary policy influences the decision-making process with respect to public expenditure. It is therefore not an essay on monetary or budgetary policies as such or on the monetary transmission process, but on the behavioural relationship between the public authorities involved.

Clearly, there is no direct relationship between monetary policy and the control of the volume of public expenditure, except for the effect of monetary policy on interest-rate levels and, hence, on public-sector interest payments (for this subject, see pp. 170–3 below). There is, however, an indirect relationship. In cases where an expansion of public expenditure is met from increases in the burden of taxation and social insurance contributions, and attempts to shift the effect of such increases lead to (an acceleration in) wage and price rises, monetary policy may have a role to play. This is also true if the expansion of public expenditure results in an increase in the public-sector borrowing requirement (see pp. 173–6 below). It is this increase which may affect the monetary outcomes, depending on a number of factors, such as the manner in which the borrowing requirement is financed (see pp. 176–9). Feedback from monetary policy to the volume of and the movements in public expenditure is created only if some form of monetary targeting is applied and budgetary policy is to be embedded in it (pp. 179–81). This feedback may be the result of consistently formulated monetary and budgetary policies or it may ensue from a conflict between the two. Whether it is the monetary authorities or the fiscal authorities who prevail in such a situation depends in part on political and legal conditions. It is, incidentally, possible to put off a conflict between monetary and fiscal authorities for a prolonged period of time owing to the variety of escape options (including financial innovations) open to the public sector.

In this chapter, attention will also be given to budgetary and monetary policy issues in the Netherlands, which, leaving aside institutional differences, are in large measure illustrative of the problems that can confront small industrialized countries with open economies (appendix II).

Finally, it is concluded that monetary policy exerts only a fairly limited influence, and an indirect one at that, on the control of public expenditure. If this control is not effected, the monetary authorities are faced with a terrible dilemma in a situation where it is barely possible to ascertain what monetary policy is least harmful for the economy as a whole under the prevailing conditions. But there is no doubt that if public expenditure cannot be brought under control, economic recovery stands little chance of having more than an *ad hoc* nature, in which case monetary guardians must risk an almost permanent collision with governments. In the longer run, this could result in a rekindling of inflation, payments imbalances and the continuation of extremely high unemployment rates as a consequence of a probably ever worsening consumption/investment mix.

RELATIONSHIP BETWEEN MOVEMENTS IN PUBLIC EXPENDITURE AND BUDGET DEFICITS

Over the past few decades, most countries have experienced a very sharp increase in public expenditure. Generally, this increase has been much more pronounced than the rise in national income. A few exceptions apart, the sharpest increase has been recorded notably by current expenditure. Within current expenditure, major growth categories have been income transfers and, particularly in the period following the first oil crisis, public-sector interest payments consequent on a sharp increase in public debt on the one hand, and relatively high nominal and real rates of interest on the other. The causes of the increase in public expenditure are many (and have been frequently analysed elsewhere), such as the development of the modern welfare state, indexation mechanisms, adverse terms of trade for public expenditure, and demographic factors. However, what we are concerned with in this chapter is to what extent the increase in public expenditure has prompted policy reactions on the part of the monetary authorities, and the consequences this has had or should have had for the control of public expenditure.

Cost-push inflation, caused by a sharp increase in the burden of taxation and social insurance contributions as a result of the development of expenditure, must primarily be checked by instruments other than monetary ones. If, however, inflation or the threat of inflation and/or (potential) external disequilibria are much more the result of an excessive supply of finance to the economic process, monetary policy has from the beginning a very direct role to play. It is this situation which is topical in most countries, owing to the large size to which budget deficits and payments imbalances have grown. Even though (the consequences of) increases in the burden of taxation and social insurance contributions may also have repercussions for monetary policy, the following deals only with the interrelation of budget deficits, monetary policy and control of public expenditure. Considering the major differences among the various countries as regards monetary instruments and their efficacy, technical matters will be left undiscussed.

An important question is whether an increase in public expenditure is automatically attended by a growing tendency towards deficit financing. The experience of the past few decades does not allow any definite answer. It is evident from table 11.1 that in the first half of the 1960s the general pattern was that the public sector was able to cover only some 55 per cent of the increase in expenditure. This was to change later during that decade and in the early 1970s: the slowing down of the growth of expenditure, which was apparent in practically all countries, was attended in the United States, Japan, Germany, Denmark and the Netherlands with a progressive increase in revenues, thus permitting the budget deficit to decline. In the United Kingdom, Belgium and Italy, however, the increase in revenues was insufficient for a decrease in the deficit to be achieved, and in the latter two countries – which are now running the highest deficits – the foundations were laid for ever further mounting budget deficits (for the figures of the major countries, see appendix I).

Table 11.1 *Public finance in the OECD area (changes in percentage points)*

	Position (% of GNP)	*Change*				*Position (% of GNP)*
	1961	*1961–7*	*1968–73*	*1974–7*	*1978–81*	*1981*
OECD						
expenditure	29.3	2.7	1.3	4.5	3.1	40.9
revenues	28.7	1.5	2.8	2.1	2.4	37.5
deficit[1]	0.6	1.2	−1.5	2.4	0.7	3.4

[1]Net lending as defined by the OECD. Expenditure consists of total public expenditure, including net capital transfers and gross investment, but excluding lending and participations.
Source: OECD, – *Economic Outlook*, December 1983.

After the first oil crisis (in 1973), the rate of growth of revenues fell in nearly all countries, attended by sometimes equally rapidly, but in most cases more rapidly growing expenditure, so that, in addition to Belgium and Italy, other countries too were confronted with mounting deficits. The turn-about which occurred during the period following the first oil crisis in the relationship

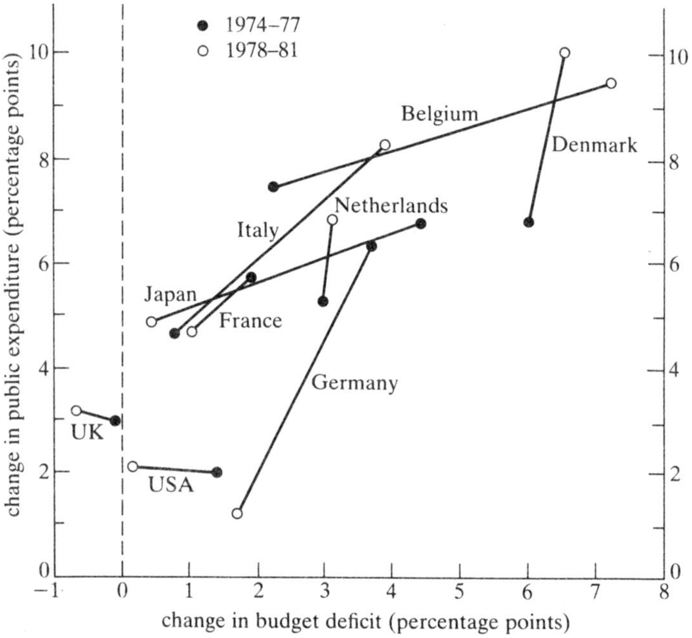

Figure 11.1 Changes in budget deficit/public expenditure in a number of countries.

between expenditure growth and deficit growth was in considerable measure the result of deliberate policy: countercyclical policy in the traditional sense in order to counterbalance the fall in demand in the industrialized world as a consequence of the first oil crisis.

At about the time of the second oil crisis (1978) a number of countries appear to have totally lost their grip on the development of public expenditure. Figure 11.1 shows to which countries this applies in particular. The direction of the arrows in the figure denotes that these countries simultaneously – some to a greater, others to a lesser degree – lost control over their budget deficits, owing in part to their inability or unwillingness to increase taxes and social insurance contributions. After 1981 (although not presented in the figure), this description also fits the United States. Developments as outlined above may, of course, have been the outcome of a political choice in favour of deferred rather than current taxation. In most countries concerned, however, this development appears not so much to have been the result of a *deliberate* policy choice as to constitute a symptom of uncontrollability, considering the very sharp rise indeed in public expenditure.

In many industrialized democracies the problems in public finance have taken on the character of a 'scissors crisis', that is, an increasing gap between public expenditure and income of the public sector. The available data suggest that this must be explained by both the effect of the recession on public revenue and, even more, by the exceptionally strong impact of established programmes, interest payments and transfers on public expenditure. In a historical perspective, the conclusion cannot be escaped that no earlier downturn in the world economy ever confronted governments with as wide a collection of activities and responsibilities as in the early 1980s. Add to this the proliferation of open-ended indexed income transfer programmes and at once the lack of flexibility in public expenditure comes into focus. Efforts to change priorities meet with strong resistance. Policies aimed at controlling the public-sector deficit through austerity are then defended and attacked with sometimes equal skill and vigour. The resulting present deficits and even more those estimated for future years are of troublesome size.

BUDGET DEFICITS AND MONETARY OUTCOMES

The question whether there is a relationship between the size of the budget deficit and the growth of the money supply is a highly controversial subject in literature. The conclusions reached, as is usual, are dependent on the models used, the countries included in the analyses and the periods covered. Within the framework of this paper, it would not be very relevant to list once more what the theoretical literature concerned has to offer in terms of agreement or lack of agreement, nor is this paper intended to add yet another study to this ongoing discussion. Where the question as to the relationship between monetary policy and the control of public expenditure is concerned, the first point at issue is whether the monetary and the fiscal authorities assume the existence of such a relationship. In other words, their actual behaviour is of primary importance, for that is what governs their behavioural reaction and it is only through this behavioural relationship that monetary policy may exert influence on the control of public expenditure. On the other hand, it must be emphasized that the theoretical literature is of great importance in testing the behavioural responses.

There need be little doubt as to the fact that generally the monetary and the fiscal authorities regard mounting budget deficits as a threat to monetary stability; through the resultant acceleration of the growth of the money supply they expect, in the short or longer run, an acceleration of the rate of inflation and/or external disequilibria. This train of thought governs their actions to a high degree.

It must be pointed out that the monetary authorities are certainly not unjustified in assuming a connection between the development and the manner of financing of the deficit and the monetary outcomes. Table 11.2 shows money creation, broken down by source, for the countries included in figure 11.1. Contrary to the usual presentation in a number of countries, the table distinguishes not only direct money creation on behalf of the government (placements of short-term debt with domestic holders of

Table 11.2 *Budget financing survey for a number of countries (percentage of money supply at beginning of year)*

	United States					*Federal Republic of Germany*					*Netherlands*					*Denmark*				
Description	*75*	*76*	*81*	*82*	*83*	*75*	*76*	*81*	*82*	*83*	*75*	*76*	*81*	*82*	*83*	*75*	*76*	*81*	*82*	*83*
Direct money creation on behalf of central government:																				
(a) at home	4.5	0.6	2.0	3.2	3.9	0.2	1.4	0.6	0	−0.3	3.2	3.4	1.7	0.8	−0.2	.	.	.	.	.
(b) abroad[1]	0.7	0.9	0.3	0.5	0.7	—	—	3.1	1.4	1.1	—	—	—	—	—	—	—	—	—	—
Total	5.2	1.5	2.3	3.7	4.6	0.2	1.4	3.7	1.4	0.8	3.2	3.4	1.7	0.8	−0.2					
Indirect money creation on behalf of central government due to increase (+) in long-term central government debt:																12.4	9.6	14.9	18.2	20.9
(a) with total domestic banking system	1.6	1.9	−0.4	0	1.6	4.7	2.6	2.1	2.2	0.9	0.8	1.2	2.2	4.8	5.4					
(b) abroad[2]						−0.3	0.6	−0.2	0.4	0.7	.	.	2.3	2.2	1.3	0.1	0.1	−0.6	−0.4	1.1
Grand total	6.8	3.4	1.9	3.6	6.2	4.6	4.6	5.6	3.9	2.4	4.0	4.6	6.2	7.8	6.5	12.5	9.7	14.3	17.8	22.0
Other money creation/ inflow	7.5	9.7	8.4	6.8	6.9	4.0	3.8	−0.6	3.2	2.9	5.6	15.7	0.3	0.4	3.8	12.6	1.2	−4.7	−6.0	3.3
Increase in domestic money supply	14.3	13.1	10.3	10.5	13.1	8.6	8.4	5.0	7.1	5.3	9.6	20.3	6.5	8.2	10.3	25.1	10.9	9.6	11.8	25.3

Table 11.2 *(continued)*

	United Kingdom					*France*					*Italy*					*Belgium*				
Description	*75*	*76*	*81*	*82*	*83*	*75*	*76*	*81*	*82*	*83*	*75*	*76*	*81*	*82*	*83*	*75*	*76*	*81*	*82*	*83*
Direct money creation on behalf of central government:																				
(a) at home	7.9	2.4	1.2	2.1	3.0	4.4	2.2	4.2	2.6	3.7	9.3	9.4	13.8	12.0	4.2	0.3	3.8	6.9	2.5	4.3
(b) abroad[1]	0	1.1	−1.6	0.3	0.5	0.1	0.2	—	—	—	0	0	0.8	1.0	0.6	−0.1	−0.1	14.8	15.1	8.9
Total	7.9	3.5	−2.8	−1.8	3.5	4.5	2.4	4.2	2.6	3.7	9.3	9.4	14.6	13.0	4.8	0.3	3.7	21.7	17.6	13.2
Indirect money creation on behalf of central government due to increase (+) in long-term central government debt:																				
(a) with total domestic banking system	2.0	0.2	−0.5	−0.1	0.5	0	0	—	—	—	7.5	2.7	0.4	3.5	7.5	3.5	2.2	−1.0	2.0	5.6
(b) abroad[2]	0	0.3	0.6	0.5	1.5	0.1	0.2	—	—	—	.	.	.	.	.	.	.	.	.	.
Grand total	9.9	4.0	−2.7	−1.5	5.5	4.6	2.6	4.2	2.6	3.7	12.8	12.1	15.0	16.5	12.3	3.8	6.0	20.5	19.6	18.8
Other money creation/ inflow	−2.4	7.0	17.0	10.4	4.0	13.5	9.7	6.2	8.2	4.7	12.3	14.9	2.8	1.5	3.7	11.5	6.6	−14.1	−12.5	−13.3
Increase in domestic money supply	7.5	11.0	14.3	8.8	9.5	18.1	12.3	10.4	10.8	8.0	25.1	27.0	17.8	18.0	16.0	15.2	12.6	6.4	7.0	5.5

[1]Mainly organized borrowing abroad.
[2]Mostly, this item is not large, as the increase in long-term external public authority debt is already counted as direct money creation as far as central government debt of bankers' currency countries or active placement of public authority debt abroad is concerned, or as the relevant transactions are not really significant or are not separately known.

1983 figures are estimates.

spending of the counter-value of liquid and 'organized' official borrowing abroad), but also indirect money creation (as counterpart of sales of non-liquid government debt to the banking system or proceeds in domestic currency of foreign investments in these instruments). It is, after all, obvious that in the event of major placements of long-term public authority debt abroad or with banks the public authorities should be held at least partially responsible for the ensuing money creation, as it is they who provide the vehicle. In this context it is noteworthy that in early 1984 the Danish Central Bank issued a general warning to the commercial banks that their large purchases of bonds (to a large extent government bonds) were fuelling the sharp increase in Denmark's money supply, and urged them to stem its growth. According to the Bank, the increase in the money supply, which far exceeds the growth in GNP, is 'unacceptable' and the banks' purchases are an important contributory factor. The Bank's policy, of course, will only result in a lower monetary expansion rate, if it induces increased government bond sales to the non-bank public (or, better yet, curtailment of the budget deficit itself), assisted by more conducive margins between deposit and bond rates of interest.

It would not, of course, be correct to hold the public authorities *fully* responsible for indirect money creation via the banking system. First, the banks themselves have a distinct responsibility of their own for their lending policy. Second, (indirect) money creation at the banking system occurs only to the extent that the increase in the banks' holdings of long-term central government paper is not financed from additional savings and to the extent that other forms of lending are not reduced. These details do not, however, alter the fact that the figures presented in table 11.2 show clearly that, in the years 1975–6 and 1981–3, the large budget deficits have in many cases had substantial monetary consequences. These consequences have been most pronounced in those countries where a continued sharp increase in the expenditure ratio was attended by (often) substantial increases in the budget deficit (Denmark, Italy, Belgium, and, to a lesser extent, the Netherlands).

MONETARY AND BUDGETARY TARGETING

The figures presented in the previous section show that in a number of countries a connection can be established between the explosive development of public expenditure, the movements in budget deficits and monetary developments. This raises questions as to the consistency of the monetary and budgetary policies to be pursued under such conditions and, considering the subject of this essay, as to the influence which the formulation of monetary policy may exert on budgetary policy and budgetary results.

In the longer run, both monetary and budgetary policy have, of course, one single objective: the realization of balanced and sufficient economic growth with an adequate consumption/investment mix at a low rate of inflation, a low level of unemployment and an external position which is more or less in equilibrium. However, in the short run, partly on account of political considerations underlying the budgetary decision-making process, the fiscal authorities tend to evince a greater interest in growth and employment than in what the monetary authorities regard as their first priority, namely, price stability and balance-of-payments equilibrium, also in view of the movements in the exchange rate.

A brief period of discord between the two authorities need not immediately lead to problems. However, if they are on a collision course for a longer period, the efficacy of both monetary and budgetary policies will be drastically reduced. This must create misgivings, since it is not desirable to finance public expenditure by means that will specifically lead to a reduction in productive investment. A tight monetary policy can lead to the crowding-out of the private sector by raising interest rates (though this depends on the degree to which the private sector can reduce its cash balances and on the volume of capital inflows thus induced), and an easy budgetary policy can frustrate monetary policy to such an extent that longer-term price stability is endangered. The possibilities of conflicting policies are naturally greater the more independent the monetary authorities are of the fiscal authorities and the less the fiscal authorities succeed in controlling their deficits. In view of the fact that in most countries the minister of finance bears ultimate responsibility for monetary policy, the central banks of most developed industrialized countries are definitely not completely independent in determining this policy (though they are often free as to its implementation). In general, it can be argued that in those countries where there is a tradition that the financial power of the state should be subject to controls – such as the Federal Republic of Germany, Switzerland, the Netherlands and the United States – the central banks are also the most independent. At the same time, these countries show the best results with respect to price stability, indicating that a clear and balanced division of responsibilities between central banks and governments is a necessary condition to prevent the latter from exploiting the advantages of their monopoly to issue money for purposes that differ from those for which the monetary monopoly was granted.

Budgetary norms are in general easier to formulate and to assess than are monetary targets. Well-known examples of budgetary norms can be seen in the United States (full employment surplus), the Federal Republic of Germany (cyclically neutral budget) and the Netherlands (structural deficit approach). If the actual budgetary developments deviate from the norm, there is therefore a compass which shows the desired direction for budgetary policy. Yet this compass gives much less certainty in judging the budgetary situation at present than it did in the past, because as a result of the large breaks in trends consequent on the first oil crisis it is now much more difficult to distinguish between structural and cyclical developments and to quantify the budgetary norm.

It is worth noting that governments in many countries now seem to be trying to (re-)introduce global norms in different shapes, both as a confidence-building signal to domestic and international markets as well as to commit the public sector itself to budgetary discipline. This, however, is not an easy task. One difficult dilemma is created by the trade-off between simplicity and adequacy, since global budgetary norms are to be used as educational tools. Quite frequently governments take the risk of revealing that their declared targets make rather sad reading in the *ex-post* situation.

The setting of *monetary targets* in practice often leads to a host of problems. In recent years, concern for the money supply led an increasing number of countries to announce aggregate monetary targets. A first problem is that, regrettably, it became apparent at the same time that the relationship between the money supply, however defined, and nominal GNP is definitely not stable, especially in the short run, as a result of the introduction of financial innovations, changes in real interest rates and inflationary expectations, cyclical factors, etc. This means that it is difficult to interpret the various aggregates unambiguously, and this has led to a stream of literature in which conjuring tricks are performed with monetary aggregates and adjustments to monetary aggregates. Undoubtedly, the monetary-control problems are more serious for a period of one or two quarters than they are for longer periods. Sadly, however, the public generally bases its assessment of monetary policy on short-term developments. On the basis of the experience of the past years, the assessment of actual developments in various countries tends towards a less mechanical view of a certain aggregate, more attention being paid to multiple targets and sets of monetary and non-monetary indicators. This development harbours risks for the credibility of the monetary authorities. If, for several years, it has been argued forcefully that, for example, the development of £ – M3 is *the* touchstone for monetary policy and the public has accepted this, it is far from easy to argue credibly that attention should also be paid to levels of interest rates, exchange rates, etc. A central bank, having made the choice for a certain aggregate, should only be prepared to accept the pursuit of a more discretionary policy by the government, if it feels that the overall policy is on the right road. This feeling will be stronger the closer the size of the actual financial deficit, in which non-recurrent and cyclical factors also feed through, is to the structurally acceptable size.

A second problem in setting monetary targets is the low-interest-rate sensitivity of public expenditure, in contrast with private investment. This means that, if the public sector does not adjust, the private sector will to a large extent have to bear the burden of the monetary targeting. (The next section deals with the impact of interest payments on public expenditure.) Consequently, the monetary authorities of countries where the real economy is developing unfavourably and unemployment is very high will be faced with an exceptionally unpleasant policy dilemma, and they will be unable to obey their monetary conscience as rigidly as they consider desirable. It must be noted that the pilot function which can emanate from monetary policy, especially by way of interest rates, can also be frustrated by the fact that the public sector to an increasing extent influences the flow of funds to industry via the budget, thereby frustrating the market mechanism.

A third problem of monetary targeting is that, as soon as a certain aggregate is chosen, the target must be given a quantitative value. In a situation of equilibrium, the obvious choice is a growth target derived from the potential rate of growth of the economy and the inevitable rise in prices. In these circumstances monetary policy can make a well-balanced contribution to economic development. However, if the rate of inflation is clearly too high and if the inflationary expectations are not yet eliminated, it will be far more difficult to express the monetary targets in quantitative terms.

In those cases where it is far more difficult than in the past to give values to monetary and budgetary targets, it is obvious that the choice of the appropriate policy mix will be characterized in part by an increasing interest in medium-term and long-term targeting, and in part by a process of trial and error.

The process of trial and error implies a very real chance that policy adjustments will have to be made more or less regularly. Such adjustments will be required not only on the basis of monetary or budgetary developments, but also on the grounds of a whole series of economic indicators. Attention has already been paid to developments along these lines. However, these developments reduce the impact that can be made by monetary policy alone on the behaviour of the budgetary authorities.

REACTIONS OF FISCAL AUTHORITIES

The fiscal authorities have become increasingly aware that there must come an end to the large financial deficits which, for some countries, have lasted a very long period. They are aware that powers have been unleashed which will be exceedingly difficult to control. In addition to discretionary measures

Table 11.3 *Public-sector interest payments in a number of OECD countries (percentage of GDP)*

	1973	*1984*
Belgium	3.3	10.4
Denmark	1.3	9.0
Federal Republic of Germany	1.0	3.2
France	0.8	3.3
Italy	3.0	9.9
Netherlands	2.9	6.6
United Kingdom	3.8	4.7
United States	2.2	5.0

increasing the deficit, indexation mechanisms and disappointing rates of growth (with consequences for tax receipts, support to industry, social assistance and unemployment benefits), the sharp rise in interest charges is playing an increasingly important role here.

Table 11.3 gives a clear indication of the increasing significance of (gross) interest charges. It should be noted that the figures relating to interest payments provide only a limited insight into the problem of interest charges in the medium and long term. For the major seven OECD countries, gross debt interest payments in 1983/4 amount to some 4 per cent of their combined GNP and some 60 per cent of their aggregate (general government) deficit. Within a few years, interest payments in these countries will at least equal, on average, the government deficit, putting additional pressure on tax rates and/or the non-interest payments of the government. If no very drastic reduction can be achieved in the short run in the size of the financial deficit, then by the end of the 1980s the burden of public-sector interest payments in a number of countries such as Belgium, Denmark and Italy will probably amount to more than 15 per cent of national income, and this might have serious consequences not only for budgetary policy, but also for interest-rate levels and thus also for private-sector investment. It is only in recent years that the realization has gradually gained wider acceptance as to what extent the departure from the balanced-budget philosophy can, under some circumstances (high real rates of interest, large financial deficits, low rates of real growth), lead to an accumulation of the burden of debt servicing. The national authorities are fully aware of this danger, but in a number of countries they barely seem to have the power to reverse the developments now in progress.

It is difficult to determine to what extent the less accommodating policies of the monetary authorities of a number of countries also contributed to the change in the attitude of the fiscal authorities. Yet it seems justifiable to conclude that the increased emphasis on monetary policy has contributed to the notion in many quarters that the growth of the financial deficits must be halted. Having already lost some of its efficacy, budgetary policy suffered a further loss of efficacy in those countries where the monetary authorities did not wish to accommodate or wished to do so to a limited degree only. This loss of efficacy took place in two ways. First, the stimulation of effective demand consequent on the increase in the deficits was checked by the effect on interest rates of a non-accommodating monetary policy. This presupposes that higher deficits result in higher interest rates. Although theory on this point is rather convincing – unless bond issues create their own demand, long-term interest rates will rise as the supply of government bonds rises – the empirical evidence is often much more difficult to interpret, especially as far as the strength of the relationship is concerned. Second, the higher rates of interest also gravely affected the budget, which thus had to be more austere than would otherwise have been the case. This second effect played a very important role in the United States in 1984. Tentative calculations show that if the 1984 real rate of interest in the United States was as high as in 1980 (for the sake of simplicity, it is assumed that the rise in real interest rates which has occurred since then has been entirely the result of a collision course between monetary and budgetary policies), the projected financial deficit in 1984 would not have been 6 per cent of GNP, but some 3½ per cent.

It should be remarked that at first the fiscal authorities tried to evade the constraints that were to some extent forced on them via monetary policy. Many new financing systems were developed initially. Some of them fitted in with the general trends, but attempts were also made to acquire funds at lower rates than prevailed in the market: a sharp reduction in the period to maturity (fairly common), placing public authority loans abroad (in various countries), low interest-rate loans issued greatly below par (in some countries), large recourse to the central bank, etc. An illustration of the extremely difficult position in which a central bank can find itself is provided by the situation in Belgium, where the total volume of funds borrowed by the central government direct and indirect from the central bank has now reached approximately Bfr. 250 billion (13½ per cent of the money supply). What was intended as a temporary support arrangement by the central bank has degenerated into a permanent source of finance for public expenditure.

However, more recently there have been indications of a turn for the better in some countries, and the high rates of interest which accompany a large financial deficit appear to be accepted to a somewhat greater extent, although it is still too early to draw firm conclusions from the scattered evidence. Not so long ago, the (unlimited) obligation imposed on the Central Bank of Italy to take up all unplaced Treasury paper was abolished; in various European countries there is clearly a reduced volume of direct placings of loans abroad (Federal Republic of Germany in 1982, Belgium in 1983); and, for example in Italy, Sweden and Belgium, a larger part of the new debt is placed for longer maturities. These developments are more or less symptomatic of the public authorities' rising concern about the monetary consequences of the very high deficits and confirm their serious intention actually to reduce the financial deficits. This notion also finds expression in the fact that many countries have now formulated medium-term targets for their budgetary policies. Alas, this insight was awakened at a time when, in some countries, a change of direction was hardly feasible.

CONCLUSIONS

The following conclusions can be drawn from the above and from the brief description of the case of the Netherlands in appendix II.

1. Although, generally speaking, it cannot be said that a strong increase in expenditure will inevitably lead to a strong increase of the deficit, such a link has been clearly discernible in a number of countries since the second half of the 1970s.

2. In those countries which were faced with vast budget deficits, these deficits and the manner in which they were financed had a very considerable influence on monetary developments.
3. The monetary authorities of a number of these countries subsequently reacted by tightening their policies, thus accentuating the inappropriateness of the monetary and budgetary policy mix.
4. Possibly partly as a result of the tightening monetary policy, but undoubtedly also for other reasons, the fiscal authorities have made it ever clearer that their position is that the budget deficits must be reduced in the short to medium term.
5. Initially, the fiscal authorities fervently sought to circumvent the problem, but lately they have increasingly been showing judicious restraint. In many cases, however, it was already too late, so that several countries have landed themselves in an extremely difficult situation.
6. In a small country with an open economy, fixed exchange-rate relationships and no restrictions on external payments, the possibilities of curbing the growth of the money supply are limited. It is self-evident that the monetary authorities in such an economy (let us disregard institutional relationships for a moment) have less power than those in a closed economy to confront the fiscal authorities (at an early stage) with the consequences of their policy with the aid of monetary instruments.
7. However, even in open economies, the monetary authorities can and have to exert pressure on the fiscal authorities where the size and manner of financing of the budget deficit are concerned. The measure of their success, self-evidently, depends to some extent on the reaction of the fiscal authorities.
8. Only in realistic consultations between the two authorities can, under the given circumstances, an optimum course be charted and an undesirable clash between the two policy instruments be avoided, so that the high-priority policy target to tilt the consumption/investment mix to more investment can be better achieved.

Present public-sector deficits have deep and strong roots in underlying changes in our societies, which cannot be cured by budgetary and monetary policies alone. The kind of budgetary policies practised in recent years appears to be inadequate for the future. The scissors between growing expenditure and declining revenues became wider than ever before, partly reflecting successful efforts of shifting the burden of economic security onto others. If public expenditure cannot be brought under control, economic recovery stands little chance of having more than an *ad hoc* nature, in which case monetary guardians must risk an almost permanent collision with governments. The result would be an upsurge in inflation and an ever-greater worsening of productive investment.

Appendix I

Table 11A.1 *Public finance in a number of countries (changes as a percentage of GNP/GDP)*

	Position (% of GNP)	*Change*				*Position (% of GNP)*	*Change*
	1961	*1961–7*	*1968–73*	*1974–7*	*1978–81*	*1981*	*1982–4*
United States							
expenditure	29.0	2.2	0.1	2.0	2.1	35.4	2.2
revenues	27.4	0.9	2.8	0.6	2.0	33.7	−0.6
deficit (+)	1.6	1.3	−2.7	1.4	0.1	1.7	2.8
Japan							
expenditure	17.4	1.9	3.0	6.8	4.9	34.0	.
revenues	20.9	−1.7	3.2	2.4	4.5	29.3	.
deficit (+)	−3.5	3.6	−0.2	4.4	0.4	4.7	−1.9
Federal Republic of Germany							
expenditure	33.8	5.0	2.9	6.4	1.2	49.3	−1.3
revenues	36.3	0.6	5.5	2.7	−0.5	44.6	0.5
deficit (+)	−2.5	4.4	−2.6	3.7	1.7	4.7	−1.8
France							
expenditure	35.7	3.3	−0.5	5.7	4.7	48.9	4.5
revenues	36.2	2.0	0.4	3.8	3.7	46.1	3.0
deficit (+)	−0.5	1.3	−0.9	1.9	1.0	2.8	1.5
United Kingdom							
expenditure	33.4	5.1	2.6	3.0	3.2	47.3	−0.2
revenues	31.5	5.0	−0.1	3.1	3.9	43.4	0.3
deficit (+)	1.9	0.1	2.7	−0.1	0.7	3.9	−0.5
Italy							
expenditure	29.4	4.3	4.1	4.7	8.3	50.8	5.7
revenues	28.2	2.8	−0.6	3.9	4.4	38.7	7.3
deficit (+)	1.2	1.5	4.7	0.8	3.9	12.1	−1.6

(continued overleaf)

Table 11A.1 *(continued)*

	Position (% of GNP)	*Change*				*Position (% of GNP)*	*Change*
	1961	*1961–7*	*1968–73*	*1974–7*	*1978–81*	*1981*	*1982–4*
Belgium							
expenditure	29.8	4.7	4.6	7.5	9.5	56.1	1.7
revenues	28.4	4.8	3.2	5.3	2.3	44.0	3.1
deficit (+)	1.4	−0.1	1.4	2.2	7.2	12.1	−1.4
Denmark							
expenditure	27.1	7.2	7.8	6.8	10.1	59.0	2.3
revenues	26.6	7.5	12.7	0.8	3.6	51.2	1.5
deficit (+)	0.5	−0.3	−4.9	6.0	6.5	7.8	0.8
Netherlands							
expenditure	35.4	7.1	6.8	5.3	6.9	61.5	3.5
revenues	34.9	5.7	9.2	2.3	3.8	55.9	1.6
deficit (+)	0.5	1.4	−2.4	3.0	3.1	5.6	1.9
Total OECD							
expenditure	29.3	2.7	1.3	4.5	3.1	40.9	.
revenues	28.7	1.5	2.8	2.1	2.4	37.5	.
deficit (+)	0.6	1.2	−1.5	2.4	0.7	3.4	.

Public expenditure (i.e. of central government and local authorities combined) includes net capital transfers and gross investment, but excludes lending and participations. The deficit is net lending as defined by the OECD.

Source: OECD, *Economic Outlook*, December 1983; post-1982 figures based on EEC estimates.

Appendix II *Budgetary and Monetary Policies in the Netherlands, 1973–83*

INTRODUCTION

The Netherlands has a rather high public-sector deficit (about 10.5 per cent of GNP, including financial transactions). It is therefore interesting to examine for this country what the relationship has been between the monetary and fiscal authorities in recent years. First, however, it is necessary to consider some of the background to the policies pursued by the authorities.

The contribution of *monetary policy* to the aims of economic policy is by way of controlling the money supply (broadly defined) and the rate of exchange. In an open economy such as the Netherlands, the rate of interest is viewed as an instrument to influence the exchange rate rather than the money supply. In order to influence the latter, use is made of public-sector debt management and of the instrument of direct quantitative restriction on the (net) money-creating operations of the money-creating institutions.

In an open economy, the opportunities of influencing the money supply are clearly more limited than they are in a closed economy. At more or less fixed exchange rates (the Netherlands is a member of the European Monetary System), and in the absence of restrictions on external payments, a tightening policy with the resultant increase in interest rates will lead to an inflow of liquidity. This means that measures to curb domestic money creation may, under certain circumstances, have to be supplemented with restrictions on borrowing abroad. It must be noted that the limited efficacy of credit-control policies in countries with an open economy entails an inherent danger, in that these countries might focus unduly on the intermediate target of exchange-rate stabilization, because a strong currency policy contributes to price stability, a declared objective of the monetary authorities. However, if the development of the money supply is ignored for too long a period, the exchange-rate target is endangered or, alternatively, its achievement must be bought at an extremely high price (in terms of interest rates).

As regards *budgetary policy*, it must be remembered that in the Netherlands a structural budgetary policy was pursued from the early 1960s until 1979. The philosophy underlying this policy is based on the assumption that the size of the structural deficit of the public sector should equal the structural savings surplus of the private sector, taking into consideration a (normative) surplus on the current account, which amounts to the development aid recorded on the capital account. Temporary (conjunctural) deviations from the structural value were permitted.

There is, in the Netherlands, a clear *link between monetary and budgetary policy*, in the sense that it is assumed that under normal circumstances (that is, when the actual deficit is more or less equal to the structurally acceptable value), the public sector can and should finance its entire deficit in the capital market. This basic starting-point has been a bone of contention in the academic world. The authorities, both the Minister of Finance and the Netherlands Bank, however, have always held the (to some extent normative) view that there is no reason why the structural savings surplus of the private sector should not be channelled to the public sector in a monetarily neutral manner. This point of view was doubtless also prompted by the consideration that, under certain circumstances, an easier way of financing the structural deficit (namely via monetary financing) would in time also corrode policy discipline with respect to the *size* of the deficit.

DEVELOPMENTS SINCE 1973

The monetary policy conducted after 1973 must be viewed against the background of the observations made above. Immediately after the first oil crisis, the Netherlands government decided to pursue a strongly stimulating budgetary policy. The financial deficit rose markedly (from 1.5 per cent of net national income in 1973 to around 5.25 per cent in 1975), while the burden of taxation and social insurance contributions continued to expand (by some 3 per cent in two years). It must be noted here that on the eve of the first oil crisis the public-sector deficit was very small (1.5 per cent), owing to a combination of circumstances. The increase which followed in 1974 and 1975, on the other hand, clearly brought the deficit to a height which exceeded the level considered acceptable in the longer term (4 per cent). This development was viewed with some concern by the Netherlands Bank. Admittedly, it could not be denied that, in view of cyclical conditions, the deficit was permitted to exceed the structural value of 4 per cent of net national income for some time, but confidence gradually waned in the government's possibilities to bring the deficit down to the structurally acceptable level within a reasonable period of time. In the course of 1976 the Bank's concern increased further, when the medium-term projections of the Central Planning Bureau indicated that the early 1980s would see a rate of inflation of 6–7 per cent and that the financial deficit could be brought down only very gradually to a level (of 5 per cent) in 1980, which was, in the Bank's opinion, still too high. In addition, there were developments in 1976 which began to indicate increasingly that monetary conditions were getting out of hand: the liquidity ratio (M2/Y) rose sharply (by about 2.5 percentage points) as a result of substantial recourse in liquidity creation on behalf of the private sector and a turn-round in the monetary outcome of public finance in 1975/6 (see table 11A.2). The Bank came to the conclusion that the financial deficit would have to be reduced faster and to a greater degree than planned in the medium-term forecasts and, furthermore, that the rate of liquidity creation on behalf of the private sector would have to be slowed down considerably. In the Bank's opinion, this liquidity creation was closely connected with the price rises that had meanwhile set in on the market for real estate.

Table 11A.2 *Monetary survey (percentage of the domestic money supply at the beginning of the year)*

	1973	*1974*	*1975*	*1976*	*1977*	*1978*	*1979*	*1980*	*1981*	*1982*	*1983*[3]
Direct money creation on behalf of central government:											
(a) at home	−4.6	−2.4	3.2	3.4	1.5	1.6	4.4	1.8	1.7	0.8	−0.2
(b) abroad	—	—	—	—	—	—	—	—	—	—	
Total	−4.6	−2.4	3.2	3.4	1.5	1.6	4.4	1.8	1.7	0.8	−0.2
Indirect money creation on behalf of central government due to increase (+) in long-term central government debt:											
(a) with total domestic banking system[1]	−0.1	−0.1	0.8	1.2	0.4	0.7	1.3	0.3	2.2	4.8	5.4
(b) abroad[2]	.	.	.	.	.	.	0.5	1.4	2.3	2.2	1.3
Grand total	−4.7	−2.5	4.0	4.6	1.9	2.3	6.2	3.5	6.2	7.8	6.5
Other money creation in flow	19.3	17.8	5.6	15.7	5.7	3.1	0.6	0.4	0.3	0.4	3.8
Increase in domestic money supply	14.6	15.3	9.6	20.3	7.6	5.4	6.8	3.9	6.5	8.2	10.3

[1]Relates to change in the portfolio of long-term central government paper held by the banks and giro institutions.
[2]Net purchases of central governments bonds in foreign markets after deduction of redemptions.
[3]Estimate.

In May 1977, the Netherlands Bank imposed credit restrictions, with the express intention of bringing about a decrease in the liquidity ratio of 1 percentage point per year. It must be pointed out that the possibility was not excluded that, in view of the disappointing trend in economic activity, it might be decided at some point to slow down the rate of reduction. Apart from admonitions that the deficit should be reduced, no measures were taken against the public authorities. Only the money-creating operations of the banking system were subjected to curbs. If and in so far as banks exceeded the predetermined rate of credit expansion, they would have to attract extra long-term funds. This would exert an upward pressure on capital market rates, which would in turn lead to additional imports (in this case a decline in net exports) of capital for the non-monetary sector.

With the benefit of hindsight, the conclusion must be drawn that the Netherlands Bank reacted too late rather than too soon to the ever more manifest disturbances in the monetary sphere: after all, 1977 saw the turn-round from a large surplus on the current account of the balance of payments to increasing deficits. By the tightening of monetary policy and the ensuing rise in interest rates, an attempt was made, on the one hand, to limit the current-account deficit by a recovery of domestic equilibrium and, on the other, to bring about compensatory capital imports.

Both table 11A.2 and figure 11A.1 show that in the period 1977–80 the goals set could not be achieved by means of the monetary policy persued. There was, admittedly, a slight decline in the rate of inflation, but the deficit on the current account of the balance of payments continued to grow until 1980, and although the net exports of non-monetary capital declined, it did not undergo a turn-round to modest net imports until well into 1979. This development was due to the vast monetary financing by the public sector. In the period concerned, the exchange rate could be maintained only through a tightening of money market conditions. This meant that monetary policy centred on the exchange rate – undoubtedly an important factor for countries such as Denmark, Belgium and the Netherlands for the realization of relatively low price increases – rather than on the development of the *total* money supply.

In the period 1977–80, the relatively high short-term interest rates led to a considerable inflow of funds through banking transactions. In the course of 1980, however, the Bank began to fear that exchange-rate expectations would consequently turn against the guilder. That was the reason why the Governing Board of the Bank wrote a letter to the Minister of Finance, on 18 December 1980, stating that 'the lifting of the restrictions on the banking system's net foreign liabilities has not helped to bring about a return to equilibrium, but has in fact worked as a mechanism by means of which excessive monetary financing by the public authorities became possible thanks to the funds attracted by the banking system from abroad'. The Netherlands Bank consequently proposed to the Minister of Finance that in 1981 direct monetary financing by the public sector be limited to fl.3 billion. The Minister

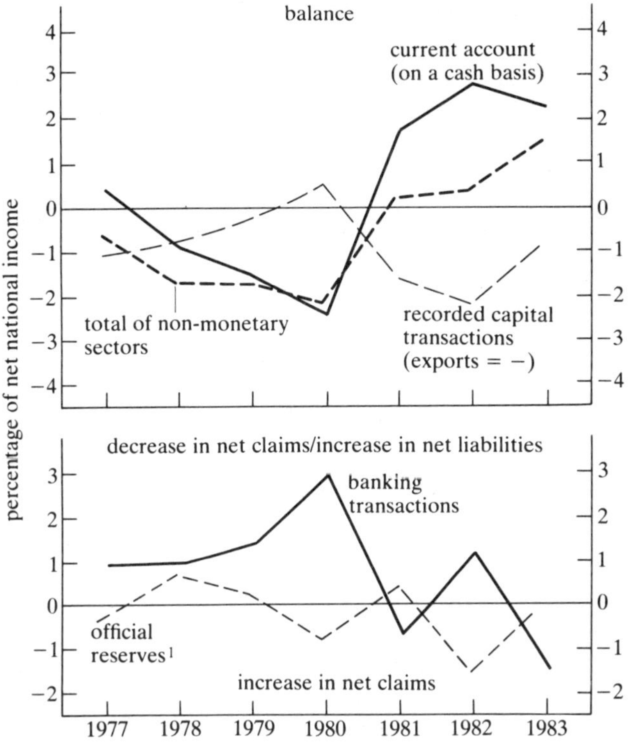

Figure 11A.1 Balance of payments, overall accounts (annual figures as a percentage of net national income).

[1]Excluding allocation of special drawing rights

agreed with this proposal, stating at a later stage that monetary financing by the public sector should be eliminated entirely. Direct money creation on behalf of the government slowed down substantially from 1980 onwards, and disappeared completely in 1983 (see table 11A.2).

The balance of payments meanwhile underwent fundamental changes. In 1983, the surplus on the current account of the balance of payments amounted to around 3 per cent of net national income, whereas the rate of inflation was about 2.5 per cent. The original argument in favour of neutral financing by the public sector was gradually replaced by another, namely, the fact that the financial deficit had more than doubled in the years after 1979. In order to prevent a loss in confidence from affecting the exchange rate, this unhealthily large deficit had to be financed in the soundest possible manner. Another policy would augment the risks of an upward pressure on interest rates to an unnecessary degree.

Although direct monetary financing by the government was eliminated gradually, there were still worrying aspects as to the financing of the public sector deficit, since indirect liquidity creation on behalf of the public sector increased very markedly in the early 1980s (see table 11A.2), mirroring the ballooning deficit. Therefore, the overall contribution of the government to the increase in total domestic money supply became very substantial (30 per cent in the period 1975–8; almost 85 per cent in the years 1979–83). So, financing in the soundest possible way does not mean sound financing, since the latter implies a reduction in the budget deficit. In the absence of such a reduction, sooner or later a conflict between the Minister of Finance and the Bank becomes inevitable.

CONCLUDING REMARKS

From an assessment of the relationship between monetary and budgetary policies during the period 1973–83 in an open economy such as that of the Netherlands, which participates in a system of fixed, but adjustable exchange rates, the following conclusions can be reached.

1. As soon as the deficit began to deviate too much and for too long a period from the structurally acceptable value, the development of the money supply threatened to be made into a dependent variable.
2. Bolstered by an unfavourable development regarding inflation in the period 1974–6 and convinced of the aptness of their approach by the considerable turn-round on the current account of the balance of payments in 1977, the monetary authorities refused to accept the growth of the money supply and imposed credit restrictions.
3. These credit restrictions pertained to liquidity creation on behalf of the private sector, and were, in the first instance, also warranted by developments in the private sector (the boom in the market for dwellings).
4. The efficacy of monetary policy was clearly undermined by the fact that the public sector did not put its house in order with regard to the budget deficit, when the credit restrictions were imposed.
5. When, subsequently, in 1980 fears arose at the Netherlands Bank that exchange-rate expectations would turn against the guilder, *no* attempt was made to impose quantitative restrictions on public-sector borrowing; instead, in conjunction with the Minister of Finance, the search was on to finance the deficit in such a manner that monetary consequences would be avoided as much as possible. This was done through government restraint in direct money creation.
6. The solution outlined above (point 5) was in fact by far the most sensible. If, to achieve its goal, the Netherlands Bank had imposed restrictions on lending to the public sector, the chances of a direct conflict between the government and the Bank would have been very large indeed.
7. Whether in the case of a real clash the government would come out on top depends on the prevailing political situation, as the Minister of

Finance could always resort to direct financing of the budget deficit abroad or put into practice Section 26 of the Bank Act, giving directions for the Bank's policy 'to be properly coordinated with Government's monetary and financial policies'.

8. Apart from preventing grave political unrest, the road chosen provided the Minister of Finance with yet another economically and strategically more relevant advantage, namely, that he was able to persist fully in his intention of reducing the budget deficit. Had he resorted to direct financing abroad or to giving the Bank directions, the fact that the barriers were down could have meant that, as regards the budget deficit, the sky would have become the limit. By (wholeheartedly) giving in to the Central Bank's wishes, the Minister of Finance therefore at the same time strengthened his position *vis-à-vis* his colleagues in the Cabinet.
9. Although, as a result of agreements reached between the Minister of Finance and the Central Bank, direct liquidity creation on behalf of the public sector could gradually be eliminated entirely, indirect liquidity creation on behalf of the public sector increased very markedly in the early 1980s (see table 11A.2). If this process is continued (and this process is to be continued without a reduction in the public-sector deficit), the monetary authorities will be confronted sooner or later with an awkward dilemma as to the policy to be persued. There is no doubt about it that the Central Bank will abide by its responsibilities under those circumstances. It must be noted that the situation described above is by no means unique to the Netherlands. In half the EEC countries, bank lending to the public sector exceeded that to the private sector in 1982 and 1983. Making headway in reducing budget deficits therefore remains of paramount importance.

12

Market and Non-Market Alternatives in the Supply of Public Goods: General Issues

Charles Blankart

PRIVATIZATION IN ECONOMICS AND POLITICS

Socialization is a well-known issue in economics and politics, but its counterpart, privatization, is rarely found. Indeed, the notion of privatization can be found neither in Webster's *New World Dictionary* (1970) nor in the *Oxford Advanced Learner's Dictionary of Current English* (1973), but it does appear in the German *Duden* (1973). Therein privatization is defined as a 'transformation of public into private property'.

It is not accidental that the notion of privatization is known in Germany, but not in the Anglo-Saxon countries–at least not until very recently. In Germany, the idea of free enterprise never gained such a large momentum as in the United States and in Great Britain. Towards the end of the nineteenth and the beginning of the twentieth century there was even a large political movement towards socialization of private property in Germany. Prussian railways urban transport, part of the coal mines, distribution of electricity and gas, street lighting, etc. were socialized. The number of government-owned industries was further increased during the First World War. This development of growing government interference in private markets reached its peak in the period from 1933 to 1945, when Germany became a planned economy. After 1945, many Germans were disillusioned with government activity in business and planning. Moreover, observations of failures of economic policy in the Soviet zone of Germany corroborated these critical views and created a new attitude towards the free-enterprise system. The theoretical underpinnings for this new view were furnished by the so-called ORDO–Liberal School. Of course, the extension of government holdings in the production sector no longer fitted into the new ideological picture. So a movement towards privatization of publicly owned enterprises (often called re-privatization) emerged in the 1950s. Major examples of partial privatization included PREUSSAG 1959 (metals, energy, transport and construction), Volkswagen 1961 VTG (a storage and transport corporation) in 1961, and VEBA (chemical and oil industries) in 1965. The privatization movement then stopped at the federal level for thirteen years, when the Social-Democratic–Liberal coalition was in power. At the local level, however, the discussion continued. Here, the main argument was that privatization would help to reduce local government expenditures.

In 1983, the privatization issue was resumed at the federal level under the new Conservative–Liberal coalition. Further shares of VEBA were sold to private individuals in the first months of 1984. New private holdings of capital were allowed in the Lufthansa corporation in 1984. Finally, proposals to sell government properties in the banking and tourist sectors have been put forward.

The recent privatization policy in the Federal Republic of Germany seems similar to that in the United Kingdom. A closer look, however, reveals that there are substantial differences. The British privatization policy is much more far-reaching. It includes telecommunications and electronic media, which are not a privatization issue in Germany.[1]

FOUR DIFFERENT VIEWS OF PRIVATIZATION

In politics, the privatization issue goes beyond the narrow field of 'a transformation of public into private property' (as defined above). Most definitions fall into four different categories:

1. privatization by application of the equivalence principle;
2. privatization as deregulation;
3. sale of government-owned industries;
4. outside contracting of government services.

These four categories are often not strictly separated from each other. Although such a mix of issues can be understood from a political economy point of view, it is not helpful for economic analysis because the *ceteris paribus* requirement becomes blurred. In order to avoid further confusion, I shall characterize these four categories of privatization.

Privatization by an application of the equivalence principle

Often a service is said to be 'privatized' if it is allocated through the price system and not the bureaucratic process. The term 'private', in this case, relates to the form of its financing over 'private' (individually paid) prices instead of public (collectively determined) taxes. The goal of such privatization measures is the application of the equivalence principle in order to attain a more efficient allocation of resources. Typical examples are the substitution of free by priced health care, schools, universities, housing, transport, day care homes, etc.

The *economic* limits to this form of privatization are given by the exclusion costs. From an economic point of view, the price system should not be used if exclusion costs are higher than efficiency gains realized by using prices. It has to be conceded, however, that the *political* limits are much narrower. Many goods and services that could be supplied privately for purely economic (allocative) reasons cannot be so supplied because of political constraints. Therefore politicians' willingness to respond to economists' proposals to apply the equivalence principle by pricing, rather than by using some other form of financing, are rather limited.

Privatization as deregulation

Another policy measure often subsumed under the notion of privatization is *deregulation*. Strictly speaking, however, deregulation only means that a good or service that has been supplied at regulated prices will now be supplied at free market prices, independently of whether the means of production are publicly or privately owned.

Free market prices will, however, only result, if free entry of private (along with public) firms is allowed. From an *economic* point of view, the problem with deregulation is therefore whether free entry always contributes to an efficient allocation of resources. Faulhaber (1975) has shown in a seminal article that free entry may lead to inefficiency in the case of natural monopolies producing under increasing returns to scale (subadditivity). Not all natural monopolies are so 'natural' that they are immune to action by market entrants to destroy their inherent cost advantages. Market entry will then lead to an inefficient duplication of activities at higher total costs. Such a situation may arise, for example, when long-run average costs exhibit a non-monotonic curvature in the relevant region of demand (see Baumol, 1982). The practical relevance of this argument is not yet clear. On the one hand, it has been shown that many regulated industries have constant or monotonically declining average costs (see Blankart, 1979). On the other hand, these studies often do not take account of the multitude of products made in one firm. Under such conditions, a combination of strong economies of scale with weak economies of scope may weaken the stability of natural monopolies.

The problem of inefficient entry, however, does become relevant when, for *political* reasons, there is internal subsidization among product groups. Then cream-skimmers can enter into the market and destroy the inherent cost advantages of natural monopolies. The economist's answer to this problem would be that cross-subsidizations should be abolished. Cross-subsidizations, however, are important elements in a politician's vote-production function. He has an interest in subsidizing some political groups at the cost of others in order to attain a sufficient majority in the elections. Therefore politicians are not likely to be willing to abandon such an instrument. The scope for politically feasible deregulation is therefore limited, at least within the institutions found in Continental Europe.[2]

Sale of government-owned industries

Some government-owned industries operate in fields not related to governments' proper activities. They produce neither inputs for the governmental production process, nor are they engaged in the production of outputs for which the government is responsible. Government investments in foreign developed countries may be subsumed under this category, or investments in the tourist industry or in department stores, etc. In such cases, the *commercial* aspect of the investment is overwhelming, relative to other goals. The political device is therefore that such industries should be privatized wherever the overall return on government investments can be increased by such a decision.

The sale of such firms, however, is not a simple matter, because the market for firms is not well developed. The number of transactions per period is small, which makes it difficult to find the market price. Moreover it is not an easy matter to assess the value of a firm or the value of packages of a firm. Stock-market information is mostly not available, because most firms' shares are not traded at the stock exchange. All these problems are further enhanced when the government pursues distributional objectives with an asset sale. In the Federal Republic of Germany, the government tried in the 1950s and 1960s to sell nationalized industries in order to create a broad-based distribution of wealth within the population (the so-called 'people's shares plan').

The problems involved in such privatizations can clearly be seen in the case of VEBA share sale in 1965. There, the initial offer of the government was first oversubscribed so that it had to increase the share supply. Later, stock prices fell, inducing the government to buy back part of the shares in order to keep the former level of the share prices constant (see von Loesch, 1983). Similar difficulties happened in the United Kingdom in 1982, when Amersham International and Britoil were privatized (see Heald, 1983). Thus privatization is tied to serious transition problems from public to private ownership which should not be overlooked.

But let me take the analysis one step further: what are these industries in which the government has only a *commercial* or *private* interest? Why have those industries ever been socialized, if there was no *public* interest? From a political economy point of view, an interest is defined as public whenever a large enough coalition can enforce that its private interests are supported by public means. Usually right-wing governments have different views to left-wing governments on how far public interests should reach.

Thus the number of industries that are regarded to be only of commercial and not of public interest to the government and that may be privatized therefore depends on the actual majorities. This can clearly be seen from the recent policy changes in the United Kingdom, France and the Federal

Republic of Germany. But even for right-wing governments, it is relatively difficult to privatize subsidized public firms such as coal mines, iron, steel and shipbuilding industries. Here, public interest means that these industries make a contribution to the fight against unemployment.

Outside contracting of government services

In the above three cases, distributive problems set a narrow barrier to privatization. This does not seem to hold with outside contracting, for a contract can be tied to the requirement to respect the distributive constraints.

Outside contracting has a long tradition in Western countries in road construction, in the provision of armament and of railway equipment. In services, the lease of the postal monopoly to private entrepreneurs (such as Thurn and Taxis in Imperial Germany) is the most popular example. Often today governments do not make formal contracts. They use subsidies or regulations to meet collective goals in private firms. Subsidies to private steel corporations to maintain historical employment levels is one case; another is regulation of private insurance companies in order to enforce, for example, the supply of low-priced third-party-liability motor insurance.

Thus (formal or informal) outside contracting seems to be a politically attractive alternative to other forms of privatization because of its adaptivity to a variety of political goals: its theoretical foundations, however, are rarely investigated. This will now be done in the following section.

OUTSIDE CONTRACTING IN ECONOMIC THEORY

Traditional theoretical views

In management science, the pros and cons of outside contracting are seen as an alternative between two ways of procurement: make or buy. Outside contracting has to be chosen when it is cheaper than own production, but when is it cheaper to contract than to produce, and when is it cheaper in the specific case of governments?

An answer to the latter question is given by the property rights theory. It says that it is *in general* cheaper for governments to contract than to produce because of the efficiency advantages of private ownership. Private ownership is supposed to supply more incentives for entrepreneurs to be efficient and to find new ways of combining the factors of production than public ownership (Alchian, 1965). In the limit, the property rights theory suggests that the government should remain merely an agency contracting for all services that the government is supposed to provide.

It is rarely asked, however, how the contracting system really works. Some answers are given by traditional price theory.[3] In this framework, contracts are regarded separately on a contract-by-contract basis. There is full information which ensures that the cheapest supplier emerges through the competitive bidding process.[4] Moreover, the existence of monopolistic contractors does not change the results substantially. The price may merely rise to an upper limit, beyond which it becomes cheaper for the government to produce than to buy.

In such a world there is no room for contract failures. Markets for contracts always work as in any other markets for goods and services. Given this result and the hypothesis of the property rights theory that public firms produce at higher costs than private firms, contracting is always superior to production within the government.

Contract theoretical views

This view has been questioned by Williamson (1975). He says that contracts cannot be fully specified in general, because of the complexity of the procurement processes. Even if there is competition among suppliers before the contract is made, the supplier and the demander are locked in a bilaterial monopoly position after the contract has been signed. *Ex ante* competition and *ex post* monopoly encourage opportunistic behaviour of the contractors, which is detrimental to efficiency. In order to avoid such difficulties, it may be more advantageous to make rather than to buy.

The Williamson approach represents a big step forward in our understanding of the make or buy alternative, but it still leaves open the question of why such complicated contracts are made at all, if they are difficult to enforce. Why are contracts not divided into less complex parts? Moreover, why are there no learning effects helping to overcome the initial difficulties with complex contracts? If Williamson's suggestion is right that complexity of contracts is a permanent phenomenon, then complexity has to be explained and not simply postulated.

In order to approach this problem, time has to be introduced into the analysis, because only then does imperfect information (complexity) make sense. This is done by giving up the assumption of single separate contracts for a model of an evolutionary system of contracts as suggested by von Weizsäcker (1980). In such a world, decisions of the government as buyer as well as those of a private firm as supplier are *overlapping*. Current decisions are not independent of the information obtained from previous decisions and future decisions will depend on information on current decisions, etc. For our analysis, it is helpful to distinguish two kinds of overlapping:

1. overlapping in the production sphere;
2. overlapping in the consumption sphere.

Let me first explain the problem of overlapping decisions in the *production sphere*. Such overlapping emerges because dispositions of the government as buyer and those of a private firm as supplier change at a different speed over time. Government's demand, on the one hand, may change relatively quickly in the course of economic growth; supplier's fixed equipment, on the other hand, is less adaptable to a changing environment. A change in government's demand may mean that the firm's capital is lost. The government therefore wishes to contract in as short a term as possible, whereas the private supplier will try to contract in as long a term as possible. A compromise has to be found among the two in order to come to a contract. Such a compromise, however, gives the private firm an incentive to behave strategically. For example, when a contract for a power company has been agreed for several decades, the firm may mazimize its profits by decreasing the service quality in the first period and increasing it towards the end of the contract period, in order to be in a better position when the contract has to be renewed. Thus the firm will build up its *goodwill* strategically over time. Its behaviour is similar to that of a government, subject to a re-election constraint, making unpopular political decisions just after the elections and popular decisions before the next elections (see Frey and Schneider, 1978).

Furthermore, the compromise on the contract period raises again the problem of sunk costs. A firm's fixed equipment will still have an economic value at the end of the contract. The incumbent firm will therefore have a cost advantage *vis-à-vis* other competing firms when the contract has to be renewed.[5] The cost advantage may be so substantial that competition for contract renewals is only a formal matter. Why, then, should a bidding procedure be organized? It is not surprising to observe that formal bidding procedures are often no longer organized in practice in such cases and that contracts are tacitly renewed with the incumbent firm.

These arguments point to efficiency limits in outside contracting wherever large sunk costs are involved. Some examples are railways and urban rail systems, cable TV (see Williamson, 1976), electricity and water distribution, hospitals, etc. Note, however, that outside contracting is still feasible, but the government has to secure its rights to interfere with the ongoing contract in order to avoid strategic behaviour by the firm. Under such conditions, however, the freedom for entrepreneurial initiative to secure efficiency is rather limited, and we would not expect much difference in the costs between public and private production.

We have seen that overlapping of planning decisions in the production sphere can weaken the efficiency of outside contracting. The contrary is true for *overlapping in the consumption sphere;* here, overlapping facilitates outside contracting. It helps to overcome the problem of *quality uncertainty*. Let me explain this point in more detail. If the good considered is a pure *inspection good* (see Nelson, 1970), there is not quality uncertainty. By definition, the quality can be inspected and evaluated *before* the contract is made. Therefore competition among suppliers will work in general. This can be seen by considering examples such as raw materials or energy supply, for which competitive stock markets exist. For these reasons inspection goods should generally be bought on the market and not produced within an organization. Many goods used by governments have important characteristics of an inspection good, such as paper and printing materials, cleaning services, office equipment, energy used by governments, etc. They are mostly bought and not made.

Experience goods, on the other hand, cannot be evaluated in their quality *ex ante*, but only *ex post*, when the good or service is used. Therefore market efficiency may be impaired by adverse selection and moral hazard effects (see Akerlof, 1970). Information derived from previous purchases, however, may help consumers to overcome these market deficiencies and to make rational choice. Consumers will extrapolate the quality experienced in previous purchases to actual purchases, and producers have an incentive not to disappoint consumers' extrapolations and to provide the requisite quality, because only by being reliable in quality can they expect to be selected again as suppliers in the future. In other words, producers invest in *goodwill* in order to increase the probability of obtaining future contracts (see von Ungern-Sternberg and von Weizsäcker, 1981).

The idea of an evolutionary system of contracts points to a large number of government services that may be contracted out, such as consulting, planning, monitoring, auditing, debt collection, etc. Limits to contracting, however, may emerge when contracts are infrequent, because the costs of obtaining experience will then be relatively high. Consider, for example, contracting for money supply with a private central bank (similar to the proposal of von Hayek, 1976). A contracted central bank may build up goodwill capital during its contract period, but in the end, just before the contract expires, it may multiply its money supply, reap the profit from customers who still believe in the previous stability and then leave the market. In such circumstances, outside contracting may not be advantageous at all. Nevertheless, it must be acknowledged that nationalized central banks, too, often did not behave differently in history (see Bernholz, 1978, 1983).

Finally, there is a group of goods whose output is so intangible that experience cannot be acquired, or where the evaluation of experience is a disputable issue itself. I shall call these goods *trust goods*. For these goods, output cannot be an indicator of a contractor's performance. Following Majone (1983) and Frey and Pommerehne (1983), the *rules* applied for producing such goods serve as a substitute for the hidden output. The activity is therefore evaluated by the rules applied with its production and not by its output.

Jurisdiction, that is, the administration of justice by courts, is a useful example for understanding the nature of trust goods. Suppose that courts are contracted out to the least-cost suppliers. How could their performance be measured and evaluated? Justice is an output both difficult to measure and to evaluate. Instead, the rules are judged which are applied in the production process. Typically, the quality of jurisdiction is evaluated by considering whether or not the law and the dogmatic tradition of law is applied correctly and not on the result or the output.

Where correct rule application is the criterion of performance, private enterprise cannot flourish, for its comparative advantage lies in finding and developing new markets. Free enterprise is not an institution that can be fruitfully employed to attain rule obedience. It is to be expected, therefore, that private firms will not work as efficiently in such a system as public enterprises or public administrations.

There is a wide variety of government services exhibiting characteristics of trust goods: armed forces, social services, general public administration and maybe diplomatic services. For these services, rule adherence is the principal criterion of performance evaluation. Privatization will therefore not induce substantial efficiency gains. It must be conceded, however, that the boundaries between trust goods and experience goods are not quite strict. The relative weights given to outputs versus rules as evaluation criteria are a disputable issue and are therefore not independent of what ruling coalitions declare to be important.

CONCLUSIONS

In the political debate, quite different aspects are subsumed under the notion of privatization, such as the application of the equivalence principle for publicly supplied goods and services; deregulation; sale of government-owned industries; and outside contracting of government services and inputs. Outside contracting is the theoretically most underdeveloped part of these four aspects of privatization; therefore the main focus of this chapter has been on outside contracting.

The crucial issue with outside contracting is whether the market for contracts works like any other market, or whether there are limits to outside contracting because this market may fail to induce efficient choices. A taxonomy of contract failures has been assessed in the above analysis. *First*, sunk-cost goods are expected to be as costly to produce under public as under private ownership, because the contract needed for the procurement of these goods has to be long term and must allow for current interference by the government. Second, inspection goods can be contracted out because competition is likely to work, given the feasibility of *ex ante* quality control. Third, most experience goods may be contracted out too, for competition may work through an evolutionary system of recurring contracts. If contracts are infrequently recurring, however, efficiency limits to outside contracting may emerge (for example, contracted money supply). Fourth, trust goods are the goods most difficult to contract because performance is judged by rule adherence. In such an environment, private enterprise is not likely to be more creative and efficient than public administrations.

Clearly, a classification of contract failures as this one does not solve the problem of privatization *per se*. This is true for all sorts of classifications used in economics. The distinction between public, private and mixed goods, for example, which was in the scientific debate some decades ago, also did not provide a solution to the public good problem, but it did stimulate invention of new ways to overcome market failures. Moreover, it clarified where research in public finance should start. Our classification of goods into those which may be easily contracted and those which may not has to be seen in exactly the same way. It is a call to economists to develop arrangements for overcoming the deficiencies of markets for contracts.

NOTES

The author is indebted for helpful comments to Monika Faber, Wolfgang Blümel, W. W. Pommerehne, R. Windisch and P. Zweifel.

1 There are some minor attempts to bring private initiative into electronic media in Rheinland-Pfalz. Also satellite television is expected to be supported by private entrepreneurship.
2 This conclusion does not necessarily hold for US institutions, where commissions and courts have an independent influence, cf. Kaufer and Blankart (1983).
3 For a survey, see Ramser (1979).
4 Risk and uncertainty are included, in the sense that risk preferences or search costs may affect choices (see Ramser, 1979).
5 This particular point can also be found for in Williamson's recent survey article (see Williamson, 1981).

REFERENCES

Akerlof, G. A. (1970), 'The market for "Lemons": Quality uncertainty and the market mechanism, *Quarterly Journal of Economics*, vol. 84, no. 3, pp. 488–500.

Alchian, A. A. (1965), 'Some economics of property rights', *Il politico*, vol. 30, pp. 816–29.

Baumol, W. J. (1982), 'Contestable markets: an uprising in the theory of industry structure, (presidential address, delivered at the ninety-fourth meeting of the American Economic Association, 29 December 1981), *American Economic Review*, vol. 72, no. 1, pp. 1–15.

Bernholz, P. (1978), Review of F. A. Hayek, *Denationalization of Money, An Analysis of the Theory and Practice of Concurrent Currencies*, (London 1976), in *Kyklos*, vol. 3, fasc. 1, pp. 136–9.

Bernholz, P. (1983), 'Inflation and monetary constitutions in historical perspective', *Kyklos*, vol. 36, fasc. 3, pp. 397-419.

Blankart, C. B. (1979), 'Die wirtschaftliche Bedeutung von Skalenerträgen öffentlicher Unternehmen', *Zeitschrift für öffentliche und gemeinwirtschaftliche Unternehmen*, vol. 2, no. 1, pp. 1–25.

Faulhaber, G. R. (1975), 'Cross subsidization: pricing in public enterprise, *American Economic Review*, vol. 65, no. 5, pp. 966–77.

Frey, B. S. and Pommerehne, W. W. (1983), '*Public vs. private production: misplaced emphasis*?' mimeo, University of Zurich.

Frey, B. S. and Schneider, F. (1978), 'An empirical study of politico-economic interaction in the United States', *Review of Economics and Statistics*, vol. 60, no. 2, pp. 174–83.

Hayek, F. A. von (1976), *Denationalization of Money, An Analysis of the Theory and Practice of Concurrent Currencies*, Hobart Paper Special Number 70, London: Institute of Economic Affairs.

Heald, D. (1983), '*Privatization of public firms: the experience during the Thatcher government*, mimeo, University of Glasgow.

Kaufer, E. and Blankart, C. B. (1983), 'Regulation in Western Germany: the state of the debate', *Zeitschrift für die gesamte Staatswissenschaft* (Journal of Institutional and Theoretical Economics), vol. 139, no. 3, pp. 435–51.

Loesch, A. von (1983), *Privatisierung öffentlicher Unternehmen, ein Überblick über die Argumente*, Baden-Baden: Nomos.

Majone, G. (1983) 'Quality in the service Sector', *Options* (IIASA, Laxenburg), no. 4.

Nelson, P. (1970), 'Information and consumer behaviour', *Journal of Political Economy*, vol. 78, no. 2, pp. 311–29.

Ramser, H. (1979), 'Eigenerstellung oder Fremdbezug von Leistungen', in W. Kern, *Handwörterbuch der Produktionswirtschaft*, pp. 437–50. Stuttgart: Poeschl.

von Ungern-Sternberg, T. and von Weizsäcker, C. C. (1981), 'Marktstruktur and Marktverhalten bei Qualitätsunsicherheit', *Zeitschrift für Wirtschafts- und Sozialwissenschaften*, vol. 101, no. 6, pp. 609–26.

von Weizsäcker, C. C. (1980), *Barriers to Entry, A Theoretical Treatment*, Berlin, Heidelberg, New York: Springer.

Williamson, O. E. (1975), *Markets and Hierarchies: Analysis and Antitrust Implications, A Study in the Economics of Internal Organization*, New York: Free Press and London: Macmillan.

Williamson, O. E. (1976), 'Franchise bidding for natural monopolies – in general and with respect to CATV', *Bell Journal of Economics*, vol. 7, no. 1, pp. 73–104.

Williamson, O. E. (1981), 'The modern corporation: origin, evolution, attributes', *Journal of Economic Literature*, vol. 19, no. 4, pp. 1537–68.

13

Market and Non-Market Alternatives in the Public Supply of Public Services: British Experience with Privatization

Ian Byatt

INTRODUCTION

In the early 1980s, the Conservative government in the United Kingdom adopted a policy of strengthening market forces in the economy by switching activity from the public sector to the private sector. What are the possibilities in this area in the UK?

The 'public supply of public services' includes:

1. public industry, especially public utilities, such as gas, electricity, transport and communications;
2. public services, whose use is charged for, but in a way not closely related to consumption, such as local authority housing, water supply and sewerage;
3. public services, provided without charge, such as health and education;
4. transfer programmes, such as social security – including public assistance (often through the tax system) to private provision of, say, occupational pensions.

This chapter does not discuss public assistance to 'market' activities such as agriculture, or the supply of services such as internal security and external defence, where market forces are inevitably peripheral.

There is no simple way to measure the overall economic importance of these activities. Value added in public corporations, central and local government accounts for 11 per cent, 9 per cent and 11 per cent of UK GDP respectively. Public corporations go wider than public utilities, however; the operation of transfer systems, such as social security, provides a service not included in GDP, and these figures include 'non-marketable' services such as defence and public administration.

PUBLIC INDUSTRY

It is useful to distinguish industries that are in competitive markets, such as coal mining, steel and shipbuilding, from utilities such as gas, electricity, posts, telecommunications, (much) surface transport and some air transport. The first set of industries have many problems: they are often facing structural difficulties, and may be over-extended and inefficient; they require extensive subsidies which governments, even those committed to a market philosophy, find difficult to reduce. But they do not pose the monopoly problems of the utilities which in many countries, including the UK, have led to their inclusion in the public sector.

In the case of the utilities, the monopoly may be either a natural monopoly, as often occurs with the 'network' industries (gas, electricity, telecommunications, rail) or with industries with a special locational advantage (airports) or one resulting from legislation (buses, posts). Often these two elements are combined. Where there are natural monopoly elements, governments have often added statutory monopoly powers as part of a package which includes the imposition of duties on the monopoly operator to ensure its operations are in the 'public interest'.

In the UK, public ownership of utilities began with local authorities and passed to central government after the Second World War. In the Nationalisation Acts, statutory monopoly powers were granted, coupled with statutory obligations. Subsequently the industries were given 'guidance', sometimes formal, but non-statutory, as in the case of the three post-war White Papers on Nationalised Industries, published in 1961, 1967 and 1978, and sometimes both informal and non-statutory, in the form of day-to-day contacts with the government on individual issues.

The municipalization and, subsequently, nationalization of public utilities turned primarily on the argument that private markets were imperfect. In the mid-nineteenth century, when water and gas utilities were developing in Britain, it had been argued that competition, or potential competition, was sufficient to achieve beneficial social results. But the unsatisfactory experience of such competition, typically a form of unstable duopoly where periods of cut-throat competition alternated with monopolistic collusion, led the municipalities to acquire water and gas undertakings and to engage heavily in the supply of electricity and the development of tramways. When larger-scale supply became appropriate, a national authority was established to integrate supply over a wider area. Hence a Central Electricity Board was established in the 1920s as the first step in the development of a national grid. More recently, the gas industry, already in public ownership, but in the form of Area Boards with a coordinating Gas Council, was centralized into the

British Gas Corporation to organize a national supply of natural gas from the North Sea.

Despite the advantages that such organizations can bring, there has been dissatisfaction with the rigidity and, in some cases, high costs that such arrangements can entail. Hence the Conservative administration in the early 1980s emphasized the desirability of reintroducing market forces. The key to success is getting the right balance between market failure, on the one hand, and bureaucratic failure, on the other. For the economist, this is not simply a question of public or private ownership, but rather one of market structure.

The Conservative government's pursuit of a policy to strengthen market forces involved:

1. examination of statutory monopoly and regulatory powers, and their abolition where this could increase genuine competition;
2. transfer of public corporations to the private sector – 'privatization'.

The situation in 1985 is thus: the monopoly of electricity generation has been abolished; courier services are now permitted to deliver letters and documents subject to a minimum fee; inter-city coach services have been deregulated; customers can now instal telecommunication equipment not supplied by British Telecom (BT); an alternative telephone service, Mercury, has been licensed to operate certain trunk routes in competition with BT.

Privatization is not solely concerned with competition in the sense of the word used by economists. Privatization may benefit the public finances; it may lead to more enterprising management and to greater internal efficiency. Under the first Thatcher government (1979–83), privatization was mainly concerned with non-utility industries. But the planned privatization of BT involves important issues of competition, as would the privatization of gas, electricity, airports and bus services.

Where there are major entry barriers, mere abolition of statutory monopolies may have little effect. Privatization of a natural monopoly may simply substitute a private monopoly for a public monopoly. The privatization of BT has been accompanied by the establishment of an Office of Telecommunications (OFTEL), and price increases will, in the early years, be restricted to three percentage points below the index of retail prices. Even where entry barriers are small, the existing corporation may dominate the industry and inhibit genuine competition. Given the evidence on the effects of regulation of private monopolies, the gain may be small, or even negative. It is necessary to analyse individual cases to see where the gains and losses arise.

It is natural for economists to adopt a structural approach to identify the natural monopoly elements, which will require some kind of regulation, and to separate them out from those parts of a service where competition could operate or where the market could be 'contestable' (Baumol, Panzar and Willig, 1982). For example, much electricity transmission and local distribution is a natural monopoly, but electricity generation is not. Local telephone networks (certainly in the absence of cable television) are natural monopolies, but competition could operate on trunk or international lines. British Gas Corporation monopsony powers in the North Sea derive from the absence of a physical link between the UK gas fields and continental Europe, and freedom to export UK gas; there is no natural monopoly in the servicing of gas appliances; but the gas pipelines possess considerable natural monopoly power. There are no significant economies of scale in the provision of bus services, but bus stations, like airports, have local monopoly power.

In cases where the natural monopoly is a 'network' (electricity or telephone cables, gas pipes, railway lines, air space) or a terminal (airports, bus stations, ports), it will be desirable to design and regulate non-discriminatory 'common carrier' tariffs. In the case of electricity, this exists in the form of the bulk supply tariff. Legislation, passed in 1982, sets out the rules for determining the price at which electricity can be sold to the grid or bought from it. But in other areas much remains to be done. For example, the rules governing the ability of other telephone operators to interconnect with the BT network and the charges made for such interconnections will be a major element in the regulation of a privatized telecommunications system. Economic theory tells us that if competition is to thrive round these networks or terminals, there must be no discrimination in charges between users.

Exposing public utilities to (competitive) market forces is complicated by the existence of widespread cross-subsidy. The subsidization of 'socially desirable' loss-making services by profitable ones is a time-honoured tradition in the public control of natural monopolies, and economists find it difficult to convince the public of the iniquity of these practices. But in many areas, notably transport, regulation combined with cross-subsidy inhibits the development of more flexible services. Yet governments fear getting sucked into specific subsidies for the unprofitable services, which they wish to see preserved, both because of the public expenditure consequences (is it worth increasing taxation to achieve resource gains?) and the difficulty of determining what subsidy payments are really necessary and what are dead-weight costs.

The issues of cross-subsidization and price discrimination are crucial both to the operation of 'common carriers' and 'common terminals', and to deregulation when 'socially desirable' services are at risk. But there are major problems involved in defining, let along measuring, cross-subsidization. Should it be defined in relation to average costs, or marginal costs; and if marginal costs, short-term or long-term costs? Or are demand elasticities relevant, as in optimal taxation theory? These are problems on which progress has been disappointing during a century of public utility operations. Accountants and economists have not managed to put their heads together. Governments have found the problems either too difficult or too inconvenient. But our inability to give useful practical answers reduces our ability to facilitate the operation of competition, which can operate through and around a natural monopoly network. Perhaps what we most need are incentives to make progress. One possibility would be to extend the notion of a legal obligation to supply services to all comers at non-discriminating prices. At present, in the UK we only have legal obligations not to discriminate between classes of consumer.

Sometimes exposure to (competitive) market forces will be best accomplished by deregulation and abolition of statutory monopoly, and sometimes by privatization. Sometimes the two will be closely linked. Deregulation of air transport in the US seems to have brought significant advantages. A similar operation in Europe might be equally beneficial and might contribute more to efficiency than the privatization of British Airways. But is airline deregulation likely, when governments own the carriers?

These issues have been systematically explored in the case of the UK bus industry (see Cmnd 9300, 1984). Following an examination of the potential for competition in stage bus services, it is proposed that:

1. Licences that formerly conveyed monopoly rights to run buses over particular routes are to be abolished and the market will be open to any competitors.
2. The dominant operator, the National Bus Company is to be restructured and privatized so as to ensure that its successor companies have no overwhelming advantages compared to new entrants.
3. Regulations will remain to meet environmental requirements, for example, on public safety and to control congestion in town centres.
4. Bus companies will be invited to tender to run services that do not cover costs, but that, for social reasons, the local authority wishes to subsidize. These direct (specific to a route) subsidies will replace existing general subsidies, as well as meet those social objectives previously covered through cross-subsidies.
5. It is recognized that to ensure fair competition, no bus operator should have sole control of a bus station, which would enable him to exclude other operators. Thus major bus stations are to be operated under arrangements that enable all operators to have equal access.

Sometimes there are short-term conflicts between privatization and increased competition. The logic of singling out the natural monopoly elements of an existing organization from those parts that could operate in a competitive situation implies the separation of the organization into different parts. Such separation would avoid anti-cross-subsidization controls imposed from outside. But breaking up organizations would impose costs which, even if they are once-for-all costs, can be considerable. Also it could slow down the process of privatization, so risking a loss of political impetus.

Two 'halfway houses' are worth mentioning.

1. Franchising is a 'leasehold' solution which permits periodic competition for the use of a facility. It seems particularly useful where existing

facilities are in existence, so that the winner of the franchise does not need to make heavy investment and can avoid the problems of disposing of the assets, should the franchise be transferred to someone else at the next round. Franchising is frequently employed in 'terminal' situations, for example, catering at airports. It could also be used in conjunction with networks, for example, separately operated, and possibly separately owned, Pullman trains. Franchising can be used with loss-making as well as with profitable services;

2. Public-sector operators could be separated into distinct organizational groups, both to reduce pressures for cross-subsidization and to provide a first step to the greater separation of authority which would be involved in the privatization of ownership.

PUBLIC SERVICES

Recent years have seen some shift towards a market approach in the pricing of two services. The nationalization of water supply and waste water disposal at the beginning of the 1970s was accompanied by a shift away from a public-service approach to one based on the style of public corporations. Assets were identified, a unified charge levied for water supply and waste water disposal, appropriate financial targets for water authorities were determined, and the metering and pricing of water became subjects of serious debate. But little use has been made of pricing in determining demand; equalization of charges geographically has long been an object of policy; there is only limited metering; and there are obvious difficulties in pricing environmental services, such as the reduction of water polution. Charges are still primarily related to covering overall costs rather than determining individual usage.

The government has embarked on a drive to sell local authority housing. Legislation has given tenants a right to buy at substantial discounts, although some refund must be made if the dwelling is resold within five years of purchase by the tenant. At the same time, rents have risen in relation to prices. Some 650,000 dwellings were sold between 1979 and 1983. Attempts have also been made to encourage a revival of privately rented housing by the introduction of short leases without security of tenure for new lettings. But the effects on resource allocation are not clear-cut. Short-distance mobility among local authority tenants is greater than among owner–occupiers, although long-distance mobility is smaller. So although some increase in mobility may be expected, it cannot be guaranteed. The prospects of reviving private renting may be small while the political risk of rent control remains and while owner–occupiers enjoy fiscal privileges.

The Conservative government has undertaken a review of the financing of the Health Service. Eventually it decided that the NHS would continue to be financed, as at present, largely by taxation. Any health insurance scheme tends to blunt the edge of market forces and the operation of insurance schemes in other countries reveals some deficiencies. The NHS is, by international standards, a relatively low-cost operation. In particular, the costs of doctors are well below those in countries with insurance arrangements. The NHS also exercises some control over the prices it pays for drugs.

Problems of imperfect markets are striking in the case of the public provision of health care, education and personal social services. But the UK government sees considerable scope for greater reliance on market forces in the provision of subsidiary services, such as hospital laundries and school cleaning, by contracting them out (that is, franchising for a limited period of time). Services such as refuse collection have also been franchised in some areas, often accompanied by considerable cost savings. There is also scope for franchising in transport services.

The use of franchising may be an effective way of exposing some elements of a public service to (competitive) market forces, while preserving the present relationship between doctors, teachers, social workers, etc. and their clients. Some of the effect is a once-for-all one, when a long-protected service has failed to benefit from innovation – perhaps because of the power of restrictive labour practices. There are instances when existing departments have tendered for a franchise at costs well below those of the existing operation. But there are difficulties – as with the franchising of public industry operations – in specifying the required service, especially standards of performance, sufficiently tightly.

As there is private as well as public supply of directly provided services such as health and education, restraint on public budgets tends to encourage the demand for private services, hence increasing the influence of market forces (not necessarily competitive ones).

SOCIAL SECURITY

The complex subject of the possible disincentive effects of social security are outside the main thrust of these comments. Two aspects are worth noting, however: the effect of unemployment and other out-of-work benefits on the level of employment and the effect on labour markets of occupational pensions.

The effect of social security on employment has been much discussed in the UK recently, but the debate has generated more heat than light. The replacement ratio (income out of work compared with income in work) was much higher during the 1970s than it had been earlier, although it has subsequently fallen. But the consequences are not clear-cut, and it is possible to derive different results from similar data. The closest to a consensus is the view that the evidence points to a negative relationship between the replacement ratio and the supply of labour which is statistically significant, but numerically rather small.

The effect of pension provision, and its effect on labour and capital markets, is attracting increasing attention. There are both public and tax-supported private schemes. The traditional flat-rate public-sector scheme is being supplemented by a state earnings-related scheme, where pensions are related to the best twenty years of employees' earnings. This was introduced in 1975 and comes to maturity in 1998. Occupational (private-sector) schemes, normally linked to final salaries, now cover about half of the workforce. They get favourable tax treatment. Employers whose schemes are thought adequate are allowed to contract their employees out of the earnings-related part of the state scheme. Employees in occupational pensions schemes retain *some* entitlement to pension on retirement, even if they move to other employers.

The present arrangements have important capital market effects and occupational pension schemes potentially impede labour mobility. A major inquiry is in progress under the personal supervision of the Secretary of State for Health and Social Security. The first subject for the investigation has been the transferability of private pension entitlements. A consultative document has been published with suggestions designed to enable employees to arrange personal pensions with their employers, with fully transferable rights, while benefiting from broadly the same tax arrangements as enjoyed by employees in occupational pension schemes or by the self-employed (DHSS, 1984).

CONCLUSION

This chapter does not discuss the general theory of the provision of services by the public sector and the alternative of provision through markets. Rather, it provides a brief summary of the attempts by the UK government to expose services traditionally supplied publicly to (competitive) market forces. Some general principles relating to the 'privatization' of public utilities are set out. But we are at an early stage of a major shift in public policy. It will be important to look at this in, say, five years' time, by when it should be possible to report on results.

NOTES

The views expressed in this chapter are those of the author, and not necessarily those of the Treasury. I am grateful to John Rickard and to those attending the seminar at Cernobbio, especially Carla Marchese, for helpful comments on the original draft.

REFERENCES

Baumol, W. J., Panzar, J. C. and Willig, R. D. (1982), *Contestable Markets and the Theory of Industry Structure*. New York: Harcourt Brace Jovanovich.
Cmnd 9300 (1984), *Buses*. London: HMSO.
Department of Health and Social Security (1984), *Personal Pensions: A Consultative Document*. London: HMSO.

14

Market and Non-Market Alternatives in the Public Supply of Public Services: Some Empirical Evidence

Carla Marchese

INTRODUCTION

This study is divided into two parts. The first focuses on the problems of provision of public services. It makes use of some suggestions derived from transaction costs theory to find cases where market production of public services, such as contracting out for a firm, is an inefficient solution. However, in order to say that public production could be more efficient, the specific organizational characteristics of the public production process and of the political decision-making process must be taken into account. Allowing for these aspects, the problem is reformulated in terms of a choice between production in a competitive or a non-competitive market, instead of between private or public production. Competition, which offers the most efficient solution, could be sought to some extent within the public sector too.

The second part of the study focuses on the problems of financing. In this case, the most important market alternative in the public supply of services is pricing. A serious hindrance to the wider use of pricing, in divisible or partially divisible services, comes from the fact that pricing reduces fiscal illusion and hence the degrees of freedom of political decision-makers. However, a wider use of prices could contribute towards limiting the growth of public expenditure. This is the suggestion of an empirical test performed on time-series and cross-section data for Italy and the EEC.

PRODUCTION OF PUBLIC SERVICES

The government can choose from among a number of different organizational forms in order to provide public services: public bureaux, public enterprises, contracts with regulated or unregulated private firms, etc. The standard literature on public goods does not shed much light on the problem of the best organization for public supply. According to some authors, however, the public sector can offer some services which cannot be produced by the market.[1] Criminal courts, for example, are generally public, because they would otherwise lack the required hallmark of legal institutions. In a democratic society, the case where public production is required occurs mainly in institutional services, such as justice or defence. In these situations strong conflicts of opinions and interests among citizens may arise, so that the compulsory nature of the intervention and the need for a lawful, public solution is more evident. Even in these cases, however, public production may to a certain extent use intermediate services bought in the market. Hence market alternatives in the supply of public services can have a very wide range of use.

Some useful suggestions about the choice between market or public production can be found in studies of transaction costs and vertical integration. In fact, direct production by the government sector may be viewed as a case of vertical integration; instead of behaving simply as a commercial intermediary (to collect information about demand, find private partners, check performances, etc.) or as a regulator, the government becomes a producer too. So one may try to explain direct production by the government sector by looking at factors analogous to those which, in the private sector, promote vertical integration. This analogy, however, as we shall see, cannot be pushed too far, because of the specific organizational characteristics of the public sector.

Studies on transaction costs have presented many cases where the market process is inefficient and a more centralized solution is needed. In exploiting the transaction costs theory,[2] I will focus particularly on the consequences of three hypotheses concerning, successively, information costs, opportunistic behaviour, and quasi-rents. In a world where information is costly and people also pursue their interests by misrepresentation, transaction costs for a firm may be in some cases higher than the organization costs of producing directly. Transaction costs are certainly high for typical public services, because of the difficulties of providing for all future contingencies in a contract which should last for a certain period of time, and because of the problems of defining and measuring the output quantity and quality. Entrusting the service to a private firm would lay upon the government the burden of writing a sufficiently well-specified contract, of checking performance and costs, of preventing the private firm from illegally using information related to the service, of remedying contractual breaches, etc. It must also be remembered, however, that when there are difficulties of measuring the output and of defining the required performance, choosing public production is often a way of avoiding the problem, instead of solving it. The autonomy given to the bureaucracy in this field can open the way to waste and inefficiency. This is a problem peculiar to the public sector, which we shall come back to later.

The quasi-rent argument is applicable in those situations in which the other partner in the contract has a degree of market power, such that (in order to avoid the possibility of an opportunistic behaviour on his part) direct production is preferred. These cases may occur in situations not commonly called monopolies, but where there have been specific investments which generate appropriable quasi-rents. In these circumstances, even if the contract is well specified and enforceable, and the quality and quantity of the service is easily measured, there is always the possibility of post-contractual opportunistic behaviour. For example, the owner of a printing press who leases his services to a newspaper publisher can capture part of the increase in the publisher's profits by imposing a higher rental price. Even if the publisher could litigate and prove his rights before a judge, even if another printer could be found at the previous price within a reasonable time, the newspaper publisher would probably avoid a rupture, faced by the threat of a production delay during litigation or during the search for an alternative (which could impose substantial costs on him). According to Klein, Crawford and Alchian (1978, p. 298), 'as assets become more specific and more appropriable quasi-rents are created (and therefore the possible gain from opportunistic behaviour increases) the costs of contracting will generally increase more than the costs of vertical integration'. An alternative to vertical integration can be that of either resorting to standby facilities that are otherwise not worth while, or to a market mechanism of contract enforcement which operates as a kind of insurance. The potential 'cheater' in a long-term relationship receives a price high enough to give him a premium, whose discounted value exceeds his potential gain from opportunistic behaviour. The costs of this alternative, however, are, probably related to the size of the appropriable quasi-rents, whereas the costs of direct production probably are not. So the higher the appropriable quasi-rents, the more vertical integration should be the preferred solution. Problems of this kind are very common in public services. The most obvious case is that of public utilities, where the network brings about specialized quasi-rents and raises the possibility of post-contractual opportunistic behaviour. While the competition 'in the field' is impossible or undesirable,[3] the competition 'for the field'[4] is not a sufficient answer to this problem. But the possibility of being 'locked in' must be considered also for intermediate goods and services. For example, leasing hospital equipment, control apparatus for missile weapons, or computers to handle tax revenues could expose the public sector to serious risks of post-contractual opportunistic behaviour.

To sum up, market alternatives are presumably costly in cases of information problems and of market relationships lasting for a certain period of time, during which the partner has dangerous blackmailing powers. In this second case, direct production could also be more innovative, since a private supplier working in a non-competitive market generally would not innovate when he incurs capital losses higher than the expected private returns from those innovations.[5]

The problems considered up to now are to a large extent common to public and private sector of the economy. Public production, however, raises specific problems because of its organizational characteristics. The property rights theory[6] has pointed out particularly that with public production organizations the costs of transferring property ar prohibitively high as they imply emigration or victorious political action. Therefore specialization in property is ruled out and capitalization of future consequences of present choices is inhibited. As a consequence, the owners (that is the tax payers) have less incentive to detect and police the performance of public organizations; on the other hand, public managers and civil servants have a wider scope to pursue their own goals, instead of the goals of the organization. Empirical studies seem to support the view that public organizations are relatively inefficient. Recently many studies have appeared comparing the efficiency of private and public production, particularly in the public enterprises field. A survey by Borcherding, Pommerehne and Schneider (1982), of more than fifty applied studies for five countries, finds higher costs for public production ranging from 10 per cent to 50 per cent. Public production, however, seems more efficient when there is competition between public and public or public and private firms. On the basis of the generally accepted postulate of rational choice by economic agents, the authors conclude that so general a use of apparently inefficient organizations (like public firms) must conceal specific reasons, connected with:

1. the specific characteristics of the desired output;
2. the savings that a public enterprise generates in transaction and control costs (that are very difficult to measure in an applied study);
3. the possibility of selecting through the public enterprise the recipients of policies aimed at redistribution of income.

These explanations, like the property rights theory, seem to confirm the hypothesis of the public enterprise as a production organization tied to specific goals, which would justify systematically higher costs than those of producing similar services through a private firm. However, some doubts arise about looking at the historical record. It is instructive, for example, to compare the Borcherding, Pommerehne and Schneider (1982) results with those reported in a classic Italian text in public finance in 1902, *Municipalizzazione dei publici servigi*, written by Montemartini. The author collected broad empirical evidence for the second half of the last century on local public enterprises in Italy, UK, USA, France and Germany. He found systematically lower unit costs in the public enterprises. Some examples are reported in tables

Table 14.1 *Private and public production in electrical utilities in the United Kingdom (£)*

Years	*No. of enterprises*	*Sales revenue*	*Production costs*	*Profits*	*Profit rate (%)*	*Sales price*
Private enterprises						
1895	27	515 533	277 371	238 162	5.49	6.08 d.
1896	29	616 382	314 996	301 386	6.33	5.77
1897	36	812 734	410 991	401 743	6.54	5.62
1898	37	897 628	480 280	417 348	5.51	5.51
1899	43	1 053 291	580 548	472 743	5.45	5.24
Public enterprises						
1895	33	206 868	119 632	87 235	4.92	5.32 d.
1896	42	310 098	172 581	137 517	5.61	5.18
1897	54	502 957	265 074	237 873	5.73	4.68
1898	61	709 335	376 381	332 954	5.55	4.35
1899	75	988 404	555 682	432 722	4.90	4.06

Source: Montemartini, 1902, p. 265.

Table 14.2 *Capital/output ratios and unit costs in electrical utilities in the United Kingdom (£)*

Years	*Capital*	*Capital/ output*	*Output*	*Unit cost*
Private enterprises				
1895	4 338 106	51.16	84 792	3.27
1896	4 761 232	44.57	106 825	2.95
1897	6 142 859	42.48	144 615	2.84
1898	6 574 374	46.49	162 909	2.95
1899	8 674 183	43.15	201 010	2.89
Public enterprises				
1895	1 773 069	45.59	38 885	3.08
1896	2 451 283	40.95	59 864	2.88
1897	4 151 361	38.63	107 467	2.47
1898	5 999 171	36.79	163 066	2.31
1899	8 831 061	36.27	243 449	2.28

Source: Elaboration of data in Montemartini, 1902, p. 265.

14.1–14.3. Table 14.1 lists data for English private and public electrical enterprises. Table 14.2 is an elaboration of data in table 14.1, which shows that public enterprises had lower production costs and lower capital–output ratios. Table 14.3 compares prices in public and private enterprises with a standard production cost in the gas sector in Italy. Even though the evidence

Table 14.3 *Private and public production in gas utilities in Italy (current Italian lire)*

		Gas produced (m^3)		*Gas consumed by households (m^3)*		*Sale price*			
Cities	*No. of inhabitants*	*Before public enterprise*	*After public enterprise*	*Before public enterprise*	*After public enterprise*	*Before public enterprise*	*After public enterprise*	*Cost price (m^3)*	*Year of municipalization*
Spezia	30 000	250 000	1 338 519	80 000	635 395	0.50	0.25	0.13–0.14	1897
Como	26 395	1 200 000	2 400 000	—	1 557 094	0.24–0.20	0.24	—	1894
Padova	70 753	1 616 905	2 060 000	902 000	1 423 000	0.38	0.20–0.18	0.11	1896
Vicenza	38 713	420 000	475 000	200 000	220 000	0.38	0.25–0.22	0.19	1897
Asti	33 518	—	1 070 000	—	650 000	0.25	0.20	0.16	1898
Voghera	16 613	350 000	660 000	—	440 000	0.325	0.18	0.13	1899

Source: Montemartini, 1902, p. 251.

presented by Montemartini should be revised, in order to bring it into line with modern standards, his book performs the service of drawing attention to the possibility of greater efficiency within the public sector, though in a different historical context. The organizational characteristics outlined by Montemartini appear to be particularly interesting. The public enterprise to which he makes reference differs in some important features from the private one, such as its strict compliance with the laws regarding accident prevention, and acceptance of negotiated wage rates with unions. However, in many respects it is very similar to private enterprise:

1. public enterprises can be and are sometimes closed down for inefficiency;
2. the management is largely autonomous in its operations;
3. employees' tenure is no different from that prevailing in a private firm.

Given its initial phase, the performance of public enterprise is easily compared to that of private enterprises, which still have an important share of the market and offer an actual alternative. These organizational characteristics appear to be consistent with some suggestions of the public choice theory[7] of public production. The cost differences between private and public production, not explicable by the kind of ownership (private or public) or by the goals specified for management (profits or public interest), may depend upon penalties and rewards for the decision-makers and the employees. They depend also on the structure of the market, which may or may not be able to inflict punishment on inefficient firms. Thus market alternatives do not need to be alternatives to public production; they can be contemplated within the public sector, by breaking the identification between public and monopolistic production, through the introduction and/or the strengthening of the competition among bureaux or public enterprises, and through the reshaping of penalties and rewards for the decision-makers and the personnel. In this context, private alternatives may operate as a means to stimulate changes in the public sector.

Today it is widely recognized that public organizations usually employ inefficient production processes, which lead, according to some authors,[8] to overcapitalization, and, according to other authors,[9] to excessive use of labour. The standard explanations of these inefficiencies refers to aspects peculiar to the organization itself: its monopoly power in offering information and services to political bodies, its property rights structure. A relatively less well researched area is that of all those elements that give political decision-makers within a representative democracy some possibility of moving away from the solution preferred by the majority of the voters. I will focus on the topics of specialized preferences and interest groups.

The production of public services gives rise to specific problems in democracy, where the citizens involved in the production process (as civil servants, or owners of enterprises looking for franchises or contracts with the public sector) can be at the same time voters and political 'entrepreneurs'. Their specific interests cannot be expressed simply through the vote on an issue (which demands just a 'yes' or 'no', and does not measure the 'intensity' of a preference). The degree of intensity must find other means of expression. The theory of the formation of interest groups predicts that, taking into account organizational costs, the people interested in public production will form pressure groups to influence government choices of production processes that make use of their service, and to increase the demand for public services. Interest groups can offer, in exchange, support for electoral campaigns and various kinds of legal and illegal 'incentives' to political and bureaucratic personnel. Several recent re-examinations[10] of this topic have shown that there are important limits to the possibility of interest groups 'capturing' public bodies, essentially due to:

1. a law of diminishing returns to group size in politics[11] (that restricts the possibility of success of large interest groups such as that of civil servants);
2. the rising opposition of other citizens as the burden on them increases;
3. the increased possibilities for clever political 'entrepreneurs' of organizing the opposition of the taxpayers in a world of diminishing communication and information costs.

Nevertheless, the role of interest groups in the production of public services cannot be ignored. A positive point of view regarding the choice between market or public production and regarding the production process (more or less capital-intensive, more or less vertically integrated) used in the public sector must take into account the characteristics of the political decision-making process.

An explanation derived from the economics of politics concerning the choice of the production process for public services has been verified in a cross-section study by Brosio (1983). The capital/labour ratio in Italian local public enterprises in the fields of public transport and refuse collection is explained by political market imperfections and characteristics of bureaucratic organizations, which influence decision-makers and can distort the efficiency by a more or less capital-intensive process. For example, the proportion of the working population employed in firms that produce capital goods for public enterprises should indicate the percentage of voters who probably prefer capital-intensive production process, whereas the proportion of unemployed people looking for their first job should indicate the percentage of citizens interested in the creation of jobs in the public sector. The statistical performance of a regression model, where these and other variables are considered, is good enough to support further research in this direction.

An analogous approach could also be used to explain the choice between public or private production of services. Neither of these alternatives can guarantee that distortions to efficiency, due to the political decision-making process, can be avoided, even if the size of the distortion can differ from one case to another. From a very general and preliminary point of view, one can emphasize that the possibilities for decision-makers to deviate from the wishes of the majority of voters has its basis in political and economic market imperfections, which are often unavoidable. Specialized preferences become more and more important, in so far as voters think that competition could not prevent them from benefiting from a particular production decision, whereas interest groups have their basis mainly in oligopolistic markets.

So the recent movement toward 'privatization' of public services in Western societies can obtain useful results, when it is a way of making use of the opportunity to introduce more competition inside and outside the public sector; on the contrary, however, it would be too naive to think that private production could always stop the 'capture' process of bureaucracy, without posing new and different problems of lobbying and capturing.

FINANCING OF PUBLIC SERVICES

Market alternatives in the financing of public services may include prices, charges, earmarked revenues and so on. They are independent of those in production arrangements: one can opt for public production in education or health services and finance these services mainly through prices; or one can opt for the converse, that is, private production and public financing. The degree of mix of the two dimensions, however, can be interesting from an organizational point of view.

Prices can be used when the government supplies services that are at least partially divisible and excludable. Today a wider use of prices or charges is often recommended as a way to hold in check the fiscal crisis of the state. These forms of revenue collection are supposed to be more acceptable to the citizen than taxes, because they are linked to specific services. This would be a partial recourse to patrimonial financing, which would not require surpluses, but which would control deficits. Suggestions of this kind have an objective basis in the growth of public expenditure in fields where individual benefits are important and services are partially divisible and excludable. Expenditure on education, health, social services, merit goods grew fast in the 1960s and in the first half of the 1970s in OECD countries, and has been faster than that of other typical public services, such as defence or justice. However, the growth of receipts that can be secured in this way is limited to some components of public expenditure, and does not touch the huge component of transfer payments, unless one wants to consider a wider use of the equivalence principle with regard to retirement or unemployment benefits. If we limit our focus to services, the possibility of increasing revenue by a wider use of prices may be impaired by the reaction of the market, in cases of a high price elasticity of demand.

On the other hand, prices and charges are a kind of receipt that eliminates fiscal illusion altogether. Therefore policies aimed at a wider use of pricing are probably not viable from an electoral point of view. For example, with many kinds of taxes the government enjoys a fiscal dividend connected with the real or monetary growth of income; a dividend which is often not seen by the citizens. When faced with prices, on the other hand, the customer always measures this sacrifice in terms of alternative uses. Thus inflation usually reduces the revenues collected through public prices, because it lessens unit prices in real terms; consequently frequent and unpopular changes are needed. The Italian case indicates that as far as the personal income tax is concerned the government is able to show its good will by redesigning the rates structure to compensate partially for fiscal drags, while still benefiting from a substantial fiscal dividend. With user charges, a similar result can be achieved only if the changes in prices that would be required to keep them constant in real terms are forgone.

By giving a wider autonomy to public enterprises in price setting one can lessen the importance of political variables, but cannot be sure that prices will fully adjust to cost changes. It may be just the typical organizational structure of modern public enterprises that does not provide sufficient incentives; this hypothesis is tested, for example, in a paper by Peltzman (1971) for the American electrical utilities. He found that they are slower in adjusting to a cost change and generally have more rigid prices than private enterprises.

A greater reliance on prices may be recommended not so much for the purpose of increasing the receipts as for that of reducing expenditure. This could be achieved because prices eliminate fiscal illusion and reduce income redistribution now put into practice by supplying the services free of charge or below cost. The advocates of pricing, as for example Bird (1976), suggest a number of different ways to deal with the distribution problem, including transfer, vouchers, etc. It must also be noted that often under-cost charges for public services do not redistribute from high to low-income classes (the standard goal of redistribution policies); they redistribute mainly among age-groups, household, etc., without any precise reference to income.

EMPIRICAL EVIDENCE

An attempt to carry out an empirical test for the existence of a link between the level of public expenditure and financing through prices is now presented. A complete model that explains the level of public expenditure taking into account all relevant aspects is not constructed, but the effects of the introduction of prices, considering all other things to be equal, is modelled. The parameters which I estimated would probably change in a complete model. Other problems of this kind of analysis come from the usually accepted definition of the government sector, which excludes the revenues

Table 14.4 *Contribution of prices to public receipts in Europe,. 1971–80*

	1971	*1972*	*1973*	*1974*	*1975*	*1976*	*1977*	*1978*	*1979*	*1980*
Federal Republic of Germany	4.85	5.15	5.20	5.59	6.23	6.32	6.12	6.23	6.18	6.33
France	6.24	6.28	6.28	6.22	6.90	5.51	5.60	5.75	5.30	5.00
Italy	3.21	2.92	2.86	2.80	2.73	2.48	2.32	2.53	2.63	2.23
Netherlands	1.76	1.68	1.66	1.79	1.64	1.68	1.82	1.83	1.78	1.74
Belgium	0.82	0.81	0.70	0.75	0.69	0.86	0.75	0.77	0.78	0.86
United Kingdom	9.43	9.89	10.17	8.52	7.68	7.92	8.10	8.38	8.48	8.31
Denmark	3.52	3.52	3.31	3.55	3.93	3.66	3.99	3.88	3.83	3.83

Percentage share of price receipts on current government receipts plus sales of goods and services at current prices.
Source: Eurostat, 1983 a.

Table 14.5 *Pricing of public services and public expenditure*

1. *The Italian case, 1962–82*

OLS estimate

COSA = 27064.68 − 2175.04 TART
(21.73) (− 12.58)

$\bar{R}^2 = 0.89$ $F = 158.193$ DW = 0.96 SER = 1121.12

Mean of the dependent variable: 11631.66

Cochrane–Orcutt estimate

COSA = 28006.82 − 3939.42 TART
(16.07) (− 92.39)

$e = 0.33$ $t(e) = 1.55$

$\bar{R}^2 = 0.91$ $F = 205.511$ DW = 1.80 SER = 937.04

2. *The European case, 1971–80*

Fuller and Battese estimate (various components model)

CONV = 0.207 − 0.393 TA
(13.29) (− 5.19)

SER = 0.048

Mean of the dependent variable: 0.20

Parks' estimate (autoregressive model)

CONV = 0.226 − 0.230 TA
(49.71) (− 3.96)

$e = 0.75$ SER = 0.10

COSA = expenditure for public consumption plus sales of goods and services by the general government sector plus expenditure by public enterprises (Italian Aziende Autonome, such as the Post Office, etc. not included in the general government sector) at constant (1970) prices.
TART = percentage share of sales revenue in the current consolidated revenues of general government and public enterprises, inclusive of sales.
For Italy the estimate has been performed with the TSP package.
The European case includes the following countries: Germany, France, Italy, The Netherlands, Belgium, United Kingdom and Denmark.
CONV = expenditure for government consumption plus sales of goods and services by the government sector as a share of GDP at purchaser's prices.
TA = share of sales revenue in current government receipts, inclusive of sales of goods and services.
The estimate has been performed with the options by Fuller and Battese and Parks of the procedure TSCREG of the SAS package. For the Parks' estimate, the phi-matrix has not been reported here because its values are close to zero. The TSCREG does not provide the calculus of the standard error of the regression (SER); it has been calculated separately fitting the estimated equations to the data.

Sources: OECD, 1984, for public consumption expenditure.
Relazione generate sulla situazione economica del paese, various issues, for other COSA data and consolidated cash budget data for 1962–71. 'Conto di cassa del settore pubblico consolidato', in Banca d'Italia, *Relazione annuale*, various issues, for the consolidated cash budget data for later years. Eurostat, 1983a and 1983b, for CONV and TA data.

from the sale of goods and services. The data for the price receipts used here include both partial payments by households for public services and public receipts from the sale of by-products, etc. For Italy, and for the period 1962–82, I used a regression model where the dependent variable is public expenditure for collective consumption and for mixed goods from the public and private sector (the latter being measured by the expenditure by public enterprises, such as the post office, railway, telephone, etc.) at constant prices. The independent variable is the percentage share of receipts from sales (at constant prices) in the consolidated current revenues by the bodies that produce the services. The relation between the two variables seems to be strong and statistically significant, in accordance with the common experience of correlation between growth of collective consumption and decrease of the share of sales. One might conclude that the practice of below-cost has produced the illusion[12] that public services are free services, and has favoured the growth of demand.

I performed a similar test for a pooling of data for seven EEC countries (Federal Republic of Germany, France, the Netherlands, Belgium, United Kingdom, and Denmark) for the years 1971–80 (see table 14.4). In this case, the dependent variable is the share in GDP of expenditures for collective consumption, puls sales of goods and services by the government sector (as defined in the ESA accounting system). I could not include the expenditures by public enterprises classified as quasi-corporate enterprises. I tested two hypotheses regarding the error structure (see table 14.5). The first – the Fuller and Battese (1974) method – assumes that the errors of the regression have three random components, one specific to the country, the second for the year and the third for both the year and the country. They have zero mean and different positive variances. The second – the Parks method (Kmenta, 1971) – assumes that the errors are heteroscedastic, contemporaneously correlated among countries and autoregressive. Both methods use generalized least squares on transformed data. The results show the expected relationship. However, a definite answer about the role of public prices in the growth of public expenditure could come only from a model of public expenditure determination.

To summarize, more empirical evidence and more statistical tests are needed to reach a conclusion on the usefulness of prices for purposes of increasing government revenues and/or reducing public expenditure. A greater reliance on prices also raises problems of equity in income distribution and of inflationary pressures on the price level, particularly when systems of indexation exist. One important consequence of pricing, however, is a reduction in fiscal illusion and an incentive to new suppliers. One can also achieve a more accurate revelation of preferences than that provided by the political process. Misuses and inefficiencies would have to face the reaction of customers through a type of 'voice' and/or 'exit' mechanism. These aspects, though far from solving all the problems involved, seem important enough to lend credence to proposals for more extensive reliance on pricing of public services, especially in a context such as the Italian one, where the problems of quality in the public services are especially severe.

NOTES

1 See, for example, Alchian (1965) and Forte (1980).
2 This theory has been developed particularly by Williamson in several studies (1975, 1979, 1981).
3 In the case of natural monopoly, competition in the field leads to higher costs than production through a single enterprise; when the instability of the natural monopoly solution or the chosen price system leaves room for competition, entry barriers should be provided by law. On this topic see Faulhaber (1975) and Schneider and Schulz (1980).
4 On this topic, see Demsetz (1968).
5 For a discussion of the innovations problem in regulated firms, see Ekelund and Higgins Jr (1982).
6 See, for example, Alchian (1965, 1979) and Demsetz (1967).
7 Starting points for this approach are Alchian and Kessel (1962) and Niskanen (1971).
8 See, for example, De Alessi (1969).
9 For this point of view, see Borcherding, Bush and Spann (1977).
10 A new analytical approach to the role of interest groups in regulation policies is developed in Peltzman (1976); see also Demsetz (1979) and Wilson (1980).
11 Because of the problems of overcoming free-riders as the size of the group increases, and of the strengthening of the opposition as its social basis narrows.
12 The expansive effect of fiscal illusion (and, in particular, of an understimation of the tax burden) on expenditure is tested, for example, in Pommerehne and Schneider (1978). The index of fiscal 'invisibility' – instead of 'illusion' used here – should, however, approach the phenomenon more simply and directly.

REFERENCES

Alchian, A. A. (1965), 'Some economics of property rights', *Il Politico*, vol. 30, pp. 816–29.

Alchian, A. A. (1979), 'Some implications of recognition of property right transaction costs', in K. Brunner (ed.), *Economics and Social Institutions*. Boston: Martinus Nijhoff.

Alchian, A. A. and Kessel, R. A. (1962), 'Competition, monopoly and the pursuit of money', in NBER, *Aspects of Labor Economics*, special conference series 14. Princeton, NJ: Princeton University Press.

Bird, R. M. (1976), *Charging for Public Services, a New Look at an Old Idea*. Toronto: Canadian Tax Foundation.

Borcherding, T. E., Bush, W. C. and Spann, R. M. (1977), 'The effects on public spending of the divisibility of public outputs in consumption, bureaucratic power, and the size of the sharing group', in T. E. Borcherding (ed.), *Budgets and Bureaucrats: the Sources of Government Growth*. Durham, NC: Duke University Press.

Borcherding, T. E., Pommerehne, W. W. and Schneider, F. (1982), 'Comparing the efficiency of private and public production: the evidence from five countries', *Feitschrift für Nationalökonomie*, supplement 2, pp. 127–56.

Brosio, G. (1983), 'La scelta delle combinazioni produttive nel settore pubblico: un'analisi positiva', *Economia pubblica*, vol. 13, pp. 565–73.
De Alessi, L. (1969), 'Implications of property rights for government investment choices', *American Economic Review*, vol. 59, pp. 13–24.
De Alessi, L. (1974), 'An analysis of government ownership and regulation. Theory and evidence from the electric power industry', *Public Choice*, vol. 19, pp. 1–42.
Demsetz, H. (1967), 'Toward a theory of property rights', *American Economic Review*, Papers and proceedings, May, pp. 347–59.
Demsetz, H. (1968), 'Why regulate utilities?', *Journal of Law and Economics*, vol. 11, pp. 55–66.
Demsetz, H. (1979), 'The growth of government', manuscript.
Ekelund, R. B. and Higgins, R. S., Jr (1982), 'Capital fixity, innovations, and long-term contracting: an inter-temporal economic theory of regulation', *American Economic Review*, vol. 72, pp. 32–46.
Eurostat (1983a), *General Government Accounts and Statistics 1971–1980*. Luxemburg.
Eurostat (1983b), *Conti nazionali SEC, aggregati, 1969–1980*. Luxemburg.
Faulhaber, G. R. (1975), 'Cross subsidization: pricing in public enterprises', *American Economic Review*, vol. 65, pp. 966–77.
Forte, F. (1980), *Principi di Scienza delle Finanze*. Turin: Boringhieri.
Fuller, W. A. and Batese, G. S. (1974), 'Estimation of linear models with crosses-error structure', *Journal of Econometrics*, vol. 2, pp. 67–8.
Klein, B., Crawford, R. G. and Alchian, A. A. (1978), 'Vertical integration, appropriable rents, and the competitive contracting process', *Journal of Law and Economics*, vol. 21, pp. 297–326.
Kmenta, J. (1971) *Elements of Econometrics*. New York: Macmillan.
Montemartini, G. (1902), *Municipalizzazione dei publici servigi*. Milan: Società Editrice Libraria.
Niskanen, W. A. (1971), *Bureaucracy and Representative Government*. New York: Aldine Atherton.
OECD (1984), *National Account*. Paris.
Peltzman, S. (1971), 'Pricing in public and private enterprises: electric utilities in the United States', *Journal of Law and Economics*, vol. 14, pp. 109–47.
Peltzman, S. (1976), 'Toward a more general theory of regulation', *Journal of Law and Economics*, vol. 19, pp. 211–40.
Pommerehne, W. W. and Schneider, F. (1978), 'Fiscal illusion, political institutions and local public spending', *Kyklos*, vol. 31, no. 3, pp. 381–408.
Schneider, H.K. and Schulz, W. (1980), 'Market structure and market organization in the electricity and gas public utility sector of the FRG', in W. J. Baumol (ed.), *Public and Private Enterprise in a Mixed Economy*. London: IEA, Macmillan.
Williamson, O. E. (1975), *Markets and Hierarchies: Analysis and Antitrust Implications, A Study in the Economics of Internal Organization*. New York: Free Press; London: Macmillan.
Williamson, O. E. (1979), 'Transactions cost economics: the governance of contractual relations', *Journal of Law and Economics*, vol. 22, pp. 233–61.
Williamson, O. E. (1981), 'The modern corporation: origins, evolution, attributes', *Journal of Economic Literature*, vol. 19, no. 4, pp. 1537–68.
Wilson, J. Q. (1980), *The Politics of Regulation*. New York: Basic Books.

The Contributors

Charles Blankart is Professor of Public Finance, University of the Federal Armed Forces, Munich and was previously Professor of Economics at the Free University of Berlin. His research interests are in public and regulated enterprises, and he is the author of *Okonomie der Offentliche Unternehmen* (Economics of Public Enterprises).

Giorgio Brosio is Professor of Public Finance, University of Turin. He has also lectured on public finance at the University of Geneva. He is an expert of fiscal federalism.

Ian Byatt is Deputy Chief Economic Adviser, HM Treasury, London. He previously worked as an economist in other government departments and has taught at the University of Durham and at the London School of Economics and Political Science.

Bruno Frey is Professor of Economics, University of Zürich. He has held Visiting Professorships at the University of Stockholm and the Institute of Advanced Studies, Vienna. His recent books, mainly on public analysis, include *Democratic Economic Policy* (1983).

Francesco Forte is Minister of EEC Affairs and previously Minister of Finance, in the Italian government, and Professor of Political Economy, University of Rome. His recent works include *The Political Economy of Taxation* (joint editor and contributor with Alan Peacock) (1982).

Victor Halberstadt is Professor of Public Finance, University of Leiden since 1974, and Crown-Member of the Dutch Social and Economic Council. Recent publications include *Public Policy Towards Disabled Workers: Cross National Analysis of Economic Impacts* (jointly with Robert H. Haveman and Richard V. Burkhauser).

Carla Marchese is research officer at the Laboratorio di Economia, University of Turin, where she has also taught public finance. Co-author with Francesco Forte of *Prezzi pubblichi e tariffe* (Public Prices and Tariffs).

Paolo Martelli is Director of POLITEIA, a centre carrying out research in the field of social policy in Rome and Milan. He is the author of *La Logica della Scelta Collettiva* (The Logic of Public Choice), which deals with models of aggregation of rational preferences.

Dennis C. Mueller is Professor of Economics, University of Maryland, and

President of the Public Choice Society. He was Formerly Director of the International Institute of Management in Berlin. Author of *Public Choice* and *Profits in the Long Run* (forthcoming).

Peter Murrell is Associate Professor, University of Maryland. Senior Research Fellow, International Institute of Management, Berlin (1982–83).

Alan Peacock is Research Professor in Public Finance, Esmée Fairbairn Research Centre, Heriot-Watt University, Edinburgh. Latterly Vice-Chancellor and Professor of Economics, University of Buckingham. He has held Chairs in Economics at the Universities of Edinburgh and York, and is a Fellow of the British Academy.

Ilde Rizzo is research officer in public finance at the University of Catania and some-time research fellow at the University of Buckingham. Recent publications have included work on the economic analysis of tax planning and on the relation between public debt and public expenditure growth.

Kurt Schmidt is Professor of Economics, University of Mainz. Until May 1984 he was a member of the German Council of Economic Advisers. Recent publications cover the economic analysis of corruption and the shadow economy as well as various aspects of tax and public expenditure analysis.

Vito Tanzi is Director of the Fiscal Affairs Department, International Monetary Fund. His most recent book is *Taxation, Inflation and Interest Rates*.

Nout Wellink is Executive Director, Netherlands Central Bank and former Treasurer-General of the Netherlands Ministry of Finance. He has published widely on different economic subjects, including public finance, European integration, investment policies and monetary policy.

Gianni Zandano is Professor of Economics, University of Turin and Chairman, Instituto Bancario di San Paolo, Turin.

Index